Scandal of the Cross
and Its Triumph

"I do not pray for them alone.
I pray also for those who will believe in Me
through their word that all may be one
as You, Father, are in Me, and I in You;
I pray that they may be (one) in Us,
that the world may believe that you sent Me."
(John 17:20-21)

Bob and Penny Lord

Journeys of Faith
1-800-633-2484

Other Books by Bob and Penny Lord
THIS IS MY BODY, THIS IS MY BLOOD
Miracles of the Eucharist
THE MANY FACES OF MARY
a Love Story
WE CAME BACK TO JESUS
SAINTS AND OTHER POWERFUL WOMEN
IN THE CHURCH
SAINTS AND OTHER POWERFUL MEN
IN THE CHURCH
HEAVENLY ARMY OF ANGELS

ISBN 0-926143-11-5

Cover Art by Diane St. Germain

Dedication

Pope John Paul II - Our Holy Father has been our inspiration. To us, he is truly our *"Sweet Christ on Earth"*. We have felt strength from his unbending commitment to Our Lord Jesus through His Mother Mary. From the moment he became Pope, he went after the enemies of the Church, with love, as a father goes after a wayward child, but firm, as a loving and caring parent must correct his children. We pray for his good health, and long Pontificate.

Mother Angelica - *Foundress of Eternal Word Television Network* - She has been a true Defender of the Faith. Fighting an uphill battle all her life, against the powers of the world, Mother Angelica has committed herself and her Ministry to save the Church against Its enemies, to preserve the traditions of our Church, no matter what the cost. She is truly a voice crying out in the desert; "Prepare the Way of the Lord."

We want to thank the many brothers and sisters who have lent their strong hands, their prayers and their resources. There are many, thank You Jesus, whom the Lord has sent us, we can't possibly name them all. But let us just give special thanks to a few, without whom none of this would have happened.

Dr. Jeffrey Mirus - Trinity Communications - We thank God for Dr. Mirus' wisdom and discernment, with regard to the Magisterium of the Church. The subject matter of this book is so delicate, we would not take the slightest chance of saying anything which could be in error.

Alex Tinant - He has accepted the mandate to volunteer his time and energies to our Ministry. He has been a faithful supporter of all the work we do. Whenever something has to be done, Alex is there to make it happen.

Debbie Callens - A special sister in Christ, who gives selflessly of herself in any way necessary to keep the Ministry going, especially when we had to go overseas to videotape the series on the Many Faces of Mary.

Diane St. Germain - Diane worked with Penny on the creation of the cover of this book. She allowed the Lord to work through her, using the talents He gave her to glorify His name. We thank Our Lord for giving us the gift of Diane. She is a contradiction to the modern world image of an artist.

Luz Elena Sandoval and Brother Joseph - These are truly willing servants of the Lord. They give completely of themselves every day in every way, not looking for glory or praise, but wanting to do the Lord's work. Nothing in our ministry would happen if it were not for these two committed laborers in the Lord's Garden. They are an integral part of our Community, totally consecrated to serving the Lord through our Ministry. Each day, with one mind, one heart, one spirit and one vision, they work side by side with us to evangelize the Church and the world.

Last, but not least, we want to dedicate this book to our beloved family, our grandson Rob and our daughter Clare.

We thank you Lord, for the gift of Your Children, who work tirelessly through the centuries to save the Church. We ask you to continually bless us and protect us.

Table of Contents

Acknowledgements

Excerpts were reprinted from the following books, with permission of these copyright holders:

Catholics and the New Age - Fr. Mitch Pacwa - Copyright 1991 Servant Publications - Box 8617 - Ann Arbor, MI 48107

The Catholic Church through the Ages - Martin P. Harney SJ - Copyright 1980 - St. Paul Books and Media
50 St. Paul's Ave. Boston, MA 02130

The Catholic Encyclopedia - Broderick, Robert C.
Copyright Thomas Nelson Inc. Publishers Nashville 1970

The Church Teaches -Jesuits St. Mary's College St. Mary, KS- Tan Publications - Rockford IL 1973

Faith of the Early Fathers - Vol 1-2-3 - W A Jurgens - Copyright 1970 -by the order of St. Benedict - published by The Liturgical Press - Collegeville, MN 56321

The Hidden Dangers of the Rainbow - Constance Cumbey - Copyright 1983 - Huntington House Publishers - PO Box 53788 - Lafayette, LA 70505

Lives of the Saints - Butler, Thurston, Atwater - Copyright 1980 Christian Classics - PO Box 30 Westminster, MD 21158

St. Jerome Bible (TEV) Copyright American Bible Society - 1865 Broadway NY, NY 10023 1966-1971-1976

Ungodly Rage -Donna Steichen - Copyright 1991
Ignatius Press 2515 Mc Allister St. San Francisco, CA 94118

Unicorn in the Sanctuary - Randy Englund - Copyright 1990 Tan Publications - PO Box 424 - Rockford, IL 61105

Introduction

In times of Crisis, God sends us special grace. This grace may come from Eucharistic Miracles, Apparitions by Our Lady, and Saints and other Powerful Men and Women in the Church. It may come in the form of Angelic intercession. It will come from anywhere the Lord deems necessary. There is only one thing of which we can be assured; it will come. He will use whatever or whoever it takes, whenever it is needed, to protect us from anything or anyone, who would bring us anywhere near the brink of hell. Very often, even if it means protecting us from ourselves.

That's really what this book is all about. And although we've said all this before, until we began the extensive research that was necessary to bring this work to you, we really had no idea how true that statement is. If not for the powerful intercession of Our Lord Jesus through Signal Graces, this Church we have today, would not exist. It would have been wiped out by Satan in the First or Second Century. There have been so many attacks on the Church, from without, from within, ongoing, overlapping, it's hard to believe that Satan could come up with so many variations on the same theme.

You name it; we as a people of God have gone through it. That is an important point - we've gone through it! We haven't gone over it or under it; we haven't tried to go to the right of it or the left of it. We haven't avoided it like the plague. *We've gone through it!* There have been extremely rough times, in which it looked like we as a church, as a people of God, would not pull through, and yet we're still here.   The onslaughts have come from non-Christian believers, atheists, pagans, as well as Christians.   We've been called everything from the Great Satan to the Anti-Christ. But as our Lord Jesus said to Peter, "*You are Rock, and upon this rock, I will build My Church.   And the gates of hell will not prevail against it.*"(Mt. 16:18)

In our first six books, we shared, the power the Lord has given us through Miracles of the Eucharist, through Our Lady's intervention, through the brave brothers and sisters who came before us, the Saints, and through our Angels, whom the Lord has given us to protect and guide us.   We've touched very lightly on *why* the Lord gave us Miracles of the Eucharist, *why* Our Lady came and continues to come to us in Apparitions, *why* He sent the Saints, and *what* was going on in our world and in our Church that made it necessary for Him to use His servants to intercede for us.

In this book, we attempt to focus in on the *what*, the *when*, the *why* and the *how*.   We want to share with you the ways, the evil one has tried to tear us asunder, through heresies and movements which have separated us, and how the Lord has fought these heresies in a two thousand year battle to keep His Church together.   The Lord has worked powerfully to build His Church, these last two millenniums. The growth has been remarkable.   But naturally, there has been a parallel track, the work the evil one has done to try to destroy the Church of God.   Now we want to track that route, which the powers of hell have taken, in their never-ending attempt to destroy all that the Lord has given us.

It was a monumental work, requiring lots of help in research, the need for quiet time for us to listen to the Lord, get out of the way, and write what He wants, rather than what we *think* He may want.   We couldn't afford any distractions, and yet that seems to be all that we have experienced. We have been very busy serving the Lord these last few months, even more than before we moved to Louisiana, and a wonderful army of earthly angels joined us, to help bring God's Holy Word to His Church. We have more help now, but we have triple the amount of work. Our television documentaries have been extremely well-accepted, praise God. We have traveled much more than usual to give talks, missions, and conferences. We are not complaining at all about how anointed our ministry has become. It just seems, every time we sat down to begin this book, we were interrupted to do some other *good* work.

One morning during Mass, at the time of the Consecration, as our priest raised the Host, the word that spoke to our hearts was: "*Go home and do nothing but begin My book. Disconnect your phone; put ear plugs in your ears. Write how I am grieving until My family is once more together, united.*" I was transported with the eyes of my heart to the very spot in the Holy Land, atop the Mount of Olives, where Jesus wept over Jerusalem. We were standing where Jesus had stood. We were looking over the walls of the Old City, only not at the Jerusalem of Jesus' day because it was no longer there. As He foresaw and predicted, His Jerusalem was destroyed thirty seven years after His Crucifixion. We've been told on Pilgrimage, that was why Jesus was crying. As we were meditating on what the Lord might want us to bring to you, the word we received was that He had been crying over the destruction of the *New Jerusalem*, His Church - He was crying over the shattering and fragmentation of His family, the Church.

There is an altar in that Chapel of Dominus Flevit (the Lord wept), on the Mount of Olives, which was built over the place where Jesus stood. In front of the altar there is a mosaic depicting a hen with her arms outstretched gathering her little chicks. "*How often have I yearned to gather your children, as a mother bird gathers her young under her wings, but you refused Me."*(Matt. 23:37)

God the Father sent Jesus, His Son and our Brother, that our sins might be redeemed and in that redemption, seeing how very much He loves us, that we might love one another. He showed us how He loves us *all*. And in every Mass, during the Eucharistic prayer we hear again *"He died for all!"* God wants His entire family to be *one*. Jesus said it plainly in Holy Scripture, in His prayer to His Father for His Disciples. Gathering all His children He prayed:

"I do not pray for them alone.
I pray also for those who will believe in Me
through their word,
that all may be one
as You, Father, are in Me, And I in You;
I pray that they may be (one) in Us,
that the world may believe that You sent me.
I have given them the glory You gave Me
that they may be one, as We are one -
I living in them, You living in Me -
that their unity may be complete.
So shall the world know that You sent Me,
and that You loved them as You loved Me."

(John 17:20-23)

Until this moment, these words did not have the meaning they have for us now, and we do not know why we never saw this before. It is very difficult to keep from crying; it is so clear. Jesus says *"I do not pray for them alone!"* The important word there is *alone*. No, He is praying also for those who will believe through the **word** of the *Disciples*. So, it was plain, Jesus was delegating the Apostles to carry on His teaching, to spread that Word given to Him and to us by the Father. He told the apostles, He would not leave them and us orphans, that He would be with us till the end of the world.

Then, in that same prayer in John's Gospel, Jesus commanded the Disciples to tell *all* the brothers and sisters that *in order for the world to believe that His Father sent Him*, they must be *united* not only with Him and His Father but with one another. Lord, forgive us; we've headed in just the opposite direction. Rather than telling the world to believe that His Father sent Him, the enemy began planting the seeds of heresy from the very beginning, putting doubt in the minds of the faithful that the Father sent Jesus, at all.

Now we find ourselves in the final days. There's so little time. The tide is turning in the other direction. Our dear Pope John Paul II tells us, by the year 2000, two-thirds of the world population will not know Jesus. It is estimated, that in eight years, there will be 6 billion people in the world. *That means that 4 billion people will not even know the name of Jesus.*

Are we so busy bickering, separated from one another centuries after the fact, not knowing why we broke up in the first place, that the world's hungry will never be satisfied by our Lord in His Eucharist and in His Word? In the Upper Room, the disciples sat huddled, petrified in fear. They were not *one* in mind, in heart and in spirit. They would not even accept Mary Magdalene's words that the Lord had risen. Even after some did, Thomas insisted he would not believe until *he* placed his hands into the Wounds of Jesus. Dear Lord, if we can't get a group of twelve together, how can we unite the whole church, and ultimately, the whole world?

We once said, "*We cheated them* (our brothers and sisters in Christ, as well as His chosen people, the Jews). *We never told them.*" If only we shared with the separated brethren *Who* is present in our Church and what goes on every day at Mass, then the tragic splinters of our Beloved Jesus' Cross would come back to their Church, the one Jesus so lovingly founded. Then we would have peace, and then we would have justice for all, and then *everyman*, no matter what race or creed, would be brother and sister to other brothers and sisters. We would become family, united as Jesus commanded in John 17:20. The lion would lay down with the lamb. And then, the world would *know* our Loving Father in Heaven.

There would no longer be a need for demonstrations, except in thanksgiving. There would no longer be people sleeping in the streets, nor parents helplessly watching their children dying of starvation. No, since everyman is our brother or sister, every child is *our* child by virtue of the unity that comes about when we are changed by the Lord, formed into a new creation, when we receive Holy Communion. By the very fact we are what we eat, then it is not *we* who love, but *the Lord* Who has changed us into His Image. As we begin to intimately know, in mind and heart, the Eucharist, as we listen to God through His Word, we see ourselves as we were originally meant to be, and then *metanoia* (change) comes about.

This was the plan. This is what the Lord wanted and wants for us. We were all born to live in the kingdom. But like our celestial cousins, the Angels, we were given Free Will. We had to make the decision, or rather our ancestors, Adam and Eve, had to make the decision in our name. *Eve ate the fruit; the rest is history.* That one act of selfishness and pride, committed thousands and thousands of years ago, changed the course of history forever. There's a truly important point to be made here. Do we really think about the consequences of the things we do before we do them? Do we consider how our actions will affect others, like that ripple in the stream? We have to borrow a poem by an English poet, which was used by Ernest Hemingway in his book, "For Whom the Bell Tolls", and then again by us in our book, "*We Came Back to Jesus*." It just fits so well with what we're trying to say here.

No man is an island, entire of itself;
Every man is a piece of the continent,
a part of the main;
If a clod be washed away by the sea,
Europe is the less,
As well as if a promontory were,
As well as if a Manor of thy friends
or of thine own were;
Any man's death diminishes me,
Because I am involved in mankind;
And therefore never send to know for whom the
bell tolls;
It tolls for thee." John Donne

Our actions are never just for ourselves. They are not even necessarily for our immediate circle of family and friends. Our son Richard used to say, *"What I do, I do to myself."* That is such a lie. He died of an overdose of drugs over twenty years ago, and his mother and I have never been the same. But I have to believe he didn't know the consequences of his actions. I can't believe he knew he was hurting us, anymore than I can believe that many of those who have catapulted us into heresy, division and destruction in the Church thought they would be hurting brothers and sisters a hundred or a thousand years after the fact. But we're dead just the same. As that Sixteenth Century poet knew well, we also have to know, *we are involved in mankind.*

Come with us now on a Journey of Faith. Join us as we find out how we allowed the enemy to get us into the mess we're in, and how the Lord continues to battle to get us out, how He keeps His Promise to us, against impossible odds: *"I will not leave you orphans; I will be with you until the end of time"*, because He, too, is involved with Mankind.

Right:
Pope John Paul II, our father on Earth. Jesus passed on foster fathership to the first Pope and to all 263 Popes who followed him, who have sat and now sits on the Chair of St. Peter.

Left:
Mary, the Mother of Christ's Church Her words,
"*I am the humble Handmaid of the Lord.*"
most exemplifies the role she desires.
In choosing St. John the Beloved, to stand in for us, Jesus gave His Mother to all.

How did we get here; why did it happen?

How did it all come about? What happened to cause the sorrowful devastation, which led to separation between brothers and sisters, that makes the war between the states (with brother killing brother) seem like a tea party? It started in *Genesis*, in the Garden of Eden.

When God created Adam and then Eve to be Adam's companion, He demanded *obedience*. He gave them a near-perfect world and a great deal of latitude. He really asked only one thing of them: *"You are free to eat from any of the trees of the garden except the tree of knowledge of good and evil."* (Gen. 2:16) God was not trying to trap them; He was not waiting behind a bush to catch them sinning. What loving earthly father would do that, no less the Perfect Father? God told them not to seek to decide good and evil themselves, like God, since they did not have this ability. God knew, and knows, that there are some things we cannot understand, and there are some we are better off not *trying* to understand. We don't necessarily have to understand; we need only to accept.

God is a Supreme Being

Satan called God a liar. God had told Adam and Eve if they ate from the tree in the center of the garden, they would die. Satan said that was not the reason. *"You certainly will not die"*, he said. *"No, God knows well that the moment you eat of it, your eyes will be opened and you will be like gods who know what is good and what is bad."*(Gen 3:1-8) [Sounds familiar, doesn't it? Very much like the heresies we will be writing about in this book.] He tempted Eve with *power* - *"You will not die! You can be like gods."* Isn't that what he's

15

telling us today? Right from the beginning, Satan tempted man with pride, power, and envy. And the tool he used was: *disobey*!

You can have it your way. You don't like the rules, change them, and if you can't, disobey! You can judge for yourself. You know what is good for you. You're not a child. If it feels good, then it's right. Leave it up to your conscience. There are extenuating circumstances. Every case is individual. God understands. There is no sin. There is no devil. You are God!

I will never forget my Science teacher in thè seventh grade. I did not have the privilege of attending Catholic School like Bob, our children and our grandson. I attended public school. But the Lord sent me an Irish Catholic Science teacher who taught me about God; yes, in a public school. She showed us a chart with the anatomy of a human body and said, "*Who but God could design anything as intricate and complex as the human body, all parts depending on the other, working together for life to flow through, feeding and sustaining the body?*"

Then, she turned the next huge sheet on the easel and there was a diagram of the Universe. She went into detail about how important it was that every planet and star remain within its own orbit, how if one were to deviate or go off course a minute fraction, there would be chaos, followed by total destruction of the Universe. It had to be God, Who is order, Who created such a perfectly planned world. I never forgot her words. I remember her name; it was Miss Shea. I cannot remember any of my other teachers, or *their* names. Miss Shea taught me, there is a Loving God Who, from the very beginning, carefully planned a world where His children, its inhabitants, would be happy. He gave them Free Will, not to sin, as Bishop Sheen said, but free will to love God freely! He loves us so, He wants us to love Him for Himself, not because we have to. And so, he gave us Free Will!

God is the perfect Creator. He left absolutely nothing to chance. If you were to look at that chart of the human anatomy, you would see that He considered every possibility. He gave us body temperatures which adjusted, based on climate variations. He gave us different blood, based on where we lived, and thickness of skin, if we were Eskimos, and on and on. Mother Angelica says that the computer it takes to operate the human body, *would take buildings to house!* That's how much He cared about us.

God Promised a Redeemer

Even as Eve was eating the fruit, the plan for our salvation was already in motion. When He threw Adam and Eve out of the Garden of Eden, He told them what our lives would be like because of their selfishness and pride. He said to Eve, "*I will intensify the pangs of your childbearing; in pain shall you bring forth children.*" (Gen 3:16) He said to Adam, "*Cursed be the ground because of you! In toil shall you eat its yield all the days of your life......By the sweat of your face shall you get bread to eat, until you return to the ground from which you were taken. For you are dirt, and to dirt you shall return.*" (Gen 3:17-19) He banished them from the Garden of Eden and the Tree of life. (Gen 3:23-24)

But even as He was doing this, as He was chastising us with His left Hand, with His right Hand, He was raising up another woman to be an instrument of our Redemption. Speaking of Mary, he said to the serpent, "*I will put enmity between you and the woman, and between your offspring and hers; He will strike at your head, while you strike at His Heel.*" (Gen 3:15) In this statement, God gave us hope. He gave us the first promise of a Redeemer.[1]

It was so obvious that the same God who spoke to Adam and Eve in Genesis was working in the life of Jesus. Everything Jesus did, had to do with our Salvation, our

---

[1]footnote to Gen 3:15 - New American Bible

Redemption, our well being. But Satan tried to block Jesus in every way.

Forgiveness of Sins

Jesus walked the earth, first saying *"Your sins are forgiven."* And through His Words, the mercy of Heaven was opened; healing came about. The blind could see, the lame walked, the deaf heard and the mute spoke. Now, *knowing that sin is a very real thing*, and without the forgiveness of the sins which separate us from God we cannot be healed, He granted the Apostles, and those to whom they would commission[2], the Faculties[3] to listen to and forgive sins in His Name[4]. *Was Satan upset!* Not only had Jesus committed the unforgivable crime of dying for His *persecutors* as well as those who wept at His Cross, but Jesus was leaving the power to forgive sins to those same Apostles who ran away and hid from the Temple Guards. How very much Satan hated them! Where did they come off to forgive sins!

And so Satan planted the seed of doubt from the very beginning, that Sin could be forgiven by Jesus through man. Early heresies rejected Confession and forgiveness.

Mary, the Mother of God, our best friend

God sent His Son to be born of a mortal! That was the first slap in the face to Satan, one of the reasons he broke

---

[2]Matthew 28:18-20 - *"Jesus said to them, 'I have been given all authority in Heaven and on earth. Go then, to all people everywhere and make them my disciples; baptize them in the name of the Father, the Son and the Holy Spirit, and teach them to obey all I have commanded you.'"*

[3]Canonical Faculties - Explicit powers granted as authorization to enable a person to act validly or at least licitly. Such powers are granted by the Holy See or by a Bishop or prelate, and must be authenticated. Most commonly, we hear faculties referred to the permission given to priests to administer the Sacrament of Reconciliation - Catholic Encyclopedia - Broderick

[4]John 20:23 - *"Receive the Holy Spirit; whose sins you forgive, they are forgiven; whose sins you do not forgive, they are not forgiven."*

away from God in the first place. That Jesus chose to be
born of a humble virgin (*"For He has looked upon His servant
in her lowliness."*), put him into a tailspin. But now Jesus, this
Son born of woman, is passing His Divine rights[5] to mortals,
to sinners, to men who would hide and run when the going
got rough, when He needed them. *This was just too much!*

Is it not strange that Mother Mary is another part of the
True Church which Jesus founded that separates us from
our brothers and sisters in Christ!   And how did that
happen! Lucifer, who is the master of confusion, has spread
lies that Catholics worship their Mother Mary. Not only is
this *not* the teaching of the Holy Catholic Church, but it is
most emphatically *not* the intention nor the wish of the
Mother of that Church. Her words, *"I am the handmaid of
the Lord"* most exemplify her desired role. She is the moon
with no light of her own, but a reflection through which her
Son's Light shines, leading *all* the children of her family to
eternal life in the Father. Again, we say *all*. Jesus died for
all, unconditionally. On the Cross, He did not say *"Here is
your Mother."* for only those few who were there, crying for
His pain. No, in choosing one of our first Bishops St. John
the Beloved, to stand in for us, He gave His Mother to *all*.

Our Lord having created us, speaks to us, guides us in a
manner we can understand simply if we do not let the Satan
of pride and confusion block our path to Him. *We* did not
choose our earthly mother. What makes us presume we can
choose, accept or reject the Mother, Jesus left us, His very
own Mother? As with our earthly mother, no even more
than with our earthly mother, although we reject her, malign
her, refuse to turn to her, Mother Mary is always present,
available, ready to catch us when we fall, hold us in her arms
when we feel all alone, and lead us to her waiting and most

---

[5]Luke 5:21 - *"The teachers of the Law and the Pharisees began to say
to themselves, 'Who is this man who speaks such blasphemy! God is the
only one who can forgive sins!'"*

loving Son. This is the Mother we love. This is the Mother we want to share. This is the Mother Satan hates.

Salvation through the Cross

There has always been the controversy of the Cross. Lucifer doesn't want us to think about the Cross. Even as he was taunting Jesus to come down from the Cross, he was plotting. He knew the Cross would always be a powerful weapon against him. He had to find a way to discredit it.

Did he say "*O.K. Fool, die for them. But You will see; they will never stick together. I will continue my work begun in the Garden of Eden. I will fill them with pride. I will make promises to them. You gave them the lesson of obedience and sacrifice, of suffering and forgiveness. All this involves pain and sorrow. All this points to the Cross. I will ridicule the Cross. Although I could not get You to come down from the Cross, I will strip You from the Cross. No longer will they appreciate the price You so foolishly paid for them. I will tell them not to look at the Crucified Jesus; look only upon the Risen Jesus. He suffered for you; it's all over; do anything you want. By His Wounds you were saved. The Cross is ancient history. You don't need to suffer. You're supposed to be happy! Don't listen to Jesus' words 'My Peace is My gift to you. I do not give it to you as the world gives peace.' That was for another time. He really wants you to be happy. If it feels good, then it isn't a sin.*

"*Sin, what is sin,*" he cajoles, "*just another way for you to be controlled by the prudish morality of a few. You are not children. That may be a viable way to try to control the behavior of children with the idea they are offending and separating themselves from a Living and Loving God when they sin, but that's not for intelligent adults, like you and me.*"

And yet, did not Jesus say unless we become like little children, we will not inherit the Kingdom of God? "*Sin, what is sin? There's no such thing as sin.*" And so, we make God a liar. Satan mockingly asks, through Pontius Pilate: "*What is truth?*" Satan tells us we do not have to accept the Cross. And yes, my precious brothers and sisters, one of the signs that separate us so much is our Lord Crucified on the *Cross.*

The shrill, piercing cry of the aging Archbishop Fulton J. Sheen ricocheted off the walls of the Church of St. Agnes, in New York City, on Good Friday, April 8, 1977.

"*If you're the Son of God, come down from that Cross. Come down and we'll believe.' Sure they'll believe; they'll believe anything, just no Cross. No mortification, no self-denial.*" He continued, "*Many say 'I'll believe anything! I'll believe He's divine! I'll believe in His Church; I'll believe in His pontiff, only no Cross! no sacrifice!' George Bernard Shaw said of the Cross; 'It's that that bars the way.' Sure it bars the way. It bars the way to hell.*"

Could our dear Archbishop Sheen, whom we firmly believe will be honored by the Church he loved so dearly, by being added to the Communion of Saints one day, have seen the future? Could he see the suffering, our Lord Jesus would have to endure at the hands of those who claimed to love Him? In Bishop Sheen's last years, did the Lord give him an insight of the *real Agony* Jesus suffered in the Garden, the *Agony of the great Apostasy,* which would claim such a stronghold in our Church towards the end of the Twentieth Century? Is that why Archbishop Sheen cried out so painfully for his Lord, who is tortured terribly, by those who love Him? Is that the third secret of Fatima?

The Holy Spirit

Jesus told the Apostles, He will suffer and die. Upon seeing their distress, He consoled them with the Good News that when He left, the Holy Spirit, the Paraclete, would come. "*It is much better that I go. If I fail to go, the Paraclete will never come to you.*" (John 16:7) He left the Church in Peter's care, even though He knew Peter would deny Him three times. Peter had answered to Jesus' "*And who do you say I am?*", "You are the Messiah." and that was enough for Jesus. He knew only the Father could have told this to Peter. And so, Jesus founded His Church. In order that Peter would have the courage to live and die for His Church, He sent down the Holy Spirit, as He had promised. The Holy Spirit empowered Peter and then the others, Jesus' followers, our first Bishops. And they would pass on that empowerment to the priests who would follow them.

The Pope, our Father on Earth

Jesus knew that a family needs a father. He had an earthly father, His foster father St. Joseph. Although Jesus' Heavenly Father is, was and will always be omnipotent, King of Kings, He sent Jesus an earthly father to whom He would be *obedient*! Jesus, Who was *God-Man*, obeyed an earthly Mother and foster *father*. God had entrusted this mortal, St. Joseph, with the awesome responsibility to care for, guide and protect His Son! Loving us, He, through the wisdom of the Second Person of the Holy Trinity, our Jesus, passed on this foster fathership to the first Pope and to all 263 Popes who followed him, who have sat and now sit in the chair of Peter. And yet, this is one of the forms of obedience that separate us. How could this be? It was one of Jesus' last acts, leaving His Church and all its Faculties to the Apostles who broke bread with Him at the Last Supper. And yet, the Pope, and the hierarchy of the Church was one of the first things attacked by Martin Luther. But towards the end of his lifetime, he said, "*I tried to get rid of one pope; I now have over 100 popes.*"

The Body and Blood of Christ, the Eucharist

Now, let us speak of another separation: the Wounds of Jesus: His Body and Blood, the Holy Eucharist. To give some in our Church the benefit of the doubt, in an attempt to foster ecumenism, we no longer mention the *Sacrifice* of the Mass. No, we call it *celebration*! Yes, it is true, that when the priest breaks off a piece of the Consecrated Host, Our Lord, present in His Body, Blood, Soul and Divinity, is Risen.

But how about His Crucifixion! We are taught that prior to this holy act, when the priest breaks the Host in half, this is the reenactment of the Crucifixion, the ongoing act of Redemption. Since our Lord is, was and always will be, since we cannot lock our Lord into the limitations of time and space, then each Mass is *ongoing* Calvary and Easter Sunday. *Bread, Blessed and Broken.* One of the key words here is *Broken.* Visualize the *snap*, if you will, the *break* that takes place when our priest breaks the Host in two. One day, a priest, ridiculing the reverence of those who try to pick up all the particles of the Host at the end of the Mass, said to us, *"Are you aware how many millions of particles that Host breaks into when I snap that Host in two? Millions of Jesus burst all over the altar?"* He was saying it in an irreverent way. But think about that image. Consider the Sacrifice, as your Lord bursts into millions of pieces.

Recently, a priest-historian told us, the early Church would not have lasted the first hundred years if it were not for the Eucharist. The Eucharist is the strength of our Church. And yet, we were told by a theologian that the Eucharist is not necessary for our Salvation. Far be it from us to doubt him, but one thing we know, it sure is necessary for our *survival!* We derive *nourishment* from the Eucharist; we derive *life's blood.* The Body and Blood of our Lord Jesus Christ is Food for the journey. In the Old Testament, the Angel brought Elijah food for the journey. Jesus gives us food, without which we will never make the Journey. Jesus is God! We are united with our God through the hands of the priest at Communion. It's not a community party; it's union with our God. St. Augustine tells us when we eat the Host, we do not consume Jesus; *He consumes us*! And as St. Paul told us in 1 Corinthians 16, *"Because we eat of the same*

Loaf, and drink of the same Cup, we are the body of Christ." It is not the other way round, as many would have you believe. Paul is telling that *the eating of the Body and Blood of our Savior* is what makes us the Body of Christ.

Naturally, this would be Satan's major target, and so it was. From the very beginning, there have been doubts as to the real presence of Jesus in the Eucharist. Heresies cropped up from the first century, denouncing the Real Presence of Jesus in the Eucharist. As we cry for those who Satan has suckered to do his handiwork, we grieve for those souls they will take with them. **Ezekiel 34** comes to mind:

"....*Woe to the shepherds of Israel who have been pasturing themselves! Should not shepherds rather pasture sheep? You have fed off their milk, worn their wool, and slaughtered their fatlings, but the sheep you have not pastured....So they were scattered for lack of a shepherd, and became food for all the wild beasts.*

"....*Therefore, shepherds, hear the word of the Lord. As I live, says the Lord God, because my sheep have been given over to pillage, and because my sheep have become food for every wild beast, for lack of a shepherd....I swear I am coming against those shepherds. I will claim my sheep from them and put a stop to their shepherding my sheep so that they may no longer pasture themselves. I will save my sheep, that they may no longer be food for their mouths.....The lost I will seek out, the strayed I will bring back, the injured I will bind up, the sick I will heal (but the sleek and the strong I will destroy).*"

But do not for a moment lose heart, folks. There is something you must know up front. For every positive move God makes, Satan tries to block it with a negative move. And every time Satan tries to block God, God outmaneuvers Satan. That is so exciting. That's what we want to share with you in the book, Check and Checkmate. Praise Jesus in all things!

Above: ***Adam and Eve being cast out of Paradise***

Right:
Jesus hands the keys to the Kingdom of Heaven to Saint Peter. Jesus said, ***"You are Rock, and on this rock I will build My Church and the jaws of death shall not prevail against it."***

Above: *The Last Supper - Vatican Museum - Jesus directed His Apostles* how *to bring Him to the Church, until He returned.*

Below*: Abraham tied his son Issac and placed him on the altar. Rock enclosed in the Dome of the Rock Mosque - Jerusalem*

While Jesus Walked the Earth

Right from the beginning, even before Christ died for us and rose from the dead, Jesus and His Church came under attack.

Jesus went about forgiving men's sins. The Pharisees and the Saducees could not accept this. How could He forgive sins; only God could forgive sins! They could not allow this to continue.

When a man is free from sin and *its* cancer, then and then *only* can he be free from *physical* pain. Jesus with His blinding Mirror of Love brought *Light* into the darkness of sin that was eating away at the society of His time, and Lucifer had to put out that Light. Sin is always done in the dark[1].

Our Heavenly Father, seeing the suffering and pain of His children, sent His only begotten Son to earth to be sacrificed, for the redemption of men's sins. When God asked Abraham to sacrifice his son out of love and obedience to Him:

"...*God said: 'Take your son Isaac, your only one, whom you love, and go to the land of Moriah. There you shall offer him up as a holocaust on a height that I will point out to you..*'"

"...*Abraham took the wood for the holocaust and laid it on his son's shoulders.*"

Abraham tied up his son Isaac and placed him on top of the altar. As he prepared to sacrifice him, an Angel of the Lord called to him from Heaven: "*Abraham, Abraham!*"

Abraham replied: "*Yes, Lord.*"

"'*Do not lay your hand on the boy,' said the messenger. 'Do not do the least thing to him. I know now how devoted you are to God, since you did not withhold from me your own beloved son.*'"

---

[1]Archbishop Fulton J. Sheen

"So, he went and took a ram and offered it up as a holocaust in place of his son."(Gen 22)

Our God, in His compassion, did not require of Abraham that which He, out of Supreme Love for us, would later do, see His Most Precious, His only begotten Son take the place of the spotless lamb and be sacrificed for the salvation of the world.

Was Lucifer angry! Die for men's sins that they might be saved from eternal damnation? He was livid! Do you remember how he tried to get Jesus to come down from the Cross? At a Good Friday Service, Archbishop Fulton J. Sheen passionately boomed the words of those who mocked Jesus *"Come down from the Cross!"* Lucifer knew the value of Jesus dying for His enemies as well as His friends. This God-Man Jesus was not in keeping with the lie Lucifer was selling, that of the God of anger, punishment, fire and brimstone, the God Who didn't care, Who left us alone except to catch us in sin so He could punish us.

And so, Lucifer went after the weak link in the chain of Apostles, Jesus had chosen to follow Him. Lucifer plied and manipulated Judas with *social justice*: *"Feed the poor's stomachs; do not be worried about their souls. Has any one ever seen a soul? But you can see a man's swelling stomach."* Does this sound familiar?

As Judas was stealing from Jesus and the Apostles, he was crying out for social justice. *Judas was a thief![2]* Recall when he rebuked the woman for anointing Jesus:

"Six days before Passover Jesus came to Bethany, the village of Lazarus whom Jesus had raised from the dead....Mary brought a pound of costly perfume made from genuine aromatic nard[3], with which she anointed Jesus' Feet. Then she dried His Feet with her hair, and the house was filled with the

---

[2]Archbishop Fulton J. Sheen

[3]nard-an extremely costly unguent.(Dictionary of the Bible-John L. McKensie, S.J.)

ointment's fragrance. Judas Iscariot, one of His disciples (the one about to hand Him over), protested: 'Why was not this perfume sold? It could have brought three hundred silver pieces, and the money given to the poor.' (He did not say this out of concern for the poor, but because he was a thief. He held the purse, and used to help himself to what was deposited there.) To this Jesus replied: 'Leave her alone. Let her keep it against the day they prepare Me for burial.''(Matt 13:1-8)

Judas, when Jesus said these words "*against the day they prepare Me for burial*", did not your heart melt? When He looked at you with His unconditional Love, did you not cry inside for the betrayal that would cause Him so much pain? Did you look away from His innocent questioning eyes, pleading for your soul: *How have I wronged you? I only wanted to love you. But fear not, I will show you the extent of My love. I will open My arms even wider to embrace you in My Love, on the Cross! Yes, even to you who have sinned against Me; just ask for forgiveness. My Mercy longs to forgive you.*

"*Then one of the Twelve whose name was Judas Iscariot went off to the chief priests and said, 'What are you willing to give me if I hand Him over to you?' They paid him thirty pieces of silver...*"(Matt. 26:14)

Judas sold Jesus for thirty pieces of silver! Had he become so enamored with the silver, so involved with the *monetary* cost of spreading the Word that he lost sight of the cost Jesus spoke of, that of complete *anawhim*, abandonment to the Will of the Father? Had he begun to worship the purse he held, and the *honor and power* connected with the holding of *the purse strings*? Have not Jesus' trusted friends been selling out Jesus to His enemies for honor and power for the last 2000 years?

Lucifer could not kill Jesus on the Cross. No grave could contain Him. Lucifer and his pawns could not erase Him from the face of the earth, whether by lies or deception. They tried to destroy every semblance of a Shrine to our

Lord and His life on earth, and still we remember Him.
They made bloody examples of those who dared not deny
Him, and still we dare to love and follow Him. The world
has forgotten His enemies; it will never forget Him!

Archbishop Fulton J. Sheen said Judas began his plot to
betray Jesus, when Jesus gave us His Eucharistic Doctrine at
Capharnaum, calling Himself the Bread of Life:

"*I myself am the living bread come down from
Heaven. If anyone eats this bread, he shall live forever;
the bread I will give is My Flesh, for the life of the
world.*'

*...Jesus said to them: 'Let Me solemnly assure you, if
you do not eat the Flesh of the Son of Man and drink
His Blood, you have no life in you.*'"(John 6:51)

Then, at the Last Supper, when Jesus directed His
Apostles, *how* they would bring Him to the faithful until He
returned, "*Judas completed his betrayal*[4]":

"*The devil had already induced Judas, son of Simon, to
hand Him (Jesus) over.*" (John 13:2)

Archbishop Fulton J. Sheen said Judas could not bear
belief in the Eucharist. Was his problem the same that we
will see throughout our Church's 2000 year history? Was
Jesus not the God he had hoped for? Jesus was a God of
Peace, a God of *turn the other cheek; love your enemies.* Was
this the God he had been waiting for, fighting for? Was this
the God Who would save the Jewish people? No, he wanted
a God who would fight and free the Jews from captivity,
physical captivity, a conquering hero kind of God.

Jesus was talking about eternal salvation - *tomorrow*
and forever. Judas wanted freedom, *now*; glory, *now*! He
knew Jesus; he walked with Jesus; he ate at Jesus' table;
Jesus taught him; Jesus *chose* him. How could he betray
Him? Are we any better being silent when we know false

---

[4] Archbishop Fulton J. Sheen

gods are being preached? Are we not betraying Jesus? When we are double-talked into believing our Lord's death and Resurrection is a *story* more than a *reality*, do we stand by and do nothing, as they did while our Lord was being nailed to the cross? When the enemy *pride* tempts us to choose the *humanistic* approach, replacing the one true God for a *power* within, and we buy it, are we any better than the Jews who rejected Jesus, and chose Barabbas instead? *We* know Jesus, in His Word, in His Body and Blood, Soul and Divinity as received in the most Holy Eucharist. He sent His Holy Spirit down upon us. We stand on Holy Ground, in a Church made holy by the blood of martyrs who died rather than deny Christ and His Church. We stand on a heritage bought by the faithfulness of 2000 years of Catholics professing, and living, the Nicene Creed:

> *We believe in one God,*
> *the Father, the Almighty,*
> *maker of heaven and earth,*
> *of all that is seen and unseen.*
> *We believe in one Lord, Jesus Christ,*
> *the only Son of God,*
> *eternally begotten of the Father*
> *God from God, Light from Light*
> *true God from true God,*
> *begotten, not made, one in Being with the Father.*
> *Through Him all things were made.*
> *For us men and for our salvation*
> *He came down from heaven:*
> *by the power of the Holy Spirit*
> > *He was born of the Virgin Mary, and*
> > *became Man.*[5]

---

[5]All are required to bow at the words beginning with "*by the power of the Holy Spirit*" up to "*and became man.*"

For our sake He was crucified under Pontius Pilate;
He suffered, died and was buried.
On the third day he rose again
*   in fulfillment of the Scriptures;*
He ascended into Heaven
and is seated at the right hand of the Father.
He will come again in glory to judge the
*   living and the dead,*
*   and His kingdom will have no end.*
We believe in the Holy Spirit, the Lord,
*   the giver of life,*
Who proceeds from the Father and the Son.
With the Father and the Son He is worshiped
*   and glorified.*
He has spoken through the Prophets.
We believe in one holy catholic and apostolic
Church.
We acknowledge one baptism for the
*   forgiveness of sins.*
We look for the Resurrection of the dead,
*   and the life of the world to come. Amen*

With the disciples at Emmaus, who said "*do our hearts not burn*," our hearts burn as we repeat these words of faith that have echoed from the Hill of Calvary to the catacombs of Rome to the bloodstained streets and jails of Christian Martyrs. Is your vision blurred by tears instead of clouded by false promises and teachings?

The attacks on Jesus began while He was still on earth. They have continued down through the centuries. Would they have stopped immediately if we had stood up for our Lord, if we had refused to participate in the bashing of our Lord and His Church? Would the attacks on our Church be going on today if we would have stood up anywhere along the line, if we would now stand up and say:

This is my God you're torturing, killing, spitting at. We have had enough! We will not stand by and see you hurt our Lord anymore! Stop! We say No! No more attacks on His Eucharist! No more attacks on His Word! No more attacks on His Mother! No more attacks on His Church!

Lord, we will no longer stand idly by like the spectators who watched You die on the Cross! We will not run from the mission You have given us, Lord, like our first Pope Peter! We, like Peter before us, ask Your forgiveness, Jesus. We, like St. Francis before us, are ready to walk through burning coals for You!

We are giving notice to the world: We are the Church; We are the Mystical Body of Christ; We will not allow anyone to talk against our Lord and His Church! We give notice to those of you who have betrayed the trust, our Lord has passed on to you, you who have betrayed His Church. Well, no more! *He* will shepherd us through His Vicar and the loyal bishops, who are in union with him. Mother Mary is rallying troops behind Pope John Paul II. With him at the head of our army, we will defend our Church! We are ready to live for our Church! We are ready to die for our Church!

Above: ***Chapel of the Miraculous Medal, Paris***
Below: ***The Annunciation - Mother Mary recognized the Angel.***
Shrine of the Holy House of Loreto, Italy

Attacks from Within

When we began writing our book, *This is My Body, This is My Blood...Miracles of the Eucharist*, we did not know we were writing a defense of the Real Presence of our Lord Jesus in the Holy Eucharist. We were just trying to share the gifts we discovered on our travels to the Shrines in Europe, the Treasure we have in our Church. No sooner was our first book published than we became aware of God's reason for pushing us to write about His Miracles of the Eucharist. We started to hear from the faithful, of the abuses against the Eucharist within and without the Church. It was as if our senses became raw. Everything we saw or heard about the Eucharist was as if there were spotlights on our Lord in His Body, Blood, Soul and Divinity. *Then*, we began to know the Sorrowful Heart of our Lord Jesus. We could see what He saw: His children, those He had died for, lambs being led to slaughter. For if our Lord is not truly present in the Holy Eucharist, then we are totally dependent on the Lord we find in our brothers and sisters. And what happens when we fail to find this Jesus we seek and need? Do we look elsewhere? That's the best of the bad news, that we seek our Lord in another church. But is that really what Satan is after? We no longer think so. We believe he wants us to feel hopeless. He wants us to believe that we are not children of the Father; that the Bible is just filled with stories, for a particular time, to govern people's behavior; that Jesus was never born, that He never died, that there is no God, that we are gods.

Where are the attacks coming from? The most unlikely places. That's what is so devious about Satan and his plan to destroy the Church. We grew up believing: if the priest said it, it is so. You could bank on his word, on his homilies that they were in communion with the Church, that they were based on the Magisterium. Now, we are hearing things like: *"What is a Magisterium?"* Referring to our Pope's Universal Catechism, *priests are saying, "He sounds like he has been asleep for the last twenty years."* I thought we were supposed to respect and obey the words of the Pope as our "Sweet Christ on earth[1]".

To give you an example of the deviousness of Satan, we believe he is using very unsuspecting priests and sisters to do his dirty work. And the poor lambs that they are teaching are mesmerized by sweet smiles and sweet words; nine good words and they are on the way to heresy with the tenth. I was giving a talk at a gathering of women dedicated to Mother Mary. The priest said that at the time of the Visitation, Mary's parents quickly spirited her out of town, so she wouldn't be stoned. Again inferring she went in fear for her life, he continued, *"You bet she went in haste."* I did not bother to contradict the priest because I knew our Mother would be defended when I got up to speak. Mary would have her day in court! I said: *"Mother Mary knew and recognized the Angel. She had been waiting for her Messiah to be born of a virgin. The scriptures had told her so. In her humility, she was amazed that it was she who had been chosen: 'He has looked upon His servant in her lowliness.'*(Luke 1:48) *But because she had spent her whole life in prayer, when the Angel Gabriel brought her the Good News, she was open to receive it, and act upon it. She did not focus on herself. She did not boast, 'I am the virgin who is bearing the Son of God.' Instead, believing the miracle that her aged cousin was with child, she went in haste to help her. Our Lady was not showing! She was not far enough along to show."*

My problem with this and other supposed *humanization* of our Lady is, we reduce her to our level of sinfulness, *she*

---

[1]St. Catherine of Siena (Saints and other Powerful Women in the Church)

who was not only spotless as the Mother of God would have to be, but who was *Immaculately Conceived*. The *rationalization* that is used about Mother Mary is so illogical! By placing this imperfection of sin upon our Lady, we are proposing an impossible scientific fact. We are alleging that you can get perfect Fruit from a diseased tree. The most humble farmer will tell you this is impossible.

One day, when we went into a Blessed Sacrament Chapel to pray, we discovered sheets of paper containing innocent prayers to God with the heading "*Mantras*". Surely, it wasn't the prayers that disturbed us. It was the word *Mantras*. The children in this C.C.D. class were young and impressionable; they will remember the word *Mantras*. After all, they learned it in church; it must be a Church teaching. And so, when someday someone tells them they can buy a Mantra[2], or teaches them a mantra, they will remember what they read in a religious education book: "*One kind of centering prayer that you might want to use is called a mantra.*" It goes on to say that: "*You have probably noticed that mantras are short prayers that start by addressing God.*" Have we not forgotten *what* the word Mantra has historically stood for, and is associated with till today! Definition of *Mantra* in the dictionary is: "*Hinduism - a hymn or portion of text, especially from the Veda, chanted or intoned as an incantation or prayer.*" Looking up the word *Veda* in the dictionary, we find: *Veda: Any of four ancient, sacred books of Hinduism, consisting of psalms, chants, sacred formulas etc.* Our eyes traveled down a couple of words in the dictionary and we found: *Vedanta - a system of Hindu monistic or pantheistic philosophy based on the Veda. Pantheism, teaches that God is not a personality, but that all laws, forces, manifestations, of the self existing universe are God.*

---

[2]A Mantra can go from $1500 up, according to who is giving you the Mantra. It is a tool of Modern day Hinduism under the title of *New Age*.

"A radical heresy, Pantheism had taken hold of most of Europe. Pantheism claims that man is on a level with God, equal to Him. God is not a Being, but is manifested in all the forces of the universe. It all began as a belief in 1705, when the term Pantheism was originally coined by J. Toland in England. Originally only the intelligentsia understood and accepted the heresy. But by the French Revolution, it had sifted down to the common man. They were led to believe, and accept, that because of the great strides being made by man, as a result of the Industrial Revolution, they didn't need God anymore.

"Pantheism is a direct contradiction of the centuries old belief of Catholics regarding the Immaculate Conception of Mary. Our belief, that only Jesus and Mary were born without sin, clashed with the new heresy of man being equal with God, which had caused confusion and division. There was need to make the truth clear to the faithful.[3]"

Mary brought the point across in the Chapel of the Miraculous Medal, when she appeared to a little postulant, St. Catherine Labouré, and declared she was *"The Immaculate Conception"*. Pope Pius IX officially proclaimed that which we have always believed, the *doctrine* of the Immaculate Conception on December 8, 1854. In case there was any doubt left as to the invalidity of *Pantheism*, Mary appeared again, in 1858, only now to a poor, simple peasant girl named Bernadette Soubirous, in a remote village of Lourdes, high in the Pyrenees Mountains, and stated once again: *"I am The Immaculate Conception"*. In 1846, our country was consecrated to our *Lady of the Immaculate Conception* and she was declared patroness of the United States. Stone upon stone have risen from the cornerstone that was laid in 1913, and now a National Shrine of the Immaculate Conception looms high in Washington D.C., in

---

[3]from chapter: "Paris, 1830: Mary and Her Miraculous Medal."-in Bob and Penny Lord's book: *The Many Faces of Mary*

the Capital of our country, the same country that allowed an atheist[4] to practically wipe out the Name of God in our nation. But she, like so many bed-fellows of Satan, cannot wipe out He Who is, He Who was, and He Who will always be. And this monument to God's Mother rises high among the national monuments of a country that promised religious freedom, and somewhere along the way got lost, to shout to all people for all time that we are really a country founded under God.

Mother Mary has been appearing[5], at different times, in different crises, bringing the same message to her children: *We have a personal God Who loves us.* Why is she appearing in countries all over the world, today? Is it because the threat of *Pantheism* is here, once again? Please read on as you turn the pages of this book, and do as St. Augustine was told to do and did: *"Tolle Lege!"* Take and read!

Pantheism negates the essential difference between God and His Creation; rather, it promotes, and we hear this so very often in our highly intellectual society: *the cosmic God*

---

[4]Madelyn Murray O'Hare

[5]Please note that if any of the apparitions are someday completely discredited, this does not mean that you or anyone else is obliged to believe that any special graces you obtained there are false. Our Lord and our Lady are infinitely capable of bringing good out of evil, and can easily reward those who seek them with a sincere heart, even at the site of a false apparition.   For example, there are people who have experienced the grace of conversion while praying to our Lady at a shrine which is considered questionable. This experience has convinced some that the visions are true, but that does not necessarily follow, and a dogmatic assertion of their veracity against the teaching authority of the Church would be a classic misunderstanding and misuse of the grace received. One must always make a distinction between one's own experiences at the site of a supposed apparition, and the specific claims made by the visionary (or visionaries) at that location. While there is obviously a correlation between the two, that correlation is neither necessary nor in itself sufficient proof of the authenticity of the larger claims.

Who *is found only in, and revealed solely through, created objects and things.* As you will read in this book, man has been trying to lower God to his sinful, lowly station from almost the beginning of time. The danger of Catholic C.C.D. books advocating terminology that smacks of Pantheism under the guise of sound Catholic teaching, is that it ultimately leads to *man*, and away from *God*.

A priest was giving a workshop on the Eucharist. He handed everyone a questionnaire; it asked the *four* necessary elements required to celebrate the Eucharist. We were having difficulty coming up with what the fourth element could be that he then placed *first!* He informed us the correct answer was: 1) the people, 2) the priest, 3) the Word, and then last 4) the Eucharistic Elements. He went on to stress that not any one was more important than the other. Is this not a heresy! Now, if I recall correctly what is essential for the Mass to be valid is the Word, the Eucharist, and the priest who summons the Holy Spirit down upon the bread and wine, and through his consecrated hands they are transformed into the Body, Blood, Soul and Divinity of our Lord Jesus Christ. In no way are we belittling the importance of the faithful participating in the Mass. We are simply stating that it is our belief that a Mass celebrated by a priest on a side Altar in St. Peter's Basilica, without anyone else present, although not preferable, is still valid and holy!

Let us quote from the documents of Vatican Council II:

"...Christ is always present in His Church, especially in her liturgical celebrations. He is present in the sacrifice of the Mass, not only in the person of His minister, 'the same now offering, through the ministry of priests, Who formerly offered Himself on the Cross', but especially under the Eucharistic Species. By His Power He is present in the Sacraments, so that when a man baptizes it is really Christ Himself Who baptizes. He is present in His Word, since it is Himself Who speaks when the Holy Scriptures are read in church. He is present, lastly, when the

Church prays and sings, for He promised: 'Where two or three are gathered together in My Name, there I am in the midst of them.'"

The priest kept referring to the Host as "*Eucharistic wine and bread.*" I beg to differ with him. For if the Consecrated Host is still wine, and not the Body and Blood of Jesus Christ, then how do you explain the following? I have been diagnosed by a doctor as being Hypoglycemic. I was told that the smallest amount of wine, for me, was like drinking straight arsenic. You see, when I drank even a third of a glass of wine, I had a reaction to it. I told the doctor my tongue would swell and I could barely articulate. Now I did not feel intoxicated, that is giddy or happy or angry or any of those signs. I felt woozy, like I was losing my equilibrium. My brain felt as if it had swelled to twice its size. The doctor assured me, my brain did swell when I had even the smallest portion of wine. I have had the joy of being a Eucharistic Minister for almost sixteen years. When I have been Minister of the *Blood*, there were times when I had to finish what was left of the Blood. *Never,* but *never* have I experienced any of the above symptoms in any shape, size or manner.

Now, I am not in any way disputing the Church's teaching that our Lord comes to us under the *appearance* of bread and wine. But I contend, *as Councils of the Church have proclaimed, again and again, that the Consecrated Host is no longer bread, that real change has come about, and that the wine is no longer wine, but real Blood, the Blood that Christ shed on the Cross.* If we call the Consecrated Host *bread,* then has change come about? If change has not come about, then, as with some of our separated brothers and sisters in Christ who contend they have the Eucharist but believe it is a symbol, it's all right for us to throw away the Hosts that are left over. Because after all, it's only bread! Then why Tabernacles? Is He present Body, Blood, Soul and Divinity in the Tabernacle?   Why exposition of the Blessed Sacrament?   Why do the faithful come at all hours of the day and night to keep the Blessed Sacrament company?   Are we worshiping a piece of bread?   Are we worshiping, as some of our non-Catholic brethren believe, an idol, as we kneel before a Monstrance?   Or are we worshiping our Lord in the Holy Eucharist Who is present before us in the Monstrance?

As we prayed for the Lord to share *His Eyes* with us that we might see His priest with *His* Eyes, the thought that came to me is "*Oh Father when did you lose the gift you were given on the day of your ordination?   Will you remain in the Priesthood, or will you leave?*" For, as Bishop Sheen said, our priests are not leaving because they are lonely, or the life is too hard, or they desire the companionship of a wife and a family.   They have lost their faith in the Real Presence of Jesus in the Eucharist.

If it is not bad enough to hear the Eucharist belittled and mocked when we hear a priest say that the words attributed to Jesus were put into His Mouth to teach the people of that time, what do we have left?   If the Word is not Jesus' Words, His Teaching to us; if these are not the true circumstances of His Life, then is the Bible true?   Was our Lord Resurrected?   St. Paul says if this is not so, we are all fools.   Was our Lord crucified for the redemption of our sins?   If not, we are not forgiven and we have no hope.   Was our Lord ever born?   Was there an Adam and Eve?   Is there a devil?   Is there a God?   Oh, sweet Jesus they have taken our God from us.   We are all alone!

The area upon which the Altar of Sacrifice stands, we have been told, is no more important than where the congregation sits.   The priest continued; he could not understand why some priests insist on special carpeting and giving it special reverence.   We cry out: *Father, is this not the Altar of Sacrifice, where our dear Lord Jesus is offered as an unbloody Sacrifice to the Father?   Is this not the altar upon*

*which the Holy Spirit descends at the beginning of the
Eucharistic prayer? Is this not the altar, as St. John
Chrysostom said, where the Angels accompany the Holy Spirit
as He comes down upon the altar, at the Priest's summoning?*
Upon this Altar, we not only have the relics of Saints[6] who
have been recognized because of their piety and faithfulness
while on earth, but Jesus in His Body, Blood, Soul and
Divinity; we have the Holy Spirit, accompanied by myriads of
Angels; we have God, the Father, because wherever Jesus,
the *Second* Person of the Holy Trinity and the Holy Spirit,
the *Third* Person of the Holy Trinity are, so is God the
Father, the *First* Person of the Holy Spirit.

As I meditate upon the Cross in back of the Altar of
Sacrifice, that so clearly depicts what is about to happen, the
song that comes to mind is *"We are standing on Holy Ground.
The Lord is present and where He is, is holy."* The Altar is
holy! And, dear priest, your consecrated hands are holy.
And you are called to be holy! We know, it is not always
acceptable to be holy [We have had priests object firmly to
being called holy.], but you are chosen to be a sign of Jesus
in this world and Jesus was, and is, holy!

---

[6]encased in the Altar

Above:
St. Paul went from town to town in the first century preaching to the Jews and the Gentiles.

Left:
Statue of St. Peter at the Church of St. Paul outside the Walls in Rome, Italy

The Church in the First Century

No sooner had our Lord died for us, risen from the dead, and ascended into Heaven, than the fighting and *infighting* began. The Lord gave us the Holy Spirit and Pentecost. Satan countered with one of the first and most vicious groups of heretics in the history of the Church. They attacked a very vulnerable sector of our Church, our Converts. This group of heretics was called.....

JUDAIZERS

The Apostles began preaching in the *Synagogues*; therefore those members of the early Christian Community known as *Judaizers*, contended that the Church belonged to the Jewish people, the *Chosen ones*. They used this argument: since Christ came for the Jews, it was necessary for *all* believers to observe the Jewish law, *the Mosaic Law*, in order to fulfill the mandate of Jesus. Therefore, if non-Jews, or Gentiles, wanted to join the church of Jesus, they would have to observe all the Jewish laws.

Judaizing dates back to the very beginning, to the early days after the death of Jesus. It was to be a major source of controversy in the first Century! It almost caused a break between Sts. Peter and Paul in the infancy of the Church. It almost ripped their relationship asunder, as it tore away at the very fiber of the Church.

Judaizing was a heresy that insisted the Jewish laws and customs, as passed down through the centuries, especially the laws of Moses, had to be observed in the Christian community. They had a ready-made following among the Jews who had converted over to Christianity. They argued, "*Why shouldn't the converts follow the laws of Moses?*" It would be a smooth transition from Judaism into their new form of Judaism, Christianity.

Members of one of the heretical sects around Jerusalem, formed by Judaizers during this time (Acts 15: 1-3), *were called Ebionites*[1]. In addition to other heresies, they taught: *"Christ was a mere man."* (This abomination has resurfaced down through the centuries, and is with us once more, in our time.)   Because St. Paul defended Jesus' Divinity and His Church, Ebionites called *him* an apostate. Now, in the early Church an apostate was guilty of *"going over permanently to paganism, the rejection, after an initial acceptance and Baptism, of the Graces of the Faith*[2]*"*. Therefore, like the *ultimate deceiver* himself, the Ebionites accused St. Paul of the crime they were guilty of committing.

The Church fights back!

Whenever there is a threat to the Church, you will discover the Lord will bring about *Miracles of the Eucharist, our Lady will appear to her earthly children, or He will raise a powerful future Saint.* The Church was in trouble and our Lord reached out to a contradictory figure. He chose Paul, a Jewish zealot, who had played a hand in persecuting the early Christians; this was the one He would use to defend His Church. But Jesus had to knock him off his prideful high horse *first*, and blind him to all the world and its prizes.

It was Saul who lost his sight, but it was *Saint* Paul who gained *new* sight, his eyes now only for the Way of the Lord.

He went into the synagogues, and proclaimed the Gospel. Anger rose up in the Greek Jews to whom he spoke. His Christian brothers pleaded with him to take it easy, not step on touchy subjects, like the Mosaic law. Paul ignored them. He spoke of Moses' law as having been replaced by the new covenant of Jesus. This was blasphemy! When the Jews plotted to have Paul killed, the Christians took this as an opportunity to

---

[1]Ebionite-comes from the Hebrew word for *"poor."*(Catholic Encyclopedia-Broderick)

[2]Catholic Encyclopedia-Broderick

get him out of Israel. They took him by night to Caesarea. They put him on a ship for Tarsus where he waited until Barnabas came for him. Together, they embarked on their first journey of Evangelization. They went from town to town, first appealing to the Jews in the synagogues, and then, not having been successful with them, the Gentiles.

Paul and Barnabas spent four years on this first missionary journey. We believe they thought they would return triumphant to Antioch in Syria. Maybe they even expected a little pat on the back, for a job well-done. What they didn't expect was what was in store for them shortly after they arrived home.

Judaizers came to Antioch from Jerusalem. They insisted that all Gentile Christians had to be circumcised, there could only be one Christian community, the Jewish converts who observed the Jewish law to the letter. They criticized Paul and Barnabas. "Unless you (Gentiles) are circumcised according to Mosaic practice, you cannot be saved."(Acts 15:1)

Paul and Barnabas went through the ceiling! These converts were not just numbers, a scoreboard. They were people! It went much farther than Hebrew rituals. There was a big question which had to be answered. Was salvation dependent on faith in Jesus Christ, and all that implied, His death and Resurrection, or was salvation contingent on following the laws of Moses? Did Jesus give us a new Covenant, or was it an extension of the old Covenant?

It was determined that Paul and Barnabas go to Jerusalem, to present this problem to James and Peter. They brought Titus with them as an example of a pagan, who had converted to the Lord.

At the council meeting, Barnabas stood up and recounted their four year missionary journey. He introduced Titus as an example of the fiber of the pagan converts. That's when the riot began. "Some of the converted Pharisees then got up and demanded that such Gentiles be circumcised and told to keep the Mosaic law.³" Paul jumped to his feet and lashed out at the assembly. He defended his converts, and his understanding of the New Covenant. Peter, James and John stepped in and called for quiet. They took Paul and Barnabas into a private meeting. Paul and Barnabas shared their last four years on the road, how the Holy Spirit had worked so powerfully, in converting pagans to the new way of Jesus.

They spoke with such certainty, the apostles could do nothing other than agree with them, congratulate them, and lay hands on them. The next day, James made the announcement to the council that the Gentiles did not have to undergo circumcision. The battle had been won, but there was still a great war to be fought⁴.

The bad news in our Church is, there is dissension among its members. The good news is there has *always* been, and the Church has survived. Is this why our Lord left one head, *one* who would shepherd His children on earth? The Judaizers came after Peter, our first Pope, and tried to create an irreconcilable problem.

"*Paul and Barnabas returned to Antioch, victorious, so they thought. But shortly after, Peter came to visit the church of Antioch. At first, everything was beautiful. Peter sat with the Gentile converts, and broke bread with them. But a contingent of Judaizers had followed, to spy on Peter and Paul. They used a great deal of peer pressure on Peter. He gave in to it; he removed himself from the Gentile Christians. He turned down invitations to be with them, so as to satisfy the Judaizers. Paul was aware of it. When Barnabas separated himself from his own people, to sit with the Jews, Paul knew he had to act.*

"*Peter was behaving contrary to the teaching of Jesus. Who was he, Paul, to dare chastise the man whom Jesus had made head of the Church? But he had to do it. He got up in*

---

³Acts of the Apostles 15:5

⁴from the chapter: St. Paul in "*Saints and other Powerful Men in the Church.*"

the middle of the assembly, and chastised Peter and the others for putting the law before Jesus. He ended on a powerful note "For if justice is by the law, then Jesus died in vain!"

Not a word was spoken. But everybody understood. A piercing silence blanketed the assembly. All eyes converged on Peter. He and Barnabas ran over to Paul, and embraced him. And while the problem of Jewish dietary laws continued to plague the Gentile converts, the lines were clearly established. Faith in Jesus overshadowed adherence to the Mosaic laws[5].

This was the first heresy the Church had to face. But, with the Fire of the Holy Spirit descending, once more, upon the Church, it was overcome. At the Council of Jerusalem in 40 A.D. the Apostles determined that the Judaizers were in error, (Acts 15) sending word to the Gentiles in Antioch:

"It is the decision of the Holy Spirit, and ours too, not to lay on you any burden beyond that which is strictly necessary, namely, to abstain from meat sacrificed to idols, from blood, from the meat of strangled animals, and from illicit sexual union." (Acts 15:28) making the way clear for Gentiles to be part of the Christian family.

And so, the Church corrected a serious error for all time, or so they thought. Satan would not give up with this heresy. If he could have successfully split Peter and Paul, the two powers of the Church of the First Century, we might have had to walk through our first split in the Church, a *major splinter*. But Jesus had made a promise. Hell would not prevail against His Church. As we walk through the brave battles that resulted in victory for Christ and His Church, we see the unrelenting, insistent Satan trying to lead the innocent lambs of the Church to final damnation.

---

[5]from the chapter: St. Paul in *"Saints and other Powerful Men in the Church."*

EBIONITES

Ebionites were originally Jews. They converted to Christianity, but held onto their earlier teachings.

The Ebionites denied the Divinity of Christ.

They rejected all the New Testament except St. Matthew's Gospel, but created their own distorted version of his Gospel in an attempt to affirm their false teachings, only to have them disputed by the truths of the Gospel. Again, with the Ebionites, Lucifer used man to promote fear and helplessness, and God in His Word revealed the truth which is the saving Grace needed to live in this bruised world.

They claimed that part of mankind was created by good Angels and the rest of mankind by bad angels.

They believed in and engaged in free-love.

They called St. Paul a heretic. Good work, Satan! You never stop calling the *holy* by your own names. You even tried with God, telling Eve that He was a liar. But, as with most heretics, Ebionites (as such) are unknown today, but St. Paul continues to influence the Church and all Christians.

The Church fights back!

As to the Divinity of Jesus Christ, **St. Justin** one of our earliest Fathers of the Church, and defender of the Divinity of Jesus, warned that there were some Ebionites who, although they profess Jesus is the Christ, insist and influence others into believing, He was a man born of a man, not of God; He was not the Second Person of the Holy Trinity.

St. Irenaeus tells us that the heretics, in trying to adjust the Gospels to bring about their own dogmas, only succeeded in *confirming* the Sacred Word of our Lord.

What modern day heretics create their own distorted version of Scripture, rather than fashioning their lifestyle after the message of the Bible? Some strong examples of this would be Jehovah's Witnesses and Mormons. But these are cults, not splinters of the Church.

It is believed that *Tertullian*, before he fell into heresy, came against those who spoke of their own authority, not that of Holy Scripture. We're told he later referred to the Ebionites, when he disputed the teaching *"that Christ was mere man, but that he had an angel in Him[6]"*.

SIMONIANS

No sooner does one snake slither under a rock, and we breath a sigh of relief, than another comes back when you least expect it. We just about close one chapter of the history of the Church, the Apostles having squelched the heresies of the Judaizers and the Ebionites, than a magician named Simon Magus, and his followers claim he comes directly from the *Divine*. Or, in other words, was he saying he was the Christ? John prophesied in Revelations:

"My children, the time is near! You were told the Enemy of Christ would come; and many enemies of Christ have already appeared, and so we know the end is near. These people really did not belong to our fellowship...anyone who says that Jesus is not the Messiah. Such a person is an enemy of Christ - he rejects both the Father and the Son."

There are those, *today*, who reject the male imagery of God the Father, insisting God is a woman. And others who claim to be the Christ.[7]

Since Simon Magus was the first person to oppose the teachings of the Apostles, he is known as *"The Father of Heretics"*[8]. St. Justin tells us, in his writings, that Simon Magus came from Gitta, located somewhere in Samaritan country. He had been baptized a Christian, but we have to wonder if his conversion was sincere. He went to St. Peter and the other Apostles in an attempt to *purchase* what he

---

[6]P.148 in chapter on Tertullian in the book: The Faith of the Early Fathers - Vol. 1 by W.A. Jurgens

[7]see later chapter on *New Age* in this book

[8]from "The Triumph of the Church"

considered their *magical power.* He did not understand their gifts of healing and preaching as coming from the Holy Spirit. Perhaps the Lord was not revealing Himself to Magus, as we read in Scripture, because he knew he would use this knowledge against Him and His Church.

The word "*simony*" means the selling of sacred things. This comes from Simon Magus and his heresy.

The Simonians claimed Simon Magus was the Christ. New Agers today claim that Lord Maitreya is God. And, the interesting thing about those who promote him, is how much they remind us of Simon Magus. Is simony dead? When people like Shirley MacLaine, charge large sums of money to learn how to get in touch with the god (you are) waiting inside you, is that not like Simon Magus who desired to buy the gifts of the Holy Spirit?

They denied that man had free will. They taught that some were born evil and others good. You had no control over your destiny. So, no matter what you did, you were saved or condemned ahead of time, before you were born.

They insisted that the world was not created by God, but by angels. Of course, they had to deny God as the Creator. As they were teaching predestination, which certainly precludes a compassionate and forgiving, merciful God, it follows He was not the One Who created the world. Now, if you eliminate God, then *who* are the angels they are giving credit to?

They believed in the transmigration of souls, that is passing from one body to another at death or, in other words, *reincarnation.* This heresy of reincarnation stems from the Hindu religion.

They denied the humanity of Jesus. But again, you can see the warped image Lucifer was trying to mold. The Simonians said the world was not created by God; therefore, is there a God? They taught reincarnation, that is a soul returning over and over again, until it is perfected. They would have us believe, since we are predestined to sin, our hope is that eventually we will come back as one of the favored and can do anything we want and still be saved. Naturally, it would follow they would teach Jesus was not human. If He was not human, then He did not take on our sins and die for us. Our only hope is that we are born, by chance, one of the favored, or can keep coming back until we get it right.

The Church fights back!

Simon Magus was so clever, he was able to dupe not only all of Rome into believing he was God, but the Emperor himself. Claudius commissioned a statue of Simon Magus to be erected, inscribed with the words *"To the Holy God Simon[9]"*.

Again, His lambs are in danger; the Lord calls His soldiers into combat. Saints Peter and Paul came upon the scene just as this scourge was reaching epidemic proportions. They were able, as authorities of the Church, to correct this deadly deception. But, we do not believe, it was really repressed until Simon Magus, like Satan, needed to show his *hoof* of Pride. As he claimed he was God, he declared he would rise into Heaven. Some say he was seen, not *ascending*, but *descending* on a cloud in a chariot drawn by demons. *Guess where he was going?*

Sts. Peter and Paul, arrived on the scene as this was happening. They did what Jesus had told them; they knelt, turning to their One and True God, and prayed. We know that when two or more are united in prayer, whatsoever they ask will be granted unto them. Did they pray *passionately*, seeing uninformed souls being misled? We believe in the power of prayer and of Jesus' promise not to allow a hair on our heads to be destroyed. We also believe that God, in His

---

[9]from *The Faith of the Early Fathers* - Vol. 1 by W.A. Jurgens, Page 354, 822c

mercy, watched as the poor boastful, prideful Simon Magus *plummeted* to earth, and, most likely, beneath to the fires of hell, unequivocally dispelling his divinity. St. Ambrose, St. Augustine and others have written that Simon Magus died in Rome trying to *ascend* to Heaven.

God exposed Simon Magus before he could do irreparable damage. Was not our first Pope there, our sweet Christ on earth? We would like to have been there to have heard the prayers offered up for those souls about to be lost. Did Saints Peter and Paul, like Jesus and the Prophets before Him, plead, offering themselves as victim-souls? We know Peter and Paul died Martyrs' deaths for the Faith.

Whenever we are upset about something in Ministry, we ask how much space we would give it if we were writing a book about the history of our Ministry. The Simonian Heresy is hardly worthy of one small line in the History of the *Church*. But you will see its false teachings crop up over and over again. The devil is persistent in his focus to have as many souls in hell with him. But God, Who is Almighty, is determined that we be with Him. Who do you vote for?

CERINTHIANS

You would think one heresy in a century would be enough, two would be too much, but here we have another! The followers of Cerinthus were called Cerinthians.

It was common knowledge that Cerinthus was an *Egyptian*. He founded a school in Asia and attracted quite a number of zealot followers. They enjoyed their greatest triumphs in Asia and Galatia[10].

What was the brand of heresies taught by this infamous bunch? *The Cerinthians denied that God was the Creator of the world.*

---

[10]ancient kingdom in Asia Minor that had been made into a Roman province - 25 B.C. - St. Paul evangelized there. One of his greatest battles against the Judaizers took place in Galatia.

Shades of Judaizers, *they insisted that the Law of Moses was critical to salvation.* They also insisted that St. Paul had no authority as an Apostle. They claimed he was a Johnny-come-lately, who had not been given a mandate from the Lord, so the Galatians shouldn't pay attention to him.

Also a part of their false teachings was that *after Jesus' Second Coming, He would establish an earthly kingdom where the just* would spend a thousand years *reveling in sexual pleasure.*

The Simonians denied Jesus' *humanity; the Cerinthians denied His Divinity.* It's no small wonder, what with the philosophy they were furthering, if they believed in the Divinity of Jesus, they would have been petrified.

As with so many today, as well as since the beginning of the world, man has believed in the *now*, in the ever-fading pleasure of the *now*, judging it much easier to deny Jesus than to live His Gospel Life. The only problem is, what happens on that day when you know you are helpless! Maybe it's an earthquake, a hurricane, a tornado, a loved one in a serious accident. What do you do, then? To whom do you pray?

Someone was interviewing a woman who claimed she was God. The interviewer asked to whom she had prayed during a most recent violent earthquake? Was it to herself? The woman was silent. It is believed she returned to her Lord, to the One True God, to the One to Whom she had prayed, the One Who could make things better.

The Church fights back!

Cerinthus lived in the time of St. John. It is said that the Apostle *St. John* wrote the Fourth Gospel to correct the errors concerning the *Divinity of Christ* being taught by the Cerinthians.

"In the beginning was the Word; the Word was in God's presence, and the Word was God. He was present to God in

the beginning. Through Him all things came into being, and apart from Him nothing came to be. Whatever came to be in Him, found life, life for the light of men.

The light shines on in the darkness, a darkness that did not overcome it.

There was a man named John sent by God, who came as a witness to testify to the light, so that through Him all men could believe - but only to testify to the light, for he himself was not the light. The real light, which gives light to every man was coming into the world.
He was in the world,
and through Him the world was made,
yet the world did not know who He was.
To His own He came,
yet His own did not accept Him.
Any who did accept Him
He empowered to become
children of God. (John 1: 1-12)

It is so sad when we read the words of John, when we think of how John must have felt. His Savior had died out of love for His own, and they were still rejecting Him. Was this the reason John wrote in this unique style? Did he have to bring across a point which his brother Evangelists had not considered? When you read John's Gospel, there is no question from the very first line, from the Prologue, that Jesus Christ is Lord. John proclaims it from the beginning, and all through his Gospel. Was part of the reason, he was so firm and so forceful on this point, because he was defending his friend, his God, against those opportunists who were only interested in their own ego?

I think of how sad our Lord must feel, as He asks us *"How many times must I die for you? How many times will you crucify Me?"* Our Lord is crying out to us, as He did to Saul, *"Why do you persecute Me?"*

Heresies of the Second Century

It was a young Church; it was an infant Church. We're sure the early Fathers, after having convened the First Ecumenical Council, thought they had put an end to any and all the problems the Church would ever have. They were most likely *sure* that what they were handing down to the next generation, was a Church free of strife and in-fighting. However, that's not what they got. Whereas the Saints of the First Century had gone on to their reward with our Lord Jesus in Heaven, Satan was waiting in the wings, training a brand new group of heretics, to destroy the Church.

The second century was to prove no better than the first with man insisting on being as smart as God, trying to outdo Him, and, as usual, falling flat on his human face.

BASILIDIANS

The Basilidian heresy got its name from its founder, Basilides. He is known to have lived in the time of the Emperors Hadrian and Antonius Pius somewhere between 120 to 140 A.D. Basilides came from Alexandria. The sins of the father very often are passed on to the son. Basilides' son would follow in his fallen footsteps, in an attempt to keep alive the deceptions his father was trying to promote throughout the whole Christian world. One of Basilides' teachings was *"Know others, but let no one know you."*

The views the Basilidians held on the *Deity* were:

They rejected Divine Revelation as manifested to us by Holy Scripture. They insisted they had received their own revelations direct from God.

They wrote a new book of Psalms. Basilides authored a new gospel under his own name. We quote John in Revelation *"If anyone adds to these words, God will visit him with all the plagues described herein!"*(Rev 18:19)

The Basilidian heresy claimed that *the God of the Jews had been only an angel.* What angel were they referring to? Could it be the work of Lucifer who wanted to be God?

They insisted that the world was created by the angels. Is that not like Lucifer who envied God the gift of Creation, to put God's Creation under his name, to receive credit for that which he could never possess?

They denied the humanity of Jesus and repudiated all the miracles attributed to Jesus. Are there not those today who would reduce every miraculous happening into human reasoning? Do we not hear; "There is no such thing as a miracle," "God gives you an intellect and the means to control your own destiny," "It doesn't pay to pray for a miracle, God is going to do what He has already planned to do"?

In our former parish, a wonderful young man got seriously injured in a car accident. The hospital was struggling to save his life. To human eyes, there was little or no hope of him living. But not to his family and friends. All the school children of our Catholic School joined the rest of the church in praying for the complete recovery of this young man. During the Homily, the young associate pastor said: "Don't pray for a miracle. God has already made up His Mind. Maybe God doesn't want this young man to live. Stop bothering God with your prayers."

The young man's daughter ran out of the Church in tears. We ran after her. We told her God loved her, her sister and her Mommy and Daddy; that He heard them. He was there, especially present in the Holy Eucharist in the Holy Mass, waiting for her to turn to Him. She could trust Him. He was listening!

We reminded her of the many times Jesus listened to the pleading of loved ones, sometime in seemingly impossible situations: When Lazarus' sister Mary turned to Jesus and cried "Lord, if You had been here my brother would never have died."

And then, when Jesus saw the Widow of Naim grieving over the death of her only son, He, moved with pity, told the mother not to cry and commanded her son to rise, and Jesus gave him to his now rejoicing mother. (Luke 7:11-17)   When a Jewish official pleaded: "My daughter has just died; but come and place Your Hands on her, and she will live.", Jesus responded to the father's act of faith and lifted his daughter from her death bed. (Matt 9:18-20, 23-26)

We asked this little girl, did she think Jesus loved them more than He loved her?   She prayed, believing in a miracle, and her father is now very active in the Church, very much alive.   According to the doctors, he did not have a chance. According to God, all things are possible, if only we believe.

The Basilidians denied the Resurrection of the body; they taught that it was Simon of Cyrene who was crucified in Jesus' place and that Jesus returned to His Father without having suffered the Passion. Think about it. If Jesus did not die for our sins then we are not redeemed, and all is lost. We believe that our sins died on that Cross with Jesus.

Basilidians believed in magic. These heretics denied the possibility of miraculous intervention of the Divine, but relied on sorcery and magic. Were they not saying that God has no power, but that evil (or Satan) has?

The Church fights back!

The lambs are about to be led to slaughter again, and the Lord sends forth a mighty warrior to fight another one of the Church's battles: **St. Irenaeus** was born around 140 A.D., probably in the area of Smyrna. He definitely came from Asia Minor. He was taught by St. Polycarp, another early father of the Church. *St. Irenaeus* became a bishop around 177 A.D., at the age of 37, after his predecessor, St. Pothinus, died a martyr's death. His outstanding life was marked by untiring defense of the Church and her teachings, as well as his dedicated role as a peacemaker.

St. Irenaeus wrote to a priest who was preaching heresy; and cautioned him that his teachings were not only unsound, but were so deadly that not even heretics outside of the Church would dare to espouse them.   He chastised him, stressing the seriousness of leading the innocent into error.

St. Irenaeus, like other early fathers, faithfully taught as the Apostles before him, never putting himself above the instruction passed down by his teacher St. Polycarp.   He stressed that all must be taught according to the tenets of the Church and that we were to proclaim, with one heart and one soul, as the Lord's one Mystical Body, *one Truth* as passed down by Jesus and by those He had chosen to teach His Church.   Although the Church is spread over all the earth, among people of different races and tongues, we are all to speak with one voice, that of the Roman Catholic Church.   Although each nation who belonged to the Catholic Church had different cultures, unique to their own country, the tradition of the Catholic Church is *universal*, one and the same for the entire Catholic world.

Basilides disputed the Divinity of God as well as the humanity of Jesus.   St. Irenaeus answered: No one, not even the Angels, had access to the mystery of how our Lord Jesus came to be from the Father, except the Father and the Son. As someone once said, when you understand the Lord, you have lost Him.

CARPOCRATIANS

Followers of Carpocratian, also known as "gnostics" or "enlightened" or "learned", lived during the time of Emperor Hadrian (117-138).   They began their apostasy in Samaria and Syria.

One of the heresies the Carpocratians came up with:
Everyone had two souls.
They believed in reincarnation.

Along with the Basilidians, *they also espoused the heresy that the world was created by angels.* Do we ever ask the question *who* then created the angels?

They denied the Divinity of Christ. Throughout Church history, heretics are denying either the Lord's Divinity or His humanity.

They promoted the practice of immorality as a means of union with God, just as those of the New Age today advocate *"anything goes"* sexual permissiveness as a means of getting in touch with the god *you* are, the one inside of you.

The Church fights back!

The *Gnostic Heresies* (Carpocratians) began during St. John's time. It's obvious, he was aware of this philosophy which was *purposely ambiguous and deceptive,* when he wrote, in Revelation, for then and now, attacking this insidious heresy that was attempting to erode the Church from within: *"But cowards, traitors, perverts, murderers, the immoral, those who practice magic, those who worship idols, and all liars-the place for them is the lake burning with fire and sulphur, which is the second death."*(Rev. 21:8)

GNOSTICISM

Gnosticism is the common name used for a collection of very dubious, misleading philosophies claiming to be religions. Although they were often structured differently, basically they all spouted much the same deadly heresies.

All forms of this heresy had one central purpose: either to infiltrate the Faith to impose their own brand of religion in opposition to the teachings as passed down by Christ and His Apostles, or to destroy it by wiping it out through persecution, starvation, genocide and etc.

Gnosticism, passing itself off as a *religion*, battled Christ and His Church for the souls of innocent, unknowing believers for a period of four centuries! Rather than preaching on the *universal truth,* revealed by the Church and the Word, **"they used** *personal revelations"* to support their errors. They were by far the worst threat to Catholicism. Depending on the pride of the *intelligentsia,* they deviously tore away at the fibers of all religions. They took parts of each of the beliefs and made them a part of *their* cult. As with today, with New Age, they had Pagan Gnosticism, Jewish Gnosticism and Christian Gnosticism.

They knew people would not deny their Faith, therefore they taught that *they* (the gnostics) were teaching the true tenets of the religion, not those faithful to doctrines of the Faith. Again, as you will see later, rather than *one* clear-cut philosophy, they had many fronts for the Holy Spirit to fight. It is the same today. Gnosticism of today is like a twelve barrel shotgun; it buckshots *widely* spreading its death. Attacking on many fronts, if the *believers* of this world do not stop fighting each other, Gnosticism of today will take over, and the anti-Christ will reign for who knows how many centuries.

The errors of Gnosticism were: *Jesus' Body was not real; it did not consist of flesh and blood, but was a ghost or an apparition! Docetism,* another heresy that cropped up from Gnosticism taught that Jesus wasn't human but a spirit.

The gnostics taught: *Divine Power took possession of a human body, and used it to do its will.* Therefore, according to their distorted theology, Jesus Christ was not One of the Three Persons of the Holy Trinity. They taught that Jesus was not God, but that Divine Power or Energy took over His Body and He became simply an instrument that was used by God to do his Will. Sadly, this form of Gnosticism is running rampant today in many segments of the Church, deluding the faithful into heresy against Jesus Himself!

Another desecration of the Truth was that *all matter was bad; therefore the body was evil.* This was another reason they gave for Jesus not being the Son of God. They ascertained since spirit was good and the body was evil, God would not become man. Since all matter was evil, the world could not have been created by God Almighty Who is all good, but of a god who is evil as his creation is evil.

Because of this, many abuses came about: either total immoral behavior, since the body was corrupt or extreme *fanatical* practices of mortification for one's sins (or supposed sins resulting from the error of scrupulosity[1]).

The Church fights back!

In the early Church, St. Peter came out against the early rising of Gnosticism's ugly head when he went toe to toe with Simon Magus (Acts 8:9-24), who some believed was the founder of Gnosticism.

Much of St. Paul's teachings are in defense of the Church against the false teachings of the Gnostics, especially when he wrote to the "Church of Corinth." He wrote that our faith does not rest on the wisdom and learning of the world, but on God's power! He went on to say that he did not speak with words taught by human wisdom, but in words taught by the Holy Spirit. When disputing the heresies that claimed at one point Jesus was not Divine, and then at another he was not human, Paul explained, *"As only a person's spirit within him knows all about him, so only God's Spirit knows all about God."*(1 Cor 2:5)

The Council of Nicea, or the first Ecumenical Council, was called by Constantine in 325. It condemned many forms of Gnosticism that had cropped up, but especially those heresies regarding Christ's Divinity. The Council proclaimed

---

[1]when a troubled conscience grieves over a sin that doesn't exist, or makes a mortal sin out of a venial sin. It is imperative that this poor soul go to a Priest for spiritual direction.

for all time, that the Second Person of the Holy Trinity, Jesus Christ, the Son was "consubstantial[2] with the Father".

There is a small remnant today in the Church who see the danger in our present time, and these dry martyrs who defend the traditions of the Church each day are willing to die for the Lord and His teachings. We may be, once again, in the time of *wet martyrs*, those who will be called to shed their blood for Christ.

VALENTINIANS

Their founder was an Egyptian named Valentine, who, when he failed to be ordained Bishop, separated from the Church. He had forgotten that our Lord, though God, did not exalt Himself; He chose to be born of humble estate, never wanting to be proclaimed King; He walked among the lowly, never looking down upon anyone; and although Superior, He called us brothers, friends; He left us His Body, Blood, Soul and Divinity in the Holy Eucharist, vulnerable to our acceptance or rejection, to our reverence or desecration.

Valentine came to Rome and remained there through three Papacies: during the Pontificate of Pope St. Hyginus (136-140), and Pope St. Pius I, right up to and including the Pontificate of Pope St. Anicetus.

Our Lord is always opening His merciful Arms toward us, calling us to return home to Him and His Church. Did Valentine hear that whisper of the Holy Spirit in his heart? For a time, he renounced the errors he had been spreading!

But we either walk toward the Lord each day, our eyes and heart firmly glued on Him, or we walk toward His enemy. Jesus told us we can only have one master; we will love the one and hate the other. Did the master of lies ploy Valentine with the rewards to be realized on earth for the

---

[2]"means being of one and the same substance, as the Three Divine Persons of the Trinity are of but One substance. Catholic Encyclopedia-Broderick

betrayal of Christ? How much did he offer you, Valentine? Did Satan up the ante from thirty pieces of silver to power?

Valentine embraced his heresies, with zeal. He never let up, spreading poison until his death, in Cyprus, in 160. Lord, when he faced You for the last time, did he see how he had been betrayed by the enemy, just as Judas did, when he went before the Sanhedrin?

The religion formed by Valentine was extremely organized and exacting in its *own* brand of heretical teachings; but, they threw in, for good (or more accurately bad) measure, additional instruction in some of the most wide spread forms of Gnosticism, as well.

There were two branches of the Valentinians: the Italian and the Oriental. The *Italian* spread through Rome, Italy and Southern Gaul; and the *Oriental* through Egypt, Syria, and Asia Minor.

Valentine conjured up a ridiculous, as well as purely fictional, genealogy of thousands and thousands of years when the religion and its gods began. Sounds familiar![3]

As Lucifer has never stopped hating Mary and the exalted position given to her by God, he used Valentine to preach that *Mary was not the Mother of God.* St. Irenaeus wrote: *"the knot of Eve's disobedience was untied by Mary's obedience. What the virgin Eve bound through her unbelief, Mary loosened through her faith."* Our Lord chose a spotless virgin to be the Mother of His only begotten Son. As Adam, by his disobedience, was causing the fall of mankind, God in His Mercy was planning the salvation of the world by the sacrifice of His only Beloved Son. As Eve our first *earthly* mother was betraying Him, God was already choosing Mary, our *Heavenly* Mother, to undo what she was doing.

Another heresy which will be copied over and over again is: *salvation is through justification by faith alone.*

---

[3]read on later in chapter on New Age

Holy Scripture tells us: "Not even faith[4] or conversion[5] or reception of baptism[6] or constancy throughout life[7] can gain for one the right to salvation, though all of these are the forerunners of attaining salvation through the redeeming sacrifice of Jesus." Right from the very beginning, the Church has taught that the faithful by and of themselves cannot bring about their own salvation.

Valentine would have us believe that God created us without free-will. Although God created us with free will to love Him, he allows us to use this same free will to reject Him. Valentine's brand of religion preached God made us mindless, unfeeling robots forced to a certain pattern devised by Him before we were born.

He cruelly espoused we are created evil, predestined to sin, therefore separating ourselves from God; *or we are pre-conceived one of the favored chosen to lead a life pleasing to Him,* united to Him. Sounds like Jehovah Witnesses to me! What an unloving God he would have us believe God is, to create His own to commit sin, and because of that sin, over which we have no control, to be separated from Him for all time. I had an earthly father whose greatest joy was to be with his loved ones. He would never have done anything to cause any one of his children to be separated from him. How can our Heavenly *Perfect* Father want less? I cannot fathom Him planning the condemnation of anyone of His children.

Jesus proved that His love is unconditional, on His Holy Cross, when He asked the Father to "*Forgive them; they know not what they do.*" He forgave His persecutors, his tormentors, the Apostles who abandoned Him, those who stood apathetically by and did nothing. He forgave those who today are speaking out against Him, as with Judas,

---

[4](Romans 10: 9-13)
[5](Acts 3:19; 5:31)
[6](Acts 22:16; 1Pt 3-21)
[7](Thes.2:10)

The Resurrection of Jesus - Basilica of the Rosary - Lourdes
The Dogma of the Faith teaches that Jesus' Body and Spirit rose
from the dead. The Basilidians rejected this and
the Resurrection of our bodies.

reaching out to them to repent and come back to the true teachings of His Pope and the Church.

Valentine rejected the Resurrection of the body.   A doctrine of the Church has always been that the body will be reunited with the soul, and through this *resurrection* the body will take on a new life, one with God the Father, Jesus Christ the Son and the Holy Spirit, for all eternity.

If, as he proposed, the body does not resurrect, was he alleging that Jesus did not die and did not resurrect from the dead? Our answer to him, and to heretics of yesterday and today who claim that Jesus resurrected in His Spirit only, comes from the angel's words to the women at the tomb: *"Do not be frightened. I know you are looking for Jesus the crucified, but He is not here. He has been raised, exactly as He promised. Come and see the place where He was laid. Then go quickly and tell the disciples: 'He has been raised from the dead and now goes ahead of you to Galilee, where you will see Him.' That is the message I have for you."* (Matt 28:5-7)

Satan mimics, but then his pride gets the best of him and he distorts the very Truth he tried to imitate.   The heresies that persist for the longest period of time are those which include *part* of the Truth. This is exactly how Satan works: says nine true things and then leads the deluded to hell with the tenth - his lie!

The Church fights back!

God goes to Africa and picks a man whose profession is rhetoric, converts him and uses him to defend his Church. *Lactantius* was born about 250 A.D. He went to a Greek city called Nicodemia at the bidding of Emperor Diocletian, to teach rhetoric. Because he was a professor of *Latin* rhetoric among Greeks, he didn't do too well and subsequently turned to writing. It's amazing how God weaves His Plan in the world, so that His Church will be saved, once again. Lactantius was forced to resign as a teacher in 303 A.D.

because he had converted to Christianity. This was the time of great persecution of Christians by Emperor Diocletian.

Lactantius, when he wrote *The Divine Institutions*, disproved not only the heresies promulgated by the Valentinians but by paganism in general. In so doing, he and his writings were responsible for the first Christian Doctrine written in Latin, reaffirming the true dogma of the Church.

Lactantius wrote that whether they call themselves Valentinians or whatever title of the world they confer upon themselves, if they are going against the teachings of Christ and His Apostles, they can no longer be called Christians. So, today, those who say they are Catholic and are teaching in opposition to the Magisterium, the accepted teachings of the Church, according to Lactantius are no longer Catholic.

Because of the heresies being taught by those who broke their commitment to shepherd the innocent lambs of God, many of the faithful were lost to the Church for centuries. The seriousness of their false teaching within the Church was clearly stated by Jesus as He spoke out passionately, warning those who would lead His children astray: *"If anyone should cause one of these little ones to lose his faith in me, it would be better for that person to have a large millstone tied around his neck and be thrown into the sea."* (Mark 9:42)

MARCIONITES

Just as we think, we've covered enough of these ancient blasphemies, to bring across how very many devious ways Satan and his army of heretics have tried to destroy the Church, I read how these errors are being repeated again and again. It's as if the Lord is weaving a history of His Church, so that you, His beloved can see the false teachings, Satan may be spreading today.

Marcion, founder of the Marcionites was born in about 110.   He was the son of a Bishop[8].   His own father excommunicated him. Marcion was a suffragan bishop, that is, a bishop of a diocese of a province. His father was a Metropolitan. For example: the Archbishop of Los Angeles is the *Metropolitan* of all the dioceses of Southern California (which is a province). The Archbishop (or *the Metropolitan*) of an archdiocese, has limited supervisory powers and influences over the other dioceses and bishops in his province.

The cause must have been quite grave for his father, *first*, as his father, to impose this, the harshest of sentences on his own son; but, *then* as a Metropolitan, since this is a limited supervisory, it is not one that he would have quickly exercised over one of his bishops. Not only did he condemn Marcion, but when he appealed to his father (bishop) to take him back into the Church, his father refused!

When Marcion saw that reconciliation with his father was not to be, he left for Rome. There, he joined *a* heretic named *Cerdo* and, with him, began to spread all kinds of errors. Marcion was an angry voice spitting out all kinds of blasphemies. Have you ever noticed how it is always those who have been part of a family, when they turn their back on the family, whether the family is a human one, or one of the Church, or of a country, the fury against the former loved ones is uncontainable.

It is written that, later on, repenting the evil he had spewed upon the Church, Marcion promised he would lead those innocent victims, he had led astray, *back to the Church*. As with so many who think they have many tomorrows to undo the harm they have done, to say I am sorry, or to say I love you, time ran out for Marcion and he died before he could carry out his good intentions.   You say, God

---

[8]In those days, priests and bishops could marry.

understands and He is merciful. In no way trying to play judge, I still wonder how heavy his heart must have been, as he carried the excess baggage of the many souls lost because of his vindictive anger, as Marcion journeyed that last time to encounter the Lord.

Marcion's false teachings include the heresy: the existence of two gods. One good and the other evil. According to Marcion, one god was creator of the material things of the world, and since he believed all matter created was evil, then this god was evil. The other god was creator of the world of *spirit*, and since the spirit is good, then that god is good. Since God is good, he would not become man which is matter and evil. So, it all adds up to the next heresy which is Jesus was not God become man.

He denied the Incarnation of Jesus Christ. The Old Testament foretells the coming of the Christ, the Messiah to be born of a virgin. If he was to refute God becoming man, then it follows he would have to discredit the Old Testament.

Marcion completely rejected the Old Testament. He had to reject the Old Testament! All the heresies he espoused are refuted in the Old Testament, which foretold the Messiah was to be born of a Virgin, or the Incarnation; that there is only one God; that Jesus would suffer and be rejected, in Psalm 22. Are not heretics, today, in an attempt to rob us of our Lord and God, calling the Old Testament *stories* and the New Testament *teachings*, words put into Jesus' Mouth to teach the people of His time? But the Church won *that* battle many times, and she will win all the battles waged against Jesus' Church till He comes in glory.

He separated Jesus the man from Jesus the Christ. *He alleged that only Jesus the man suffered, not Jesus Christ our Lord, God and man.* Therefore, did God the Father and Jesus the Son agree He would be the spotless sacrificial Lamb for the salvation of the world?

The Church fights back!

The Church raises up a Father of the Church and **Saint, Polycarp.** As we can see, Christ's Church has been under crisis. God, true to His promise, sends a future saint to the earth. St. Polycarp was born in Smyrna. He was instructed by the Apostles themselves and got much of his knowledge from those who had seen and heard Jesus. He was also a disciple of St. John the Evangelist. Known for his holiness, he influenced and was responsible for the training of such faithful early Fathers of the Church as St. Irenaeus. Because of his authenticity, St. Polycarp was appointed Bishop of Smyrna by the Apostles in Asia.

His precepts were always faithful to the teachings he had received from the Apostles. He followed the accepted doctrines passed down by Mother Church. His teachings have weathered the test of time, as they are still carried on by successors of the proclaimers of Jesus' Good News.

As St. Ignatius of Antioch was passing by to be martyred, St. Polycarp kissed his chains, and in turn St. Ignatius delegated him to write to his church, advising them he had entrusted St. Polycarp to take charge of his church.

In the sixth year of Marcus Aurelius' reign, a bloodthirsty persecution spread throughout the kingdom. They hunted down Christians young and old, trying to persuade them to deny Christ or suffer the brutal attack of starving beasts or other forms of torture and death. Most preferred death to betraying their Lord. When they came for St. Polycarp, he invited them to sit down to dinner, during which time, he requested, he be allowed to pray. He stood for two hours praying. His prayers were so selflessly offered for his church and the whole Church, that many of the soldiers could not stand it and left him.

Herod and his son tried to dissuade him, coaxing: *"What harm would it do to call Caesar - Lord Caesar?"* What they didn't bother to say was, what St. Polycarp knew, that this would be received as a proclamation of Caesar as God. And St. Polycarp knew he was not only responsible for his own soul, but those who respected and followed his teaching, knowing it was passed down from the Apostles themselves.

Using his advanced age, they tried to convince him, "*Just point to the Christians and say 'Away with the atheists!*[9]'" Instead, he pointed to the pagans in the stands and cried out: "*Away with the atheists!*" The proconsul pleaded "Revile Christ!" St. Polycarp's response was that for all his life the Lord had not betrayed him, and he would not betray Him! St. Polycarp went to his death praising the Lord for the privilege to die as a martyr.

We were attempting to conjecture on what Marcion could have done, for his father and Bishop to have not only excommunicated him, but to have refused to take him back into the Church. When St. Polycarp and Marcion met, Marcion asked St. Polycarp: "*Do you recognize me?*" Saint Polycarp replied: "*I recognize you as the firstborn of Satan!*"

What a condemnation. What a way to be remembered. What kind of earthly reward is worth this? If you know anyone today who could be responsible for the loss of souls to Jesus, by their false teachings, you are obligated, with love, to instruct them of the seriousness of their acts, lest you share in their sins before the Throne of God.

We have two powerful examples here: a humble, obedient servant of God who died a glorious death, and a proud man who is remembered by few, for his attempt to destroy the Church by heresy. Better to die for the Faith than to spend the rest of eternity separated from God.

---

[9]Butler's Lives of the Saints-Thurston and Atwater

CERDONIANS

Cerdo, the heretic whom Marcion joined up with, came from Syria and arrived in Rome about the year 139. He was to spread his heresies during Hyginus' Pontificate.

Cerdo denied the One True God, claiming there were two gods: one good and one evil, *denied the Resurrection of the body, prohibited marriage, and completely rejected the Old Testament.*

So, old Marcion, the rebel was not the free-thinker he thought he was, but just another dumb sheep being led by another Judas goat to slaughter.

The Church fights back!

As to the Divinity of Jesus Christ, *St. Justin,* one of our earliest Fathers of the Church, warned those, who although they profess Jesus is the Christ, insist and brainwash others into believing, He was a man born of a man, not of God. [The Mormons who have borrowed from every heresy to blaspheme against the Lord, claim that when God was Adam he had sexual intercourse with the Blessed Virgin Mary and the result of that sexual union was Jesus Christ.[10]]

St. Irenaeus said that the heretics, in trying to adjust the Gospels to bring about their own dogmas, only succeeded in confirming the Word. He said he spoke with the authority passed down to him by St. Polycarp who *knew* St. John. He argued if the Gospel writers were not Mark, Matthew, Luke and John, St. John would have told him so. Right from the beginning, the Gospels were known as having been authored by the four Gospel writers, and never anyone else. They had lived in the time of Jesus, had heard Him, and had not only *first hand* knowledge of the happenings, they had Mother Mary and others who had known Jesus, who recounted to them the words and happenings surrounding Jesus' life.

---

[10]Journal of Discourses, Vol 1, 50-51

DOCETISM

Clement of Alexandria wrote, Docetism was most definitely a religious sect in opposition to the teachings of the Church.   Little is known about its founder, Julius Cassianus, except that he was a disciple of Valentine, who not only spouted Valentine's heresies, but added a few himself.

Docetism leaned heavily on spiritualism.   It denied the Incarnation: "In the beginning was the Word ...and the Word became man." (John 1:14)   It flatly rejected the Church's teaching that Jesus was born, lived on earth, suffered, died and was buried, and on the third day rose from the dead. (Note: The modern Docetist of today, still denies the *human* Jesus Who lived, suffered and died for us, and with Him the Church who was given its authority by Him to be the visible and final word of His on earth.)

As heretics before them, *this sect taught that the Body of Christ was a mere apparition or ghost.*   They denied Jesus' human appearance, insisting possibly He was there in His Spiritual Body.   They limited Jesus to being not Body and *Spirit*, but of Spirit alone, as God had created Angels.

They denied Jesus was truly present in the Holy Eucharist.

The Church fights back!

St. John Chrysostom wrote: When the Evangelists described the Passion and Death of Jesus Christ, they most intimately shared His Incarnation, His *human* as well as *Divine* nature.   In the garden of Gethsemane, it was a very human Jesus Who sweat blood as He faced the rejection, the betrayal, the abandonment of His friends at His last hours. Do you remember, in the garden, when He asked His friends and disciples to stay awake and watch with Him, He said *"My heart is nearly broken with sorrow."*   It was a *human* Who asked the Father, if it be His Will, to let His cup of agony pass from Him.   Jesus suffered pain and disappointment like all of His creation, sparing Himself nothing we have ever or will ever suffer, except sin.   On the Cross, it was a *human* Jesus who asked His Father why He had abandoned Him.

Another early Father who upheld the dogma passed down by the first Apostles was **St. Ignatius of Antioch.** As he was awaiting death at the hands of the Romans, St. Ignatius left letters to his parishioners in Smyrna, warning them of the *Docetic heresy* which denied Jesus was both Body *and* Spirit when He walked the earth, and that His Body, Blood, Soul and Divinity was truly present in the Eucharist. Again, we can see a faithful servant following His Lord's mandate.   What was important to our Lord Jesus was important to St. Ignatius. *The night before Jesus died, He felt it so important to leave us His Body and Blood in the Holy Eucharist, He furnished the means by which we could always have Him truly present among us - He instituted the priesthood and directed His first Bishops to bring His Body and Blood in the Holy Eucharist to His children, during the Holy Mass in remembrance of Him.*   Here, we encounter one of Jesus' Bishops, on the verge of a torturous death thinking, like the Lord, of the lambs the Lord had left in his charge.

When St. Ignatius was born, he was given the name Theophorus which means God-bearer, and God-bearer he was.   It is believed he was a convert, and a disciple of St. John the Evangelist.   He was chosen by Saints Peter and Paul as Bishop of Antioch, and served *loyally* for forty years.

When Emperor Domitian died, Christians had a respite from persecution.   But sadly, it was short-lived, for, fifteen months after his death, they not only renewed their oppression of the Christians they added new tortures, cruelty and brutality.   No one was free from the tentacles of hate and fury generated against Christians and their refusal to worship Roman pagan gods.   As Bishop, St. Ignatius could do no less than refuse to worship these false gods.   And refuse he did!   He was removed from his episcopate in

Antioch, and after grueling cross-examination, was shackled in chains to stand trial in Rome. But his sentence had already been decided: he was to be the sport of the Roman spectators in the Arena, as wild beasts devoured his body.

As he travelled by sea to Rome, and the ship stopped at ports along the way, the outpouring of love by the people, was the only physical consolation he received to counterbalance the extreme night and day cruelty of his captives. They took delight in seeing how far they could go before he would crack and deny his Lord. But St. Ignatius did not submit. We know, it was only the *Signal Grace* bestowed on him by the Lord that could account for the strength he had. God does not take away the pain; He gives the martyrs, dry and wet[11], the strength to endure it.

St. Ignatius was suffering. He was on his way to be martyred for the Faith, and like Jesus and Paul before him, he was leaving instructions to his charges on earth. He begged his followers not to step in, in an effort to halt his execution, but to allow him to have this gift of dying for the Faith. He was imitating Jesus Who told *His* followers to not fight His persecutors, *"Put back your sword. Do you not suppose I can call on My Father to provide at a moment's notice more than twelve legions of angels?"* (Matt 26:52-53) Saint Ignatius' only request was:

"Only pray for me that God may give me grace within as well as without, not only to say it but to desire it, that I may not only be called, but be found a Christian. Suffer me to be the food of wild beasts through whom I may attain unto God. I

---

[11]Those who shed their blood for the Faith are called *"Wet Martyrs"*. Bishop Sheen wrote, *"since the enemies of Christ do not always kill, but instead torture, the dry martyrs suffered over a period of years pain that far exceeded that of the brief interval of the Wet Martyrs."* from chapter on Archbishop Fulton J. Sheen-Saints and other Powerful Men in the Church-Bob and Penny Lord

*am God's grain and I am to be ground by the teeth of wild
beasts that I may be found the pure bread of Christ.*"[12]

He wrote to the Philadelphians, praising their Bishop,
and begged them not to fall into heresy. Whenever you talk
of the greats of the Church, it always goes back to our Love,
our Lord Jesus in His Holy Eucharist. St. Ignatius wrote:
*"Use one Eucharist; for the Flesh of the Lord Jesus Christ is
one, and the cup is one, to unite us all in His Blood."*

He not only *lived* faithfully the tenets of our Faith, but
died a martyr's death rather than deny them. St. Jerome
wrote that when St. John Chrysostom preached in Antioch
on St. Ignatius' feast day, October 17th, he told the faithful
that although the soil of Rome was drenched with his (St.
Ignatius) blood, it was Antioch who would have his relics for
all time.[13] St. John Chrysostom added, *"You lent him for a
season and you received him back with interest."*

Tertullian, before he adopted the heresies of
Montanism argued against Docetism. When he answered
their heresy, that Christ had no real Body, that He was a
phantom who appeared to have a body, Tertullian ridiculed
it by saying: *"If Christ had no Body, then when He said, at the
Last Supper, 'This is My Body', he was referring to a piece of
bread and that piece of bread was nailed to the Cross."* As we
write this, it is such a perfect answer to those who claim that
the Holy Eucharist is still a piece of bread and not the Body,
Blood, Soul and Divinity of Christ. But, we must admit, tears
come to our eyes for this beautiful disciple of Christ, who so
brilliantly defended the Church until he fell into error. We
would like to believe that when Tertullian approached the
gates of Heaven, Jesus came forth and said to Tertullian, *I*

---

[12]Butler's Lives of the Saints-Thurston and Atwater

[13]A soldier, seeing the valiant way St. Ignatius died, placed his body
on the fire and had it burned to ashes. After which, the ashes were
scooped up and sent to Antioch-from Butler's Lives of the Saints-
Thurston and Atwater

welcome you because I remember the many times you defended Me and My Church.

MONTANISTS

Their founder was Montanus, a Phyrgian who appears to have been a *priest* of Cybele[14]. Montanus converted to Catholicism in around the year 150. Those who are new in the Faith, often are wooed by the Lord. When you convert to the Lord through His Church, you feel the Lord close to you; you have inner thoughts or what you believe are inner locutions from the Lord (and they can be), you experience emotions you have never known before. We call that the honeymoon experience. Montanus probably began to receive similar gifts. He claimed he was having visions; he claimed he was receiving messages or revelations straight from the Lord, contrary to Church teaching. People began to flock around him. We always seem to be attracted to anyone who claims to be seeing or hearing the Lord or His Mother. He began to prophecy. *Note: The greatest mystics, and those showered with gifts always tested the spirit, obediently waiting upon the Church's decision.* Possibly, the greatest sign that a vision or inner locution is not authentic is disobedience to the Church. Montanus placed himself above the authority of the Church!

As we said before, prophets, real or unreal, always attract followers, or opportunists. Maximilla and Priscilla, two wealthy women, socially prominent in the area, heard Montanus, and subsequently joined him. They not only helped to spread his heresies, with their influence and power, but soon *they* became "*prophetesses*" of his sect.

Refusing to desist from his heretical teaching, Montanus was expelled from the Church; he set up *his* own

---

[14]Cybele-a nature goddess of Asia Minor; identified by the Greeks with Rhea (Greek Mythology-the daughter of Uranus and Gaea, wife of Cronus, and mother of Zeus...). (Webster's Dictionary)

church, around the year 156. Armed with *trained* preachers, and supported by his faithful, though deluded followers, he set out to destroy the Church. Tertullian who had so ably and faithfully defended the Church, became an *apostate*, when he became a Montanist in 207.

What were the heresies of the Montanists?

Montanus claimed to have received a new revelation direct from God: According to his twisted mentality: since the Commandments of Moses and those of Christ had failed, God was now revealing to him and his followers *a new way* (or can it be called today, a New Age?).

Having claimed their revelations superior to those of the prophets of the Old Testament and to that which had been passed down in the New Testament, they set themselves up as prophets. They maintained, their revelations placed them *above* the authority of the Church and her bishops. With their own brand of truth, separate from Mother Church and her guidelines, they were responsible for leading many away from the Church. This heresy finally lost its followers and its impact after its leaders were excommunicated.

The Montanists expected the Kingdom of God to come, any *day*. Therefore, they came to the conclusion that since *all mankind was sinful*, it was essential, they (the Montanists) live by themselves, away from everyone. We wonder, was it for this reason or were they, as many cults today, isolating their followers so that they could completely brain-wash them? You can imagine the destruction of this society, under their authority, resulting from such seclusion, especially for the young growing up without the companionship of other young people.

Montanus became dictatorial. He forgot the Gospel teaching of Jesus to first love God and then to love your neighbor as yourself. He did not *love*, but instead he ruled with harshness. At first, Montanus *demanded* his followers fast for one week, twice a year. When they submitted to that, he imposed an additional week of fasting per year.

He did not allow second marriages under any circumstances. The Catholic Church has always allowed second marriages after the death of a spouse. Even before Vatican Council II, the Church has always, in her endless love and desire to have all her children part of the Family of Christ, allowed annulments under certain conditions. The Church has always judged that some unions which appear to be marriages really do not meet the conditions, and so are null and void from the first. Grounds for annulment include:

(a) One partner never intended to have children.

(b) One or both partners were not free to marry.

(c) One or both partners were incapable of understanding the nature of the contract or commitment (either from being too young, or because of psychological reasons).

There are, we are sure, grounds possibly that we have not outlined here, and if you are considering an annulment, please seek the advice of your parish priest.

These grounds are much abused today, with people believing, if a marriage did not work out, it was never a marriage, and that was justification for an annulment.

He denied the Sacrament of Penance. Not believing in forgiveness, he refused to accept back into the community anyone who had been guilty of murder, adultery or idolatry (even after they had repented). We always ask ourselves when a situation comes up in our own lives, *Is this the way Jesus would act? Do I see Jesus in this situation? Am I reflecting Jesus in my action?* Our Lord said we must forgive 70 times 7 or *indefinitely*. When you are trying to discern if someone or something is of the Lord, possibly these guidelines can help. Montanus' followers did not discern and so they would experience much pain and disillusionment as their false messiah began to show his clay feet.

He required that all virgins wear veils in church. This custom is passed down by our Jewish brothers and sisters. Their Law requires *women's* heads to be covered at all times. It goes back to the Jewish belief that to see God was to die; therefore not only women but men covered their heads, shielding themselves from gazing upon God.

In addition to his *precepts*, many of which were in direct opposition to Church teaching, the fact that they were to be followed in blind obedience to a *new*, *personal*, direct revelation from God to Montanus and his *prophets*, was a clear attempt to *circumvent* the absolute authority of the Church and all Jesus taught in His Word.

As it denied the importance of man's works and denied the forgiveness of sins, people soon became aware that *Montanism* was a very *no hope*, despondent, cruelly severe, compassionless way of life, and it did not last very long.

The Church fights back!

St. Irenaeus described the difference between the concepts of the Montanists, and the true teaching of the Faith, as passed down, faithfully to us from the first Apostles. Unlike the Montanists, he said that the bishops who taught in the centuries following the deaths of the Apostles of Jesus did not teach their *own personal views* or raise themselves up to be like God, but held fast to the doctrines of their predecessors, that we were called by Jesus to be of one Faith under one headship.

It is said Montanus died, like Judas before him, by hanging himself.

ENCRATITES

We said that whenever Mother Church has been under severe attack, God has raised up Saints and other Powerful Men and Women in the Church, has sent His Mother to earth or brought about Miracles of the Eucharist.

We have one of those Powerful Men in **St. Justin Martyr.** Famous among those who died for the Faith during the reign of Marcus Aurelius, was a *layman* called Justin Martyr. He is known as the first Christian Apologist to write a defense (of any considerable length) defending the Church and its teaching.

He was most likely a Samaritan as he came from Nablus. But he spoke no Hebrew, and his parents, who were *pagans*, seemed to be of *Greek* origin. They provided their son with an extensive education including the greek philosophers. But, as with St. Augustine, these scholars failed to satisfy him.

One day, while St. Justin Martyr was walking in a field, he met up with an old man who spoke of a philosophy nobler and more fulfilling than anything St. Justin had ever heard of, even in Plato's Science. When he asked the old man where it came from, the old man told him that God first revealed it to the Hebrew Prophets and then, when His Son came, *He* fulfilled it. The old man urged him to pray. Inspired by his words, and very possibly the urging of the Holy Spirit, St. Justin was led to study Holy Scriptures. As Justin had already been drawn to the Christians, this filled him with a desire to learn more about them. He wrote:

"Even at the time when I was content with the doctrines of Plato, when I heard Christians accused and saw them fearlessly meet death and all that is considered terrible, I felt that such men could not have possibly have been leading the life of vicious pleasure with which they were credited.[15]*"*

He was baptized into the Faith at age 30. Up to the time of St. Justin there were few apologists or defenders of the Faith. The early Christians were very simple people and for the most part unlearned. Their focus was primarily to protect the Eucharist from being profaned. Therefore, even

---

[15]Butler's Lives of the Saints-Thurston and Atwater

when their spirits were disquieted by the teachings they were hearing and even when they judged that Jesus' teachings were being misinterpreted, they were willing to put up with these hurts. Justin, on the other hand, because of his own call and walk into the Church, believed and insisted, if people learned about the true Faith, more would join and *remain*. He felt, as we have, the terrifying responsibility we all share for those lost because they had never been taught the True Faith. His words echo through our Church today:

"It is our duty to make known our doctrine, lest we incur the guilt and punishment of those who have sinned through ignorance.[16]"

Since he was a philosopher, he was able to travel extensively from land to land, dialoguing with pagans, heretics and Jews, as well as tirelessly defending the Church in his writings. He eventually ended up in Rome. There, he debated a cynic whose name was Crescens. He showed him not only to be ignorant of the Faith, but to be willfully perverting its Dogma. Although St. Justin and the Church were victorious this round, Crescens waited, then when St. Justin came to Rome for the second time, it is popularly believed that Crescens was the one responsible for the authorities apprehending St. Justin.

We have often repeated what someone wisely asked: *"If you were standing trial for being Christian, would you be found guilty?"* St. Justin boldly proclaimed he was a Christian. When he refused to deny Jesus Christ and His Church, and sacrifice to the false gods, he was condemned. He and six other Christians, five men and one woman, were beheaded.

In 167, Justin Martyr chose to die a martyr's death rather than live and worship pagan gods. St. Justin Martyr had what Mother Angelica calls *"Signal Grace,"* that which she said the early Christians possessed as they faced the

---

[16]Butler's Lives of the Saints-Thurston and Atwater

lions, who charged toward them in the arenas, and did not run.

Now, St. Justin Martyr had had a friend called Tatian. Upon St. Justin's death, Tatian chose not only to worship false gods but to lead others away from Jesus and His Church. We have included the life of St. Justin Martyr to show the paths that are laid before us. Two friends - one dies a martyr and is proclaimed a Saint; the other chooses the world and its false promises and is remembered as a heretic!

Tatian began as a Christian apologist[17]. He was born in Assyria in about 110 A.D. He went to Rome where he taught rhetoric[18]. There, he met and became the friend of St. Justin Martyr. He studied under St. Justin Martyr. St. Justin Martyr was responsible for Tatian's conversion to Christianity in about the year 152. Tatian wrote *"An Address to the Greeks"* which was one of the earliest writings (apologetics) *defending* the Church, against the pagan philosophers.

What happened? Tatian was most assuredly no light weight! What could have changed his heart from protector of the Church to heretic? After St. Justin Martyr died, in about 167, Tatian went to the East. There, he was exposed to Eastern religions and picked up some very strange ideas resembling *Gnosticism*. This is where he founded a gnostic sect of Encratites who went by the name of *Aquarii*. Very possibly they had this name because they fanatically

---

[17] This title of honor was given in the early days of the Church to writers among the fathers who defended the Church and its teachings. Now it's applied to one verse in fundamental theology, or one who teaches, speaks, or writes in defense or clarification of the teachings of the Church. (Catholic Encyclopedia-Broderick)

[18]rhetoric-the art or science of using words effectively in speaking or writing.(Webster's Dictionary)

prohibited the use of wine in any form; even during the Mass, they used water instead of wine.

He and his followers based their teachings on the same erroneous idea of heretics before them, *that matter is evil.* Those practicing this error were **Encratites** who also went under the name *Aquarii*, but in actuality they were just the Gnostic heresy under another name.

We are never satisfied to go to Hell by ourselves. Tatian proceeded to use the gifts of persuasion that God had given him and began to spread his new found heretical philosophy to the unsuspecting believers who had known him as a defender of the Faith.   He did not lead the poor sheep to the butcher's block by himself. As is usually the case, there is always some deluded *judas goat* ready to help.

One of Tatian's closest disciples and supporters was a Bishop named **Severus**. His diocese was in Gabala, Spain. By virtue of his *authority*, Severus lent credibility to this heresy. Do we not expect our Bishops to pass on the Faith as Jesus commanded, faithful to the first Bishops? Yes, we do, and how condemned are those who betray that trust! As Severus was a very forceful speaker, he could and did draw many to *him*, and away *from* the true teachings of the Church.   With his highly dramatic preaching, he brought excitement and power to the Encratites.   But that wasn't good enough to satisfy his ego. The ego is a leaky pot which cannot hold its contents but needs to be constantly filled.

Not content to follow and spread this abomination as it was, he changed some of *Tatian's* key concepts and added some of his own. Could it have been a little pride? But, think of it, how else would he have been able to lure them away from Tatian? Had he not done to Tatian what Tatian had done to the Faith *he* had promised to obey and follow?

Those who followed Bishop Severus formed a *new* group calling themselves *Severians* after their new master. Can we not again see Lucifer at work? A priest once said,

"*Satan can counterfeit any virtue except obedience.*[19]"
Disobedience breeds disobedience.   What did the chief
priests do with Judas when he went to them, after he
betrayed Jesus? Right! They betrayed him.

With the early *Encratites*, we heard that *all matter is evil.*
Now *Severus ascertained that matter was uncreated and
eternal.* Does this sound familiar? Is this not part of New
Age and Pantheism[20] where they espouse: God is nature;
God is the trees, the sea, etc; God is not the Author of
creation, He is diffused and one with creation. It sounds so
ridiculous, it has to be a case of intellectual and spiritual
blindness, almost as if we are being drugged into a stupor,
and cannot discern any longer.

Severus laid the ground work for Pantheism and New
Age. He conceded that God had a hand in creating *some*
things, but only through a *power force* He received from an
inferior creation of His. What New Age is teaching is that
Jesus was only able to perform miracles when He could tap
into *someone* possessing the same power he had[21].

We see apostates within the Church, down through the
centuries, attempting to weave the same lies into the
garment of The Church, over and over again. But because
they are not the same material as the garment Christ left us,
this new cloth made of deceit, like new wine skins rips away
from the old and has to be restitched over and over again.

---

[19]Father George Kosicki

[20]Pantheism-...the negation of an essential difference between God
and all (His) created things.

[21]"*Rosemary Haughton said:'She is pointing to a new physics...and to
the wisdom of the east as a means of recovering that which has been
lost...a new social order.' She began to explain how Jesus was able to work
His healing miracles: 'He (Jesus) perceived in others the operation of the
same divine energy that was His own motive power. He knew people...as
possessing the same power He had.'*"(The Unicorn in the Sanctuary-
Randy England)

Severus did not throw out every lie of the apostates before him. *Severus and his followers held on to these heresies:*

He denied the Resurrection of the dead;

Like heretics before him, *he denied that man has free-will;*

He rejected the Law of Moses, as never having existed.

Having to top the other heretics, and looking for something new to deny, *he condemned Matrimony and its sanctity.* Whereas some of the heresies denied second marriages, the Aquarii or Encratites or Severians rejected all marriage as evil.

The Church fights back!

Referring to Jesus, St. Irenaeus wrote in answer to gnostics of his time:

"He came to save all through Himself, - all I say, who through Him are reborn in God, - infants and children, and youths and old men. Therefore He passed through every age, becoming an infant for infants, sanctifying infants; a child for children, sanctifying those who are of that age, and at the same time becoming for them an example of piety, of righteousness, and of submission; a young man for youths, becoming an example for youths and sanctifying them for the Lord. So also He became an old man for old men so that He might be the perfect teacher in all things, - perfect not only in respect to the setting forth of the truth, but perfect also in respect to relative age, - sanctifying the elderly and the same time becoming an example for them. Then He even experienced death itself, so that He might be the firstborn from the dead, having the first place in all things, the originator of life, before all and preceding all."[22]

---

[22] Vol.1 p.87-section 201-The Faith of the Early Church Fathers-Jurgens

Left:
*The alabaster window
in St. Peter's Basilica
in Rome
The Dove over the chair
of St. Peter represents
the Holy Spirit, Who
inspires the Church.
The Monarchians
denied the Holy Trinity.*

Right
*The Blessed Virgin Mary,
the Mother of Jesus*

*The Valentinians
preached that Mary
was not the Mother of
Jesus.*

MONARCHIANS

We especially mention this heresy because *Tertullian* was one who penned this name for a group of heretics who went by the names of *Patripassionists* in the West and *Sabelians*[23] in the East. In later more modern times, it was made to include a group of earlier heretics known as *Theodotians*. This list of names, in later times, was expanded to include even more titles, and groups. An all-encompassing name for these heretics could be *Antitrinitarians* as they denied the mystery of the Holy Trinity. They promulgated the heresy that *God the Father and God the Son were One and the same Person.*

Praxeas, their founder, started out by fighting another heresy, that of the *Montanists*. Praxeas was probably the first Monarchian to visit Rome. Having been well received by the Pope between 190 and 198, he used his influence *against* the Montanists. Here, he was fighting one heresy, only to promote another. We know of Praxeas only through the writings of *Tertullian* in his book "Adversus Praxeam[24]", where he accuses Praxaes of heresies against the Holy Trinity. Tertullian held Praxaes responsible for the Pope's condemnation of the Montanists and their prophets and prophetesses.

Do we not see this happening today, within our own Church, *good people* fighting each other, trying to gain power on earth, very often without knowing it, and all in the name of Jesus and His Church?

What was the belief of these heretics? They, along with other heretics *denied that there are Three distinct Divine Persons in God.* They taught that "*God was one in Person*

---

[23]"those who unified the Persons of the Trinity and completely did away from the real distinction among Them"-from The Church Teaches-Jesuit Fathers

[24]This was written by Tertullian after he succumbed to the errors of the Montanists.

and one in Nature, and that the different Persons were merely different manifestations of the same Divine Being.[25]"

The Church fights back!

The Church has always taught and insisted that the Three Divine Persons in the One God are equal and yet distinct in form from each other.

In Genesis 1:26, "*Then God said: 'Let us make man in our own image, after our likeness. Let them have dominion over the fish of the sea, the birds of the air, and the cattle, and all over the wild animals and all the creatures that crawl on the ground.'*" God said "*our*" not *my;* Was He not referring to the other Two Persons in the Holy Trinity?

Jesus replied to Judas'[26] question, "*Lord, why is it that you will reveal yourself to us and not to the world?*":

"Anyone who loves me
will be true to my word,
and My Father will love him;
We will come to him
and make Our dwelling place with him.
He who does not love Me does not keep My word.
Yet the word you hear is not Mine;
It comes from the Father Who sent Me.
This much have I told you while
I was still with you;
the Paraclete, the Holy Spirit
Whom the Father will send in My Name
will instruct you in everything,
and remind you of all I have told you."(Jn 14:22)

Jesus is referring to Himself and His Father when He says "*We will come to him and make Our dwelling place with him.*"

---

[25]chapter-The Triune God from The Church teaches - Jesuit Fathers-

[26]not Judas Escariot, but Jesus' cousin St. Jude Thaddeus.

And then in John 15, Jesus again speaks of the Father and the Son and of the Holy Spirit, the Paraclete Who will come from Them:

"When the Paraclete comes,
the Spirit of truth Who comes from the Father-
and Whom I Myself will send from the Father-
He will bear witness on My behalf."(Jn 15:26)

We hear Jesus speak of the Holy Trinity when He commissions the Apostles:

"Jesus came forward and addressed them in these words:
'Full authority has been given to Me
both in heaven and on the earth;
go, therefore, and make disciples
of all the nations.
Baptize them in the name
of the Father
and of the Son
and of the Holy Spirit.'" (Mt 28:19)

The Third Century

TERTULLIANISTS

This sect began in Carthage, and continued to advance its errors for 200 years after the death of its founder, *Tertullian*. They are definitely a shoot that sprouted up from that sick tree called *Montanism*. Some writers claim that after Tertullian became a Montanist be was even more rigorous than the Montanists, and that's when he founded the Tertullianists. Whereas others believe, his followers did not use the name Tertullianists until after his death.

Tertullian was born in Carthage of pagan parents anywhere between the years 155-160. He was highly esteemed as a lawyer. When he converted to Christianity in 193 A.D., he used the talents and the knowledge he had acquired as an attorney, to defend Mother Church. St. Jerome tells us Tertullian was later ordained to the Priesthood. Although there are split opinions on this, either he was a priest or he had a veritable treasure house of information at his disposal that he used over the years to write his highly respected apologetics defending the Church. With the sympathies he showed toward the laity on theological matters, there are those who have equally valid arguments that he probably was a layman.

Whatever his walk, he has been one of the most quoted of the early Christian writers. When Greek ceased to be the accepted language of the West, Tertullian was the first to write in Latin. For twenty-five years of his life, his writings and loyalties fit into three time periods: The Catholic, the semi-Montanist, and the Montanist.

Although the *semi-Montanist period* wasn't considered a heresy or schism, it is the *wide road* Tertullian floundered on between Catholicism and Montanism. As you read Tertullian's writings during this time, you can see, he is beginning to demean the role of the priesthood and hierarchy, as he *inflates* the priestly role of the layman. Even before he splits from the Church, you can see his sympathies are with the Montanists and their prophets. *Today, do we not hear those who call themselves Catholics speaking against Mother Church; they insist on remaining in the Church, although they refuse to obey the Vicar of the Church, our Pope John Paul II.*

When he was writing in his **Catholic period**, he was "*Super Catholic*". He was truly orthodox in all his teachings, faithfully following all the guidelines set down by the Apostles before him. Tertullian was respected as "*the most esteemed Latin ecclesiastical[1] writer of the early Church[2]*" before he fell into error. What happened? Had Tertullian grown proud? After all, he was famous. He was looked up to by his peers. Had he forgotten his gifts were just that - gifts from the Lord? Sometimes, if we are not careful, we can be fooled into believing we are "*more Catholic than the Pope*" and are above the Church's teachings. Our Religion is not to be practiced or taught according to our consciences or what *we personally* believe. That is why the Lord left us a "*Sweet Christ on Earth[3]*" our Pope and Vicar as our teacher and guide.

By the year 213 A.D., it is pretty safe to assume that Tertullian fully entered his Montanist period. For the next seven to ten years his writings became more and more extreme, more and more distant from the truth, he had once defended. *His stern, unrelenting, heartless attitude toward sinners who had repented*, was one of the areas that would cause him to split with the authority of the Church, he had so powerfully defended, and plunge him into *Montanism.*

Tertullian's errors insisted *the Church could not absolve adulterers.* This is contradictory to Holy Scripture. The Lord

[1]ecclesiastical - of or pertaining to the Church - Catholic Encyclopedia-Broderick
[2]Triumph of the Church-Rev. John P. Markoe, S.J
[3]St. Catherine of Siena

Himself, Founder of our Church, deemed it *merciful and just*, to forgive an adulteress. When they brought a woman accused of adultery before Jesus, instead of condemning her, He challenged her accusers:

"*Let the man among you who has no sin be the first to cast a stone at her.' They all drifted away one by one, including the elders.* Jesus then said to the woman: *'Has no one condemned you?'* When she replied: *'No one, Sir',* Jesus replied: *'Nor do I condemn you. You may go. But from now on, avoid this sin.'*"(John 8:7)

"*Nor do I condemn you.*" Jesus forgave this sinner and it is believed she may have been the one who bathed Him with her tears and anointed Him with precious oils. Our Jesus said, this woman, who everyone had refused to forgive, loved Him to the magnitude of the sin He had forgiven. With that in mind, what a travesty it would have been if Mother Church had not corrected this heartless heresy.

When the crippled, the mute, the blind and the helpless asked for healing, Jesus first said "*Your sins are forgiven.*", before healing them of their physical ills. It had to be very important to Jesus, and yet this man Tertullian presumed to make *himself* master by really disagreeing with *the* Master. Does this not remind us of that time when the Pharisees grumbling, challenged Jesus, demanding who was *He* to forgive sins?(Matt 9) Jesus, knowing their hearts and minds, and fully knowing this could lead Him to His walk to the Cross, spoke up:

"*Why do you harbor such evil thoughts? Which is less trouble to say, 'Your sins are forgiven' or to say, 'Stand up and walk?'*"

Tertullian taught that *those who married a second time were adulterers.* Did this include widows and widowers? Mother Church, who so many view as being stoic and unbending, goes out of her way, loving Mother that she is, to welcome her children back into the Church family. She has made available, to those who have been divorced and wish to remarry, a Tribunal to judge the merits of their case, to see if there is just cause for an annulment of the first marriage, so that the couple can fully participate in the Sacraments.

Tertullian also stated that *it was unlawful to attempt to escape from persecution.* Let us pray on what *kind* of persecution. Could it have been Christians fleeing for their lives? It was not until the fourth century that Constantine stopped the persecution of Christians. Before his legitimizing Christianity, Christians went through one of the saddest and bloodiest periods in the history of the Church. Not all, but some emperors set themselves up as chief persecutors, instituting edicts which were designed to bring about the total extermination of all Christians and Christianity throughout the entire Greco-Roman Empire.

In the ten years following the year 205, *Emperor Diocletian* waged a campaign which was designed to totally exterminate every Christian on the face of the earth. This went on for ten years!

Emperor Septimus Severus proclaimed: Conversion to Christianity was forbidden by law.

They persecuted Bishops. In the year 235, *Emperor Maximian* thought by doing away with those who had come down from the original Apostles, the Church would die. How foolish they were. Did they not learn from the greatest attempt to abolish Christianity, the Crucifixion of our most beloved Lord, that not even the forces of hell will destroy Christ's Church?

Emperor Decius, in 250, waged the most horrendous, massive blood-bath against anyone *suspected* of being Christian.

In 257, *Emperor Valerian* confiscated all Church property and that of those *suspected* to be Christian.

One emperor more cruel than the one before him and we survived!

But to try to get into the mind and heart of Tertullian, how could a fellow Christian be so lacking in mercy on these brave brothers and sisters who risked their lives, every day, as they tried to live the Gospel life of their Lord? Was their crime, that of attempting to escape from inhuman incarceration in pitch-black, foul, filthy prisons? Many Christians were exiled to prison camps located in the middle of malaria infested swamps. The strong were subjected to forced labor in metal and salt mines, from which only one in every ten survived.

The Romans considered the crime of being a Christian a capital crime. Judges, like Tertullian condemned them to separation from the Church, they loved, if they tried to save their lives. If there was ever a time for the faithful to leave the Church, it would have been then. And yet, they stayed. They stayed to die from either beheading, crucifixion, being burned at the stake, or facing lions, tigers and leopards frenzied to the point of fury by starvation. And with the *Signal Grace* from God they did not turn and run; they stood firm, and they died that they would live *eternally* with our Lord in Paradise. Writers and historians agree that it's safe to say that over *one million* martyrs died, rather than deny the Faith.

And this was the victory, the triumph of the Cross. This is the Church we enter, the Church whose foundation was built on a lake of martyr's blood. Some modern theologians called them ignorant fanatics. When those theologians stand before our Lord and His Judgment, will they beg from these Lazarus' some water to cool their fevered tongues[4]?

St. Zephyrinus was known as a Pope who leaned heavily on his archdeacon for advice. Since the Pope had originally accepted the Montanists, when he then condemned them, Tertullian judged that Praxeas had exerted political pressure

---

[4]Luke 16:20-25

on the Archdeacon, who then influenced the Pope. Could Tertullian have been harboring a resentment against the Pope? In any event, he angrily came out against the Pope, lashing out at him, for his leniency toward sinners, for accepting them back into the Church after they repented.

Lord, You Who forgave all sinners; You, Who would have forgiven even Judas, if he had asked for forgiveness, did You turn and gaze at Tertullian as You had Peter? How sad; that he should choose to sacrifice Your Love for the god of pride and importance.

Where do we go wrong? How does a defender of the Faith turn against the very Church he loved, fought for and espoused? Tertullian would have been considered a *Father of the Church*[5], had he not fallen into error, consequently becoming a formal heretic or apostate[6].

Although much of his writings are invaluable in part, and are used till today, Tertullian *is not* among those trail blazers, who faithfully interpreted and defended the teachings of the Church, and would for all time be remembered as *Fathers of the Church.*

-----

[5]There are four requirements to be called a Father of the Church:

(a) The writer lived during the period preceding the year 800. The last Father in the East was St. John Damascene (676-700); and the last Father in the West was St. Bede the Venerable (672-735).

(b) The writer followed the orthodox teaching, faithful to the True Doctrines of the Church. His work was free of heretical teaching; however he would not have been excluded if his work contained a few inaccuracies.

(c) Sanctity- All the great Fathers and most of all the minor Fathers, having lived virtuous lives, were canonized *Saints*.

(d) The sanction of the Church. It was not necessary to be formally approved; a general acceptance was sufficient.

[6] In the early Church, a formal heretic or *apostate* was one who was guilty of "*going over permanently to paganism, the rejection, after an initial acceptance and Baptism, of the Graces of the Faith.*" (Catholic Encyclopedia-Broderick)

The Church fights back

What happened to the followers of Tertullian? St. Augustine met up with a sect known as Tertullianists in Carthage at the end of the fourth century. It was St. Augustine who converted the last of this sect in Africa and brought them back to the Mother Church who we are sure, welcomed them back with open arms.

ORIGENISTS

This cult was named after **Origen**, one of the most gifted and learned men of his time. He was born in Alexandria in 185. His father, St. Leonidas, died a martyr's death and was proclaimed a Saint by Mother Church. This son who had such promise, this son for whom he had such high hopes, this son whom his father *knew* would defend the Church, would be condemned as a heretic.

Unlike Tertullian, whose early writings were powerfully authentic and are being quoted till today, Origen's work was always interspersed with strong hellenistic teachings, making it difficult to distinguish truth from heresy. What were some of Origen's teachings that left the Church no other recourse but to declare him a heretic?

Origen contended that *from their very beginning, all rational (human) creatures[7] were pure spirits.* The Church's teaching, from the very beginning, was that the Angels *alone* were created pure spirit; animals were created with only body, and *humans* with both body and spirit[8].

Origen claimed that **after the** *universal restoration, following the second Crucifixion of Jesus Christ, even those suffering eternal damnation in hell would become pure spirits.* We, in the Roman Catholic Church teach and believe that the damned are just that, now and forever. This came about

---

[7]rational-able to reason
[8]Heavenly Army of Angels-Bob and Penny Lord

when they made the decision to break off all relationship with God. Fallen humans, as with fallen angels, having made that final decision, are *eternally*, no turning back, condemned to the ever painful fire of hell. Origen's self-made theology (heretical belief) was that hell is only a purging like that of purgatory and therefore temporary. He insisted, all persons would be saved at some time in the future.

On the other hand, *he insisted that Saints, canonized and non-canonized, or Blesseds who are in Heaven can still be thrown out of Heaven for committing a transgression there.* Now, *in the Church*, we believe that those who were tested, and chose to lead a virtuous life, are now enjoying the gift of *eternal life* in the Presence of God, in Heaven, in perfect happiness. As with the Holy Angels who were tested before the Saints, and chose for God, this is final and irrevocable. There are no more tests for them. They came out with A+.

How did Origen get to this point? He had been given the finest education. His father believed in educating his son in affairs of the world of the flesh, as well as the those of the *real* world of the Divine, so he carefully orchestrated his learning to include both worlds. On the one hand, Origen was influenced by Sacred writings encompassing all that pertains to our Lord and the Faith He passed down; and on the other hand, literature not pertaining to the Divine but to that of the world and its secularism. Much of this worldly *humanistic* knowledge, he derived from Greek philosophers and their paganistic viewpoints.

As a youth, his love for Christ and His message, was so powerful, he begged his mother to allow him to join his father in prison so that he, too, could shed his blood for our Lord and His Church. All his years of hard work and faithful pursuit of education paid off. His reputation as a dedicated teacher spread to such a degree, that priests and doctors sought his wisdom in their varied walks of life. Some say, Origen would have been considered the greatest theologian up to the time of St. Augustine, if he had not given into error.

Although he was a layman, Origen was asked to preach in Caesarea[9], on Scripture, by the *two* Bishops from Caesarea and Jerusalem. But Origen's bishop, Bishop Demetrius of Alexandria took exception to him preaching, and insisted he return to Alexandria.

Fifteen years passed. Origen found himself passing through Caesarea, once again. But this time, the two Bishops of Caesarea and Jerusalem ordained Origen to the Priesthood. *Furious*, Bishop Demetrius of Alexandria called two synods at Alexandria. Origen was relieved of his Priesthood and, if that was not enough, excommunicated! The Bishop charged canons were broken; he insisted, according to these canons, a man must be ordained by the Bishop of the Diocese where he lived.

Origen left Alexandria. He went to Caesarea where he found solace and acceptance. He opened his school there, once more. He and his school received immediate approval and were highly acclaimed.

There is no doubt that there were decided problems in much of Origen's teachings. Had Origen learned too well the philosophy of the *earthly* world? In his zealous quest for knowledge, did he forget that the greatest good that ever came about was through *obedience*, that of Jesus' Yes on the Cross?

In being ordained did Origen know he was being a party to disobeying canon law? Remember, he was extremely learned. Was his being ordained out of his diocese, the cause of Origen being excommunicated from the Church? Or did the Alexandrian council so declare because of his willful disobedience in this matter? Or was this infraction an indication of his general disregard of the authority of the

---

[9]in Palestine, or as it is also known: the Holy Land

Church in matters of the Faith? Or was the problem the Bishop knew of the dangerous heresies Origen had been interspersing in his teaching and that is why he would not allow him to preach in the first place? Was the last straw when he refused to obey?

Not even the seriousness of his excommunication from the Church, and his being released from his priestly duties, stopped people from following his teachings. Only our Lord and the *enemy* know how many souls were lost because of his pride, that evil which first led him to espouse his errors, and then led him to influence others to espouse his heretical teachings. Again, disobedience knowing no boundary, spreading and eroding, attacked the very foundation of the Church. But the House did not crumble. The Lord's Mansion on earth still stood!

His fame and accolades were to come to an end. Emperor Maximinus' persecution of Christians forced Origen to flee to Cappadocia. When he received news that Maximinus had left Caesarea, Origen returned. There, he once again, resumed his preaching against the Church's teaching. His triumphal return to Caesarea was short-lived. Emperor Decius, during his reign of terror and persecution had waged the bloodiest warfare against all Christians and those *suspected* of being Christians. Origen had suffered, along with so many others, the most horrendous and painful torture. His weakened physical health was to take a toll on his life. He died at Tyre in 254.

Tertullian and Origen were given great gifts from the Lord. They were born in a special time in a special place, under special circumstances, of special parents who afforded them special opportunities, all special Graces from God that they might glorify Him and His Church. They were given special intellectual and Spiritual skills. Much of what they wrote was in keeping with the Church, and has been used over the centuries. What happened to result in their falling into heresy? By their wisdom and opportunity it is quite plain they were specially chosen to do God's work. How did they use that which they had not earned but had been bestowed upon them by God to have and use?

In addition to their other iniquities, these men take their place in Church History among those judged the most guilty of *hellenizing* the Church, that is *the weakening of the Judaic roots of our Church* as passed down to us from our first Pope, Peter, and Jesus Himself. Jesus chose to be born of the Jewish people. He said, He had come to fulfill the (Jewish) Law, not do away with it. Tertullian and Origen, with their errors, attempted to undermine or subordinate the teachings of the Church that was built on our *Jewish* foundation to that of the philosophy of Greek writers and their paganistic rationale. Sadly, part of what History will remember of them is that they sacrificed the Truth of Divine Revelation to that of Greek Philosophy, with its false gods and its prideful lies and promises. They listened to those whom God had created rather than live by the inspired Word of The *Creator*.

The Church fights back!
Controversies on his teachings did not come about during Origen's lifetime, but surfaced three different times, in 300 A.D., in 400 A.D. and in 553 A.D.

In the Fourth Century, the Lord raised up a new saint, *St. Methodius* to defend His Church. This bishop became a formidable defender of the Faith against the Origenists. When St. Methodius, Bishop of Philippi, wrote his treatise *"The Banquet of the Ten Virgins"* he was still an admirer of Origen. But, later, around 300 A.D., he rescinded his former support and came out against Origen's teachings, declaring them heretical.

What caused St. Methodius, once an advocate, to become one of his most formidable adversaries? As we have said so many times before, Satan is the concealer, hiding the truth and Jesus is the Revealer Who will always bring all things to light. This bishop went beyond his own previous evaluation of Origen, when he discovered his teachings were heretical. He did not, as sometimes we have a tendency to do, allow his personal feelings and prejudices to interfere with his God-given mission to uphold the Truth!

In 553, the Second Council of Constantinople *condemned* Origen's writings. It charged they were a contradiction of Holy Scripture.

NOVATIANISTS

We go to Rome. It's around the year 250 A.D. There we find a priest Novatian (or Novatus as he is also known) who is so highly respected by the entire Roman clergy, he is chosen to represent his fellow Roman priests. He will not only go against his Church, he will set himself up as antipope.

Novatian like so many others of the early Church had not been baptized as a baby, but was waiting until he was at the point of death. He *was dying* and a priest was called in to administer the Sacrament of Baptism. When he recovered, he never received any of the other Sacraments of the Church that are essential to be fully a part of the Church. He was never confirmed by a bishop! It boggles the mind how he ever became a priest without having received first the Sacraments of Penance, Holy Communion and Confirmation. Without the gifts of the Holy Spirit, it is understandable how he could have fallen into prideful error.

Instead of being joyful and thanking God for having given him gifts of intellect and the charisma to powerfully proclaim the truths of the Church, he often appeared moody and despondent. His bishop, St. Cyprian, said Novatian tended to become easily agitated; he was arbitrarily rebellious and was obsessed with an *insatiable* appetite for glory and praise.

At this time, there was a great persecution going on, under Emperor Decius. Many Christians apostatized in order to avoid being part of the bloodbath. When the persecution slackened, many apostates wanted to return to the Church. This caused a great deal of bitterness among those who had stayed faithful to the Church, and suffered persecution. A heated debate arose as to whether the apostates should be accepted back in the Church. Novatian joined dissenters who believed Bishop St. Cyprian should accept those wishing to return to the Church back, at once, with little or no penance.

Pope St. Fabian was one of the first victims of the horrible persecution brought about by Emperor Decius. The Pope was arrested and was among the first to be martyred for his Faith. The clergy postponed voting for a successor because some of their number who were still in jail, were needed to vote. The bishops ran the Church for fourteen months, with Novatian as their spokesman.

When all the bishops *finally* convened to vote, Novatian fully expected to be elected Pope. Imagine his bitterness when Bishop St. Cyprian, instead, nominated Cornelius, a very humble priest who had always been grateful to serve the Church in any capacity, no matter how small. In March 251 A.D., St. Cornelius was elected Pope and remained Vicar of Christ until the year 253. Novatian contested their decision and had himself declared a bishop.

As no one would ordain the disobedient priest bishop, it is believed, he found three Bishops to do his dirty work. Because their Dioceses was located in a very remote part of Italy, the bishops had not heard of his defiance of the Pope. When he befriended them, they were completely unaware of his devious plan. He dined and wined them. He kept pouring wine until they were intoxicated to the point of stupefaction. He covertly had them consecrate him bishop.

When he was pope, Pope Fabian ordained Novatian to the priesthood, and chose him to represent the college of presbyters[10]. When he became pope, *St. Cornelius* questioned Novatian's priesthood, claiming he had been *uncanonically ordained, despite the strong opposition of clergy and laity*[11]. He said "*Novatian was possessed by Lucifer for a period of time, most likely when he was a catechumen*[12]".

Whereas Novatian had disagreed with St. Cyprian, arguing he had not shown enough *clemency* to those who had fallen away from the Church, now, he completely reversed his position, with Pope St. Cornelius, and took on a severe religiosity, devoid of all compassion toward those who desired to return. This was called the heresy of *rigorism. Novatian* attacked St. Cyprian for not being lenient enough and now, he was attacking Pope Cornelius for being too *lenient.* He disagreed with the Pope who wanted to accept them back after they had done appropriate penance; Novatian would not accept them back under any conditions. He wrote to all the bishops stating his case *against* the pope. His arguments were brilliant, as he was highly proficient in letter writing. He believed, if he could win support against St. Cornelius on this matter, he could sway the bishops to elect him pope. Although at first it appeared, Novatian would have some followers, among the presbyters, they all rallied around St. Cornelius. Novatian was condemned.

Novatian set himself up as anti-pope. He left the Church, causing a Schism. He modeled his new Church after the official Church. But that was where it stopped.

---

[10]a member of a group who advises the Bishop

[11]chapter on Novatian - Oxford Dictionary of Popes -J.N.D.

[12]In the early Church, when a pagan sought to become a Christian, he was basically instructed and became an "inquirer" and was permitted to be present only during the first part of the Mass.-(Catholic Encyclopedia-Broderick)

Although he claimed to be Orthodox, *he insisted that sins could not be forgiven after Baptism.*

Before he became ambitious and broke with the Church because he wanted to be pope, Novatian's writings were brilliant and right on target with the teachings of the Church. One in particular, his treatise on the Holy Trinity, written in 235 A.D., is considered the first great theological work to come out of Rome. (Most of the writings of the early Fathers of the Church had heretofore come from the East.) As with many of us, when we are recognized for our talents, we forget it is ours only by the Grace of God; nothing we have reason to brag about, as St. Paul said.

In 251 A.D. a council of sixty Bishops had been called by Pope Cornelius. Novatian was excommunicated! Novatian reigned as *anti-pope* from 251 A.D, until he died in 258 A.D. But the Schism he founded did not die with him, but spread to Spain and Syria. It was to strongly remain and influence the Church of Syria for several centuries!

The Novatian Schism was caused not so much because of differences in the Faith, but in the *rigoristic attitudes toward those who had either left the Church and returned, or had lapsed from the Faith, in some way, and had repented.*

As with other heresies, *they also took a very hard, unloving approach to second marriages,* forbidding them under any circumstances. Jesus' Church has never, being the great mother she is, wanted anything but that her family be united.

Another of Novatian's heresies was that *no sin was to be forgiven after Baptism.* This may be part of the reason Catechumens did not want to be baptized until the point of death. St. Augustine would, in the Fourth Century, fight this heresy. But, the Novatian Heresy would last in parts of the world until the Fifth Century!

MANICHAEANS

The Manichaean heresy was named after Manes, a heretic born in Babylon around 216 A.D. Manes (or Mani) was a Persian. When he was 28 years old, he tried to teach religion to his fellow villagers of Mardinu! They remembered when he had been born; they had watched him grow up. And now, he was setting himself up as a teacher? They did not accept him! He wandered aimlessly for forty years, proclaiming, he was the *"Messenger of the True God"*, and to Christians, the Paraclete[13], Jesus promised He would send[14].

Evidently not making an impact in his travels, he returned to Persia. He manipulated King Ormuzd I into believing he was all he claimed; but as the saying goes, all good things come to an end, or, as in this case, all bad things. His time of glory was short-lived. King Ormuzd I occupied the throne for only one year and with the new king came persecution for Mani. In about the year 276 or 277, the new ruler, Bahram had Mani crucified. He had Mani's body stripped of its skin and had the skin stuffed. He then ordered it placed on display, at the city gate, a horrible, inhumane warning to his disciples. Bahram then hunted down Mani's followers and mercilessly persecuted them.

The Manichaean heresy was based on two principles of good and evil, that Satan is no less eternal than God, and he is God's rival. Imagine, them proposing God's imitator was His *equal!* They did not believe that the devil was first a good angel created by God, and that his nature was the work of God. They claimed that the devil came forth from the darkness and was not created by God the Creator. They taught that he was himself, the beginning and the essence of evil.

---

[13]Holy Spirit
[14]Triumph of the Church-Rev. John P. Markoe, S.J

They believed that the devil formed the human body, and that a child is formed in its mother's womb by the devil. And because of these errors, they do not believe in the resurrection of the body. They said that all flesh was created by fallen angels, not created by God.

They espoused: our world is divided between good and evil, and our very nature is the battlefield between good and evil, between God and Satan. One of the most deadly conclusions one would draw from this false philosophy is since we are not responsible for this conflict within us, we are powerless to control or change it. Therefore, is there chance of conversion or change of heart? This would be dredged up again and again in pre-destination heresies that surfaced throughout the history of the Church.

The Manichaean heresy *rejected the Old Testament completely,* and only kept that part of the New Testament that had been dissected, reworded and redesigned by Mani to suit *his own* brand of heresy.

They also ascertained that there were two gods, one of the Old Testament and one of the New Testament.

Again, we find old Satan repeating the same tired lies. The only problem is that the unsuspecting have not known that these lies were dispensed with centuries before.

Another tired old heresy the Manichaeans advocated was that *Christ had no body; that He was pure spirit.*

Mani did away with the Sacrament of Baptism and of Matrimony.

Some of the heresies promoted by the Manichaeans may sound familiar. For example, *they believed that human souls as well as angels are composed of the substance of God.* That is being peddled today under the dirty banner of New Age.

His followers believed in Reincarnation. So do those who espouse New Age.

And again, the copy-cat brings up another tired error, *man has two souls.*

They believed that human souls had previously sinned in Heaven and because of this, the human bodies were cast down on earth.

Something they believed in (very suspiciously sounding like the feminist *goddess* approach to Creation Spirituality, today), was that *man was cut of the Father through the Mother of Life*[15]. As Christians, we believe that only God gives us life and that Jesus was "*conceived by the Holy Spirit and born of the Virgin Mary*". Mother Mary herself would tell you that she has no power, but that all life is through God, alone.

The Church fights back!

St. Athanasius, when responding to the errors of the Arians, concluded that the heresies of Arianism can be traced back to Manicheanism (and not only this heresy but those of Valentine and Marcion):

In answer to these heresies he wrote that we do not worship a creature (and Mother Mary is a creature).

"*For such an error belongs to heathens and Arians. Rather, we worship the Lord of creation, the Incarnate Word of God. For if the flesh, too, is in itself a part of the created world, still it had become God's Body. Nor, indeed the body being such, do we divide it from the Word and adore it by itself; neither, when we wish to worship the Word, do we separate Him from the flesh. Rather, as we said before, knowing that the Word was made flesh, we recognize Him as God even after He has come in the flesh*[16].

As with all of Lucifer's persistent evil, Manicheanism would be revived in 13th century France under a new name, *Albigensianism*, which we will study in a later chapter.

---

[15]Catholic Encyclopedia-Broderick

[16] P.345 -St. Athanasius - The Faith of the Early Fathers, Volume 1 - William J. Jurgens

Right:
St. Ambrose baptizes
St. Augustine.
Both St. Ambrose and St.
Augustine were early
Fathers of the Church
and Doctors of the Church.

Below:
The Blessed Mother hands
St. Augustine
and St. Monica
her cincture.

As we repeat over and over again, when the Church is under attack, God raises up a Saint or two. This Saint who once espoused this heresy would spend the rest of his life correcting the very errors, he once had promulgated.

St. Augustine was born into a time of schism and heresy. On the 13th of November, 354 A.D., a child was born to a pagan father, Patricius, and a Christian mother, Monica, in Tagaste, North Africa.

His pride not allowing him to walk in the simple Truth, Augustine was to grope through the darkness for answers to questions he did not know. In his chase, he embraced one of the more deadly heresies, that of the Manichaeans. He was not to find his way out of that black hole for nine years.

Monica prayed and cried while her son tried to sway her in his direction.

How heavy was Monica's cross as she saw her son, not even attending church with her. She stood by, helplessly, for the next nine years, as he became swallowed up by the false teachings and promises of that dangerous sect of the Manichaeans. I am sure it took all the faith she had, to believe he would come back, and more to live that belief. And so, she prayed!

Augustine's pride kept blocking him from admitting his mother was right. With the Manichaean sect, he could have his cake and eat it, too. They assured him he could lead a life of sin, yet still be saved through the merits of those elect, who lived a life of abstinence and total chastity.

In addition to the power of his mother's thirty years of prayers, an instrument God used to save Augustine's soul, was his thirst for the truth. What the Manichaeans taught him, no longer satisfied him. He was having a problem with their evasiveness as he dug deeper, searching for answers. Augustine had been so in love with the beauty of the word, he had not gone beyond to the meaning behind the word.

Augustine, having doubted God, now doubted man. His friends, the Manichaeans and his new-found friends, the Academics had betrayed him; their talking in circles tired him. Their worldly attempts to explain the unexplainable, did not satisfy the gnawing questioning inside of him.[17]

St. Augustine started to read Holy Scripture. A man, another Saint you will be reading about in our chapter on Arianism, St. Ambrose would be the instrument through which St. Augustine would finally come back to the Church of his mother, the only true Church, the Catholic Church.

As St. Augustine caused so many to follow this heresy, he would spend the rest of his life defending the Faith and the faithful of that Faith, against this and other heresies.

And, dear St. Augustine and St. Monica, the battle rages on, as mothers faithfully follow the Faith of their fathers, and their children, like St. Augustine the sinner, *refuse* to become Saints. But, we all stand on the promise made to St. Monica that God could not resist a mother's tears; her prayers would be answered. And they were! And ours, dear mothers, will be, too!

From the beginning of the Second Century right up to the Fifth Century, the Church was busily engaged in battling **Christological heresies** that were either denying the nature of Jesus the man, or His Divinity as Christ, the Second Person in the Holy Trinity; or **Trinitarian errors** about the Holy Trinity, and the equality of each of the Three Persons in the One God.

Forms of Manicheanism kept surfacing in Mother Church like festering abscesses. Manicheanism had spread through Africa to Spain, using the early writings of St. Augustine before he converted to the Catholic Faith. Imagine his broken heart, as he saw men of guile using what he had unwittingly espoused. St. Augustine not only

---

[17]*Saints and other Powerful Men in the Church*-Bob and Penny Lord

corrected those errors, but battled heretics and heresies that threatened his Church, the rest of his life, attacking not only the Manicheans, but the Arians, the Donatists, the Pelagians[18], and others.   As he wrote, in defense of the Church, he gave us invaluable teachings on the many dogmas, the true tenets of our Church, as passed on by the Apostles.

The Eleventh Council of Toledo, based the creed on the Holy Trinity read there on November 7, 675, on only one of many treatises written by St. Augustine on the Church which earned him the titles of Early Father and Doctor of the Church.

In 561, some bishops convened in the town of Braga, Spain which is now located in Portugal. Priscillan, a follower of Manicheanism, had helped to spread the errors of Manicheanism throughout Spain, France and Northern Italy. At this Synod, both Manicheanism, and the Priscillanists who had been promoting these heresies, were condemned.

Manicheanism crops up its ugly head once more.   In 1215, **Innocent III convenes The Fourth Lateran Council** in response to the heresy of Albigensianism which was simply Manicheanism under a new name, a new snake that had slithered from under a rock.

On February 4, 1442, the Council of Florence condemned Manichaenism with this profession of faith, which clearly stated the Church's teachings on Creation:

"The holy Roman Church firmly believes, professes, and preaches that the one true God, Father, Son, and Holy Spirit, is the creator of all things visible and invisible. When God willed, in His goodness He created all creatures both spiritual and corporeal. These creatures are good because they were made by the Supreme Good, but they are changeable because they were made from nothing. The Church asserts that there is no such

---

[18]you can read about it in a later chapter.

thing as a nature of evil, because every nature insofar as it is a nature is good. It professes that one and same God is the author of the Old and New Testament, that is the law, of the Prophets, and of the Gospel because the holy men of both Testaments have spoken under the inspiration of the same Holy Spirit. It accepts and reveres their books as here listed, (There follows the canon of books.) [19]

---

[19]P. 143 - The Council of Florence, 1438-45 from book: The Church Teaches by Jesuit Fathers of St. Mary's College

Right:
***After the
Baptism of
Constantine,
Christianity
spread rapidly to
all parts of the
Roman Empire.***

Below:
***Arch
of Constantine
erected in
memory of
Constantine's
Victory at the
Milvian
Bridge***

Fourth Century and Arianism

It is popularly believed *Arius* was born in Libya, in 270 A.D. He is credited with having started one of the most deadly heretical sects to attack the Early Church that of Arianism. It has continued assaulting the Church until today, under many titles.

Our first encounter with Arius is somewhere between 300-311 A.D., when he joined up with a group of heretics called *Meletians*. Evidently, he did not find what he was searching for; he left them.

He then managed to get himself ordained a *deacon* of the Catholic Church by Peter of Alexandria who was Bishop at the time. Evidently his *loyalties* were still with the Meletians, because when they were censured, he bitterly criticized the Church, and came out against her. He was excommunicated by the same Bishop who had ordained him deacon, Bishop Peter of Alexandria!

Arius later regretted his outburst against the Church. Mother Church not only forgave him and accepted him back into the Church, he even maneuvered himself into being accepted into the priesthood! This was done by Bishop Peter's *successor* Bishop Achillas. Then Bishop Achillas' successor, Bishop Alexander, thought so highly of Arius, he assigned him his own parish!

A killer kills; a heretic spouts heresy; a dissenter dissents. Arius became involved with *another* heretic called Lucian. Since God will ultimately reveal, we find Arius again in hot water. He just could not resist spouting his *new* mentor's (Lucian) errors. The dogma he was preaching not only brought him in conflict with his Bishop, the very one who had entrusted him with his own church, it created a tidal wave that threatened to sink the ship of *the* Church.

Arius drew many to him and his false concepts. The enemy is so clever! In our time, in the sixties, the Satan of drugs came into the lives of our young through *music*. He has been able to induce the innocent into every form of perversion and act of violence through music. It's nothing new!

Arius came upon a scheme to use *many* to spread his lies. Use music! He tirelessly substituted *his* words (heresies in direct conflict with the teachings of the Church) and set them to popular music of the day. He cut quite a figure as he went about, the troubadour priest, singing catchy lyrics to tunes everyone had already been humming. He had a slick delivery. He would sing and then speak. He even accompanied himself with a musical instrument as he spoke. Dramatic! What a charismatic figure! He was passionate! He was zealous! He was a pied piper!

Before you knew it, his doctrines were being sung by priests, fishermen, storekeepers, and farmers; mothers were caroling these little ditties to their children on their knees; everyone was singing, but it wasn't the Lord they were praising. And most of them didn't even know what they were doing or Who they were betraying.

Arianism denied the divinity of Christ. It taught that Jesus was not God the Son, that He was created out of nothing; He did not exist with the Father together with the Holy Spirit before the beginning of time. By its nature, it also had to deny the Trinity.

This is a serious heresy. Our Church teaches that Christ always was, is and always will be. *"Glory be to the Father, and to the Son and to the Holy Spirit, as it was in the beginning, is now and ever shall be world without end. Amen!"*

We believe that Christ, being One with God the Father, is One with the Creator. Now Arius was careful to say that Christ was not *just* a creature like other creatures, but that He was the highest creature; He was God, but He was not the One True God; He taught that Jesus was *a less*er God.

If, as Arius was saying, Jesus, the Second Person of the Holy Trinity is not equal with God, The First Person of the

Holy Trinity, or is subordinate (or subservient) to God the Father, then why could there not be other gods like this, as in pagan days of yesterday and today? In these, possibly the last days, there are those who are promoting just that, that we are gods. As Catholics, part of our Judeo-Christian belief which goes back to Genesis, is that there is only one God. How can Christ be God and not be One and equal with God our Heavenly Father? Surely Arius had to be digging up the old heresy denying the Trinity, that of *Subordinationism*[1]! In saying that Christ was not the One true God, was he not denying Jesus, the Second Person of the Blessed Trinity? Exactly!

He also dared to teach that *Christ became a part of the Divine Nature of God as compensation for having died for our sins, or in repayment for having redeemed the world.* This tied in with his other heresies that stated Jesus was not of one Nature with God, He did not exist before the creation of the world, and would not be with us till the end of the world. In other words, Jesus was not immortal like God the Father; He had a beginning and an end.

†

Not only had he deceived the faithful at large, but he had hoodwinked a powerful hierarchy, mainly from the East and to a small degree from the West. It got so bad that the Emperor Constantine called the Council of Nicea in 325 to bring about peace and unity once and for all.

We have to remember that Constantine was not that spiritual. He really inherited this whole problem from his father, and he wanted it over. At the beginning of the Fourth Century, his father, the monster Emperor *Diocletian* had attempted to wipe out all Christianity, whether *by torture, death or intimidation.* But violence has a way of backfiring. The terror he spread throughout his kingdom

---

[1]heresy stating Jesus was not equal to the Father

blew up into the possibility of widespread *insurrection*. In an attempt to avert civil war, he stepped down from the throne. His empire was split between the East and the West.

"The best laid plans of mice and men often go astray." The war which *Diocletian* wished to deter was to be waged for the next twenty years. That was how Constantine ultimately inherited the West from his father. But in those days, as for all time, people envy and covet, and are never satisfied. Power is a demon whose thirst cannot be quenched. Therefore, neither Constantine nor Maxenthius[2] were satisfied with the share of the kingdom they had inherited from their fathers.

Constantine converted to the Catholic Faith. However he did not give up his pagan gods; he continued worshiping Apollo (or Helios the sun god). He just believed that the Christian God was more powerful and through Him, he (Constantine) would triumph over his enemies. Bishop Eusebius later wrote that Constantine had a vision where he saw a Cross in the sky with the words: *"By this conquer."*

Therefore, although Constantine did not understand the reason for the devastating breakdown of the Church that was resulting from Arianism, for *political* reasons, he called the first Ecumenical (universal) Council. He gathered Bishops from all parts of his empire, from the East *and* the West. The Council convened in Nicea, in 325 A.D. For Constantine, the first Ecumenical Council, or as it is also known *The Nicean Council*, might have been for worldly reasons, but for the Church, it was called to bring about unity and most specifically to combat the heresy of Arianism. The Council proclaimed for all time that *"Christ shared the same Divine Nature as His Father.*[3]*"*

---

[2]who had inherited his portion of the kingdom from *his* father
[3]"The Church Teaches-Jesuit Fathers- TAN Publications

The Council condemned Arianism; it gave us the Nicene Creed, our Pledge of Allegiance to the Church, which we continue to pray every week. Everything was fine for about three years until an Arian Bishop, Eusebius, returned from exile, and insisted that Arius be reinstated in the Church. The whole thing started all over again. Arianism gathered strength in Egypt. Constantine, who had called the Council in the first place, now went against it, and supported Arianism. Again, to give him credit, he was not being vindictive, nor had he switched loyalties. He wanted peace and unity in a very large kingdom.

Constantine supported Arianism militarily, forcing this heresy where the faithful would not acquiesce. Bishops loyal to the Church, who did not buckle under the pressure, were relieved of their Sees; and some died martyrs' deaths rather than betray their Lord. St. Athanasius was banished five times because of his undaunted courage in writing and preaching against this deadly heresy. St. Hilary of Poitier lost his See and was exiled for many years. The See of Constantinople was held by an Arian for forty years. And, we do not understand the danger we are in, today?

We sometimes grieve, meditating on the waste of talent and effort by some very gifted people who insist on using their God-given gifts to fight God, instead of defending Him! Arius was so deviously convincing, in 336 A. D., he was able to manipulate Emperor Constantine into believing he was, and had always been authentically teaching the true dogmas of the Church. You may ask how was he able to accomplish this, what with all the censures that had been placed on Arius, by Bishop after Bishop, over and over again? His silver tongue got him by once more, as he met with Constantine, *privately*. The emperor issued an order; Arius was to be re-instated in the Church.

Arius strutted triumphantly back towards his quarters. Having failed to use the toilet facilities at the emperor's castle, he decided to relieve himself in the streets of Constantinople. As he was so doing in back of the Forum, suddenly his bowels burst, and he died the ugly, disgraceful death, indicative of the life he had led.

Although Arius was dead, his heresy continued to flourish while Constantine was in power. After Emperor Constantine's death the following year 337, Arianism started to lose some of its support. When Emperor Theodosius condemned Arianism in 380, you would have thought that was the end of it, but it is like a boil that stays below the surface until it can erupt once more. It was the national religion of the Germanic nations for one hundred and fifty years.

This heresy was adopted by Hitler who set himself up as god, completely outlawing Christianity, imprisoning, torturing and killing bishops, priests, and religious who would not deny Christ. The "*Heil Hitler*" replaced the Heil Jesus and the Heil Maria. Hitler told the people they were a master race, an Arian race. And the world did not know how deadly this title and philosophy would be. It is frightening when you contemplate how close Hitler came to dominating the whole world. It has been said, only the fact he was anti-semitic stopped him from using the Atom Bomb, because it was developed by a Jew!

The Church fights back!

Now, *many* of the Bishops had been won over by Arius. But, thank God, there were those who remained faithful to the Church. Whenever there has been an attack, there has always been a remnant of the true fabric of the Church who will follow the Pope and the Magisterium. *A battle ensued* between bishops loyal to the Church and those bishops who were in heretical accord with Arianism.

When Arius came out with his heresy that Jesus was not equal to the Father, the Lord raised up a defender and a future Saint and Doctor of the Church, **St. Athanasius.** He defended the Church against the Arians, arguing: "*If Jesus and God the Father were not One, eternal and unchangeable, then all is futile.*" We are lost! He cited the opening of St. John's Gospel:

"In the beginning was the Word[4];
the Word was in God's presence,
and the Word was God.
He was present to God in the beginning.
Through Him all things came into being,
and apart from Him nothing came to be.
Whatever came to be in Him, found life,
life for the light of men.
The light shines on in darkness,
a darkness that did not overcome it."

The Arians fought back brutally. There was such an uproar that it spilled over from the hierarchy of the Church to the man in the streets! There was a steaming anger brewing. The Arians instigated even dock workers at the waterfronts. It was the same as it had been, in the days of Jesus, when Pilate asked the crowd who to spare, and the few well placed rabble rousers swayed the masses against our Lord. The history of the world has always been the same, from the mob turning on Caesar right up to today, the *few* dissenters stronger than the *many* faithful.

It looked as if the controversy between Arianism and the Church would not only split the Church but pull down the state, as well. And this, the emperor could not allow. That's when he stepped in. At first, he tried to resolve matters between the Arians and the followers of St. Athanasius, peacefully. And when that did not look as if were to come about, he used force, to no avail. Those for,

---

[4]John refers to Jesus as the Word

St. Jerome (center) studied the Word of God.
"Dispute on the Blessed Sacrament" by Raphael
from the Vatican Collection
The Blessed Sacrament has been attacked all through the centuries.
Our Lord has provided proof of this Doctrine by providing defenders
of the Faith and Miracles of the Eucharist.

and against the Church would not budge! The battle continued!

The Council of Nicea (or the Nicene Council) had clearly stated the position of the Church as far as this heresy was concerned. Yet, with the support of many of the *Bishops*, twenty years later Arianism had spread throughout much of the Roman Empire. After Emperor Constantine's death, not only had Arianism gained tremendous strides in the *Church*, it had affected and infected every aspect of life. The world had stepped in and because of the wide support of those in *political* power, Arianism was choking the life out of the faithful.

Satan wasn't satisfied with the progress Arianism was making. He would deal *the* death blow to the Council of Nicea and its creed, or so he thought. In around the year 350 A.D. the Nicene Creed was accused of *contradicting* Holy Scripture. But we know, as powerful as we humans allow Satan to become, God always has a quarterback there on the sidelines, prepared to enter the game at the eleventh hour, and *win* for the Lord and his Church. St. Athanasius wrote a powerful defense of the Nicene Creed! He said:

"God creates by calling into existence that which did not exist, requiring nothing in order to do it; but men work with some existing material, first praying and obtaining the ability of making, from that God who fashioned all things through His own proper Word...men have no capacity for self-existence, are in fact, circumscribed in place, and exist at the pleasure of the Word of God...God, however exists of Himself, transcends all things, and is circumscribed by none."[5]

When, between the years 340 and 370 A.D. the disease of Arianism turned into a wide spread plague, God called

---

[5]Pg 323 - Sec 754 - St. Athanasius - *The Faith of the Early Fathers,* Vol 1, W. A. Jurgens, Liturgical Press, Collegeville, MN

upon another champion, *St. Jerome*[6]. St. Jerome cried out that which I fear will happen someday in the not too distant future, "*The whole world awoke and groaned in astonishment to find itself Arian.*"[7] Although the Church was suffering the wounds of division, with the many who were following the false teachings of Arianism, St. Jerome wrote the following to Pope St. Damasius:

"*I am joined in communion with your Holiness, that is with the chair of Peter; upon the Rock I know the Church is built. Whoever eats the Lamb outside of that house is a profane person. Whoever is not in the ark, shall perish in the flood...Whoever gathers not with you, scatters; he who is not Christ's belongs to Antichrist...Order me, if you please, what I should do.*"

As with today, and as with all those periods in history when whole nations left the Church, it was not the desire of majority of the people. *The laity have always been faithful to the Church*, and all too often have been sacrificial lambs through the hands of those they have trusted. Heresy and division have always spread through either *religious* who had gone astray or those in power using dissension within the Church for their own personal gains. In all war, whether between principalities or nations, the end result is always the same; the innocent suffer! In the past, it was because we were not educated. But today, the Lord is gathering together an army of *St. Jeromes, St. Athanasius', St. Hilarys, St. Ambroses, St. Augustines* and on and on. The names are

---

[6]St. Jerome-doctor of the Church. Learned in Holy Scripture, he translated the Bible into the everyday speech "*vulgate*" of the people of Rome which was Latin. He also translated the New Testament and the Psalms and wrote countless books on our Faith for which he was declared one of the Four foremost doctors of the Church. The Vulgate Bible of St. Jerome is considered the official Latin version of the Bible in the Roman Catholic Church.

[7]from "The Proper Context: An Introduction by the Author-from the book "Report from the Synod" by Richard Cowden-Guido

different but the hearts are the same, those immersed in the Sacred Heart of Jesus and the Immaculate Heart of His Mother.

The Lord raised up another defender of the Faith, **St. Ambrose**.

"...*Milan was being torn apart by dissensions between Catholics and Arians. Surprise you? Arianism had been gaining a foothold in the East and had spread to Milan. Bishop Ambrose had the difficult and unpopular mission of maintaining unity within the Church and peace in the city, and all this, without compromising the Faith.*

"*The Church was in danger. The forces of hell were being waged against her, and she was calling upon our Lord for a Saint. That Saint was, at this time and in this place, St. Ambrose. Our precious Church was being split in two by schism, and was bleeding. Empress Justine, who once belonged to the Arian sect, demanded that Bishop Ambrose turn the church, attended by Catholics (believed to be the Cathedral of Milan), over to the Arians. St. Ambrose refused! The Empress sent in troops to forcibly take over the Cathedral. She and they were not ready for what they encountered; St. Ambrose was preaching to a church full of worshipers. As some would leave to go home to their families, they were quickly replaced by others.*

"*Tribunes came with a summons for the Bishop to relinquish the Church to them. His important reply was a lesson to us,*

'*If the emperor demanded what belonged to me, even though everything I own belongs to the poor, I would not refuse. But the things of God are not mine. If anyone wants my patrimony (legacy), let him take it! If anyone wants my body, let him seize it! Do you want to put me in chains and lead me to death? I shall obey, and shall not allow my people to defend me. I shall not kiss the altar, begging for life. I prefer to be immolated on the altar.*'

"Nothing shook Ambrose. He sang the Psalms with his people and order was maintained."

By 370 A.D. through the faithfulness of many unsung heroes and heroines who remained with the Church, often at a great price, the Church was victorious. In 381 A.D. the *Council of Constantinople convened* to reaffirm the Council of Nicea, and to reinstate the rightful bishop of Constantinople. The Council restated Jesus' Divinity. In answer to a heresy (an offshoot of Arianism), which attacked the Holy Spirit, the Council not only confirmed our belief in the Holy Spirit as the Third Person in the Holy Trinity, but added to the Nicene Creed *"with the Father and the Son He is worshiped and glorified."*

The Pope and his faithful Bishops hoped this Council would unify the Church which had been split apart by *Arianism*. At times, we judge ourselves hopeless and helpless to combat the evil that is spreading throughout the world and throughout our Church. The bad news is, it's happening and has happened on and off for two thousand years. But the good news is, we're still here. *Jesus and Mary always triumph!*

When we are confused, when we find we cannot read a teaching of one theologian that does not contradict that of another, we have only to recall that it all happened before, and we survived. When in doubt as to what to believe, just follow what a Priest faithful to the Pope said recently: *"When you do not know who or what to believe, you can rely on the headship that Jesus left us, a succession of Popes guided by the Holy Spirit and the Magisterium.*[8]*"*

---

[8]Magisterium is the authority passed down by Jesus to the Church, in communion with infallibility with which the Church teaches authentically Holy Scripture, carrying and upholding through tradition the truths of our salvation.(Catholic Encyclopedia-Broderick)

The Fifth Century - Man can be God

PELAGIANISM

"It's still the same old story....." Here we go again, back to Adam and Eve in the Garden of Eden. The serpent says *"You can be like God."* (Gen 3:1-6). As God raises a Saint to combat one heresy, the devil is busy unearthing one more founder to revive an old heresy with a new name. In the Fifth Century, we find a new version of Pantheism, called Pelagianism. Pelagius was the founder of this heresy. Because of its deadliness, he would earn the title *Archheretic*. It is believed, he was born around 345 A.D., in the British Isles, very possibly Ireland. He came to Rome in 384 A.D. He led the model life of a monk and recluse from that time until he was forced to leave Rome, to avoid persecution. The Visigoths, a Teutonic people[1], had invaded the Roman Empire late in the 4th Century A.D. and torched their way into France and Spain, leaving smoking desolation everywhere they went. Pelagius, with one of his pupils, Caelestius, fled just before the Visigoths captured and ravaged Rome.

Pelagius and Caelestius arrived in Carthage, North Africa, and it was there, in 411 A.D., his teachings on the Faith were first opposed. There is not much known about Pelagius except that St. Augustine had, at one time, called him *saintly*, and then later wrote apologies exposing the errors of Pelagius. There was a time he was looked up to, considered a *good* man of high ideals. He had been recognized for his admirable, moral character. He had gained the respect of many for his grasp not only of matters of the world but of the spiritual life.

His pupil, Caelestius, is thought to be of Italian heritage. He went to Rome about 405, and it is believed

---

[1] Teutonic people - northern European tribes who included German, Scandinavian, Dutch or English people

Pelagius was responsible for his conversion to Christianity. He became an ardent disciple of Pelagius. Was that part of the problem? Was his focus *Pelagius*, rather than the Lord? Had Pelagius increased, and the Lord decreased? [I always worry when someone speaks more about a visionary than the Lord or His Mother, who is reportedly appearing to that seer. Are we not called to be disciples of Christ, not of man?]

Pelagius and Caelestius succeeded in getting themselves excommunicated at the Council of Carthage. Pelagius left with Caelestius and journeyed to Palestine. Pelagius was able to delude and enlist the support of many bishops in the Eastern part of the Church, John of Jerusalem being one of them. That did not stop the Councils at Carthage, and Milevis in 416 A.D., from censuring Pelagius and his teachings. Upon considering all the arguments, **Pope Innocent I** condemned Pelagius and his writings. The Pope who followed, **Pope Zosimus**, after vacillating, listening first to one advisor, and then changing his mind after listening to another advisor, condemned Pelagius, in 418 A.D.

It's difficult to understand, but even after Pelagius and Caelestius were condemned by the Councils of Carthage as heretics, Caelestius was ordained to the priesthood in Ephesus! He went to Constantinople, but was called back to Rome where he was condemned, along with his teacher and mentor. In 418, an imperial edict was issued ordering Caelestius to leave Rome. He was banished to Constantinople, along with Pelagius, and nothing is known of him after 429 A.D. Although he wrote considerably, there is little trace of his writings today. They have not lived after him, but his and Pelagius' errors still do.

It is believed Pelagius died, around seventy years of age, old and quite alone, in a remote little town in Palestine. There is nothing written about him after 418 A.D. Although it seemed as if he had disappeared from the face of the earth, his heresy had not.   It was not until 431 A.D. that Pelagianism was, at last, condemned by the Ecumenical Council of Ephesus, once and for all.

What happened to Pelagius and his protege Caelestius, who were called to holiness, to possibly saintliness?   What or who took them off the narrow road to sanctity?   We read that Pelagius made the acquaintance of a Syrian Priest called *Rufinus*.   Little is known as to the battles he may have fought and lost, the temptations he faced, the *small* differences with which he might have half-heartedly agreed.   What wide road did he follow that led him ultimately to deadly separation from the Church?

Heresies that rocked the Church
and how the Church fought back

Pelagius was able to gain support from such authorities as St. Augustine by claiming he was quoting Pope Sixtus, when he wrote: "*God has given men freedom of will so that by purity and sinlessness of life* (a life without sinning), *they may become like God*." and "*A man chaste and sinless has received from God the power to become a son of God*[2]."[3]   Pelagius exaggerated the natural powers of man, claiming man was the master of his own destiny. *He taught that God cannot do anything that man cannot do.*   He denied the existence of a supernatural condition; he denied the existence of God! [Do we not hear this today, under a new name, *New Age*?]

Believing Pelagius' source to be the Pope, St. Augustine originally defended him.   However, two followers of Pelagius, who had seen the light, came to St. Augustine and told him these were not the words of the Pope, but that Pelagius was using a Pythagorean[4] philosopher's teachings as

---

[2]The Faith of the Early Fathers - W.A. Jurgens

[3] part of today's New Age philosophy

[4] a follower or student of Pythagorus who was a Greek philosopher who lived 500 years before the birth of Christ.   One of the strangest beliefs he imposed on the brotherhood, he founded, was that *after men*

his source.   St. Augustine retracted his support and apologized, not for *what* he had written, because what he espoused was in keeping with the dogma of the Church, but that he had unwittingly used these arguments to promote a heretical teaching. In 416 A.D., St. Augustine wrote a letter to Pope Innocent I, attacking Pelagius' teaching, exposing it for what it was, a heresy.

Pelagius and his followers claimed from the very beginning, *Adam was not created by God to live eternally*; God had pre-established that Adam would die, even if he had not disobeyed Him and sinned in the Garden of Eden. Does this not make a lie out of Holy Scripture in Genesis?

He went on to say that man was not affected by the Fall; *the sin of Adam was not passed down to us*; we the offspring and children of Adam and Eve did not inherit Original Sin; Adam and Eve's disobedience only affected them. [This is the lie that Satan has been feeding our world for centuries, only now in major doses: "*What you do, you do to yourself, alone. You only hurt yourself.*"]

Therefore, according to this heresy, *we are born free of sin,* just the way Adam was before he fell. It only stood to reason, according to their false doctrines that the final hypothesis would have to be: *man* will not die as a punishment for the sin of Adam, even if he is not Baptized.

They indoctrinated the faithful of the Fifth century with one lie which led to another lie and then to another. Since Adam's sin only condemned him, and we are not born with the sin of Adam on our soul, then what must follow! *Unbaptized infants as well as baptized infants will go to Heaven.* Since we are not robbed of salvation because of the sin of Adam, *Original Sin*, then there is no need for the Sacrament of Baptism which cleanses us of this sin.

---

died their souls go into other bodies, sometimes returning in the bodies of animals; sounds like Reincarnation, to us.

Another heresy they presented was: *there were men who were without sin before Christ.* Then, are we redeemed by the Sacrifice of Jesus on the Cross? Were they not coming against the very reason Christ was born, to be the Sacrificial Lamb Who would redeem the world of their sins?

We once heard a priest say that Jesus would have died on the Cross, even if we had not sinned. I responded: *What kind of God would have His Son die so cruelly on the Cross for no reason?* He answered "It's Franciscan theology." I was really upset, until we asked a Franciscan priest about this. He smiled and said: "*He is misquoting John Scotus who said Jesus would have been* **born** *whether we had sinned or not.*" But he added, "*St. Thomas Aquinas and Saint Augustine would not have agreed with him.*"

They would wipe Jesus from the face of the earth with their pronouncement: *The Mosaic law is sufficient for us to live a life that will lead us to eternal life in Paradise; there is no need of the Gospel.* Then is there a need for Christ? The Gospel is the Word of our Lord and Savior. Our Incarnate Lord, the God Who became man, is the *Word* made Flesh. Jesus said "*I am the Way, the Truth and the Life; no one goes to the Father except by Me.*"(John 14:6). No one could go to the Father except through Him! By setting aside the Gospel, were they not calling our Lord a liar?

They had to deny the Gospel because they were teaching that *there is no need for the redemption of the sins of Adam and Eve.* But in acknowledging the Old Testament, what they did not say was that the Old Testament is *fulfilled* by the New Testament. All that came to pass, in the New Testament, was foretold in the Old Testament. Then what was the plan? *Don't let the world know who Jesus is calling us to be?* Every step our Lord took, we are chosen to follow: His Humility, His obedience to His Mother Mary and His foster father Joseph, His unconditional Love for all mankind to the point of death on the Cross. Were they not proposing: "*Do not allow the children of God to know that there is another path they can take, one that the world does not know or desire.*" If Mosaic Laws are sufficient for Salvation, then why are the Jews still waiting for a Messiah to come to redeem them? Why was Christ born and why did He die? Or was that the point: *You do not need Christ's Sacrifice on the Cross*? They taught that Christ did not come for man's salvation, but to teach.

As the spider weaves his web, catching unknowing flies, so did this heresy, as they added, *man will not rise because of the Resurrection of Christ.* If there is no resurrection of the body then we are all lost, as St. Paul said.

Another Pelagian error was that *we do not need God's Grace; all we need is free will.* Then, he contradicts all he said before by saying *God's Grace justifies mankind through our Lord Jesus Christ, but Jesus only has power for the remission of those sins already committed, and has no power to help to prevent sins from being committed.* If this sounds confusing, how about the nonsense that is being dished out to us today? Sometimes, I believe we're living in the time of the "*Emperor's clothes*" where everyone kept admiring the Emperor's clothes[5], until an innocent child said he was naked. Is this why the Mother of God always appears to children? Something that always comes to me is, Jesus spoke in simple language, so we could understand and live. Today, as in the past, our Theologians speak for the very few, the intelligentsia. Well, as a very holy priest[6] said, the Church will be saved by the laity.

The Pelagians, all the heretics of the past and of today, would have us believe in *man*, and who is the man? Themselves! How can anyone buy this? Why would I follow

---

[5]He wasn't wearing any clothes, but everyone was afraid to tell him, so they all said he was wearing beautiful clothes.

[6] Archbishop Fulton J. Sheen

sinful man's word, man who would not even die to his pride, rather than follow the One Who died that we might live?

Pelagius claimed that Peter was not granted any more authority than Jesus bestowed on the other Apostles; therefore he was not the head of the Church because Jesus did not appoint a head or Vicar of His Church. Does this not remind you of some modern day heretics who refuse to obey the successor of Peter, our own Vicar Pope John Paul II? If Peter was not proclaimed the rock upon which Jesus would build *His* Church, then the Word of God is a lie[7]. [This is the lie Satan has been telling from the beginning of our Church.]

The Church fights back

The Church doesn't like to arbitrarily condemn people and excommunicate them. They gave Pelagius every possible chance. He was called before synod after synod, in an attempt to exonerate him from charges of heresy. On July 30, 415, Pelagius was summoned to appear before a synod in Jerusalem. He and his teachings were condemned. In December of that same year Bishop John of Jerusalem called a synod in Diospolis, in an attempt to allow Pelagius to justify himself and his concepts. Pelagius presented his teachings, one more time, and he was able to get himself exonerated. History is quite mixed on this synod. Were fourteen good bishops unwittingly deluded by Pelagius'[8] explanations, or did they exonerate him because he disavowed his teachings[9]? As all things will come to pass through Jesus' Light, in 417, Pelagius was condemned by Pope Innocent I in Rome. After Pope Innocent died, in 418, the bishops convened in Carthage. They drew up canons

---

[7] Matt.16:18-"*And so I tell you, Peter, you are a rock, and on this rock foundation I will build My church, and not even death will ever be able to overcome it.*"

[8] St. Jerome called it a miserable synod

[9] St. Augustine said, if Pelagius had not condemned the errors attributed to him, he would not have been exonerated.

condemning the Pelagian heresies, and the new Pope Zosimus not only confirmed their canons, he condemned Caelestius along with Pelagius. They were ordered to leave Rome, and banished to Constantinople where it is believed they died. The Pelagian Heresy was finally condemned at the Council of Ephesus in 431.

St. Jerome was one of the early Fathers who defended the Church against Pelagius and his heresies. In 415, St. Jerome attacked Pelagius and his heresies. When St. Jerome wrote his apology against Pelagianism, he went easier than he had on other heresies. Evidently, the Pelagians did not think so. A year after St. Jerome wrote his discourse against Pelagianism, they sent a band of thugs to Bethlehem, who terrorized and brutalized St. Jerome's Nuns and Monks. In addition, in reprisal for his treatise against them, the Pelagians burned down his monasteries and threatened his life, forcing him to hide in a tower.

St. Augustine was another of the Church Fathers who came out against Pelagianism, although he had held Pelagius in high regard prior to his disobedience to the Church. St. Augustine, like his mother St. Monica, put no one before the Lord and His Church that he had promised to defend. He had no choice but to come out against Pelagius, no matter what his personal feelings had been.

These two great men, along with the countless unnamed and unsung heroes, popes and bishops who deliberated and then condemned these heresies, even though they were not always popular, were just a part of the many role models we have, who died to themselves rather than betray the trust the Lord had placed in them when He chose them as His Disciples. They were true to the Lord's commandments as they proclaimed their *fiat*, their *yes*, to His words:

"Jesus drew near to them and said '*I have been given all authority in Heaven and on earth. Go then, to all peoples everywhere and make them disciples; baptize them in the name of the Father, the Son, and the Holy spirit, and teach them to obey everything I have commanded you. And I will be with you always to the end of the world.*"(Matt. 28:18)

NESTORIANS

Our Church and the world has always been in turmoil with some good and some not very good Christians endeavoring to bring about unity! As the Saints of the first four centuries went to their reward with our Lord Jesus in Heaven, Satan remained in the wings, waiting to train a brand new group of heretics, how to destroy the Church.

Sadly, the Church of the Fifth Century found itself being split apart in 428 A. D. between those who followed the newly ordained Archbishop of Constantinople Nestorius, and those who loyally obeyed the proclamations of the Council of Nicea.

The Nestorian sect was founded by *Nestorius*, a priest and monk chosen by Emperor Theodosius as Archbishop of Constantinople.   Constantinople was a powerful See, a major stronghold of Christianity; it was important to the Emperor as a means of unifying the Roman Empire. When Constantinople fell to the Moslems centuries later, it caused a separation of the East from the West, a wound that has not been healed to this day.

At first, it appeared Emperor Theodosius had acted wisely, assigning this important task to Nestorius. After his consecration as Archbishop, in 428, Nestorius *immediately* showed himself to be an ardent defender of the Faith. He waged valiant battle against heresies. God had graced him with a persuasive tongue and the faithful followed his every word. What a powerful soldier and shepherd he was!

But the gifts that God had bestowed upon him, he soon used against Him and His Church. The year had not ended when he began spouting *heresy*. He and priests loyal to him, were teaching, *there were two distinct persons in Jesus Christ,*

Jesus died for our sins.
Pelagius preached
"You do not need Christ's sacrifice on the Cross."
Padre Pio was praying before this Crucifix
when he received the Stigmata.

autonomous of each other and different, One Who is God and one who is man; the One Who is God dwelling within Jesus the man, the man Jesus merely a temple. By so doing, he denied the Incarnation, that God became man. [This is not unlike the philosophy which is being taught today by the heresy, encompassing many heresies, called *New Age*, that there is a god within us that is waiting to be discovered; the god that Jesus discovered within Himself.]

As Nestorius claimed that Jesus had two individual and unrelated natures, in other words a split personality, and that the Divine was merely living within the shell of the man Jesus, it stood to reason that their next assumption would be: *Mary was solely the Mother of the human Jesus, not of the Divine.* Therefore, she was not to be revered as the Mother of God. He further contended, he could not envision God making Himself dependent on a human for human nourishment, like an ordinary *human* baby, feeding at His Mother's breast. Doesn't this sound like pride and its advocate, the devil?

God is the Perfect Sign of Humility. What would Nestorius' answer be to God àllowing Himself to be humiliated or humbled by the very creatures He had created? Or was he saying that it was the *human* Jesus *alone* Who suffered and died for our sins, and not the Divine? In so doing, was he not mocking the sacrifice that God the Father made as He witnessed and accepted the last bloody sacrifice for the Redemption of man's sins by His only begotten Son? As Mohammed studied the Church with the idea of forming a new religion that would unify all the Arabs of the world, is this where he picked up the idea that Jesus was simply a prophet like Mohammed himself, no more no less, but not Allah (or God)? The Moslems (followers of Mohammed) have a problem, till today, believing Christ, the only begotten Son of God could die on the Cross. They consider this a weakness. Our St. Paul said that it is in our weakness that we are strong, *"For when I am powerless, it is then that I am strong."*(2 Cor 12:10)

The Council of Nicea had declared Jesus to be of One nature with God the Father. The Apostles' Creed clearly professes Christ's *Divinity*, as it maintains and most emphatically proclaims His *humanity*! Nestorius, by contending that there were *two* distinctly different, separate and unrelated *persons* in Christ, One human and the Other Divine, was in defiance of both the teachings of the Council and the Creed which we, as Catholics, are required to profess and live, that is there are two natures, one human and one Divine, in the *One* Person who is Jesus Christ, the Second Person of the Holy Trinity.

Archbishop Nestorius caused an uproar within the Church as his heretical homilies began to spread. St. Cyril, Bishop of Alexandria, remembering the zeal with which his fellow Bishop had defended the Church, at first gently corrected him, hoping this would allow him to correct his errors. Nestorius replied with disdain and contempt for Bishop Cyril and his attempts to reconcile him to the Church and its Magisterium. It looked as if the two were at loggerheads. When he saw that he could not reason with him, St. Cyril came out against Nestorius, strongly denouncing him and his heresy.

Nestorius and Cyril appealed to **Pope St. Celestine I**. After carefully looking over the documents presented by both Bishops, the Second Council of Constantinople was called by the Pope. *Nestorianism* was condemned as a heresy, and Nestorius was given ten days to either rescind his false teachings publicly, before the faithful he had misled, or suffer *excommunication* and be relieved of his See. St. Cyril was chosen to carry out the Council's decision. The Pope sent twelve propositions with anathemas[10] to be approved by Nestorius, as a sign of his loyalty to, and total communion with, the Church and her teachings. Sometimes, especially when we have been graced with a position of authority, and have people looking up to us, it is difficult to say we are in error. Frequently, saving face becomes more important than the salvation of our soul. Or, what often happens, we begin to believe the lie so completely, we cannot accept that we were in error. That's when we must rely on the headship left by the Lord Himself, the Pope. He is our guide. We do not need to understand or reason, only obey. Often, that is too difficult. *Nestorius refused to bend.*

The Third Ecumenical Council was called in Ephesus in 431. Two hundred bishops were present, with St. Cyril representing the Pope. The Council clearly stated that Jesus was God-Man, Jesus the eternal God being One with Jesus the Man. It restated that the Virgin Mother Mary gave birth to Jesus the God-Man, condemning Nestorius who claimed she was *only* the Mother of the human Jesus, not the Divine. It went on to condemn the Pelagian Heresy that declared that man was saved by his own actions, without the Saving Grace of God. Although Nestorius was there in Ephesus, he defied the Council and refused to appear. The doctrines he had been teaching were condemned and he was excommunicated. As he had refused to abide by the decision of the Council, the Emperor had no other recourse than to relieve him of his See.

There were some Bishops who had not arrived in time for the Council, and although they did not agree with Nestorius, they turned on St. Cyril, accusing *him* of heresy.

---

[10] anathema-In the Old Testament it was something that was to be set aside because of the danger of its inherent evil to the people. In the New Testament, St. Paul uses it as a total separation of a person from the Kingdom of God, or excommunication. It was later used for the declaration of excommunication by the Pope, as in this case.

The Bishops, those who had been present at the Council, and those who had missed it and were in opposition to its findings, all appealed to the Emperor. Both Nestorius *and* St. Cyril were placed in prison. Thank God, representatives from the Pope arrived; St. Cyril was exonerated, and the opposing Bishops declared their loyalty to the Pope and the findings of the Church. Nestorius returned to his monastery at Antioch. Later, having been exiled to the Egyptian desert, he died, alone, in 451 A.D., without the comfort of Mother Church.

St. Cyril, although he suffered imprisonment, and the accusations waged against him had to have wounded him *deeply*, lived and died true to his Church.   Although Pelagianism and Nestorianism spread to the far ends of the Church, and were very much accepted in the East, because of holy men like *St. Cyril*, Christ's promise to His Church keeps her standing, awaiting His Second Coming.

Where does a man such as St. Cyril get his strength? It seems no matter what we write, it always comes back to the Holy Eucharist! St. Cyril said that when we receive our Lord Jesus Christ in Holy Communion, *"we are made concorporeal with Christ*[11]*,"* that is, we become one in body with Christ, by God's Grace. No matter how many times we hear or read this, it does not fail to cause tears of joy and awe to come to our eyes and hearts; we are made one with our Lord Jesus Christ! When Catholics fully realize that they become one with their Lord and Savior, we will have to build larger and larger churches to contain the body of Christ, rather than stadiums to contain sports exhibitions and civic rallies.

In his letter to Nestorius, St. Cyril most exemplifies his doctrine on the Lord in His Most Holy Eucharist, and the fullness of the Truth that must follow. He writes:

---

[11] Butler's Lives of the Saints-Thurston and Atwater

"Proclaiming the death according to the flesh of the only begotten Son of God, that is, Jesus Christ, and confessing His Resurrection from the dead and His ascent into Heaven, we celebrate the bloodless sacrifice in our churches; and thus approach the mystic blessings, and we are sanctified by partaking of the Holy Flesh and Precious Blood of Christ the Savior of us all. And we receive it not as common flesh (God forbid), nor as flesh of a man sanctified and associated with the Word according to the unity of merit, or as having a Divine indwelling, but as really the life-giving and very flesh of the Word Himself (Migne, PG.,lxxvii, 113)[12]."

To those separated brethren, who declare that Jesus is truly present at the point of consecration, but leaves the consecrated Hosts after the Mass is ended, St. Cyril wrote to a fellow Bishop:

"I hear that they say that the sacramental consecration does not avail for hallowing[13] if a portion of it is kept to another day. In saying so they are crazy. For Christ is not altered, nor will His Holy Body be changed; but the power of the consecration and the life-giving grace still remain in it (Migne, PG.,lxxvii, 1073).[14]" In essence, this is in response to those who say that Jesus is no longer present; therefore, it is foolish to venerate the Blessed Sacrament, as in Eucharistic Adoration, or to preserve the consecrated Hosts in the Tabernacle to be distributed to the faithful in the future.

We would like to say that was the end of it. But evil never sleeps. As Archbishop Sheen said, all evil is done in the dark. And so, when the faithful were breathing a sigh of relief in the Light of Jesus' Truth that was defined by the Council of Ephesus, Satan was scheming.

The warfare continued; therefore, one of the most important Councils was called. *In 451, The Fourth*

---

[12] Butler's Lives of the Saints-Thurston and Atwater
[13] The word hallowed means sacred, consecrated, holy, blessed
[14] Butler's Lives of the Saints-Thurston and Atwater

Ecumenical Council of Chalcedon was convened.   It
reaffirmed: Jesus Christ had two natures in One Divine
Person, both Divine *and* human.   The fact that He was
human as well as Divine, did not take away from His being
the Second Person in the Holy Trinity Who always was and
will always be *eternal*.   It declared *unequivocally* that our
Lord Jesus, the Only begotten Son of God, the Father, was
conceived by the Holy Spirit and born of the Virgin Mary.
As we have believed from the beginning, as Jesus was and
will always be Divine and eternal, *Mary was and is the Mother
of God.*

The Miracle of the Eucharist in Siena
Upon adoring the Miracle of the Eucharist, Pope John Paul II said,
"It is the (Real) Presence!"

The Moslem Conspiracy

The Church has always been under attack. As we have seen, the first six hundred years were devastating. If it were not for the gift of Our Lord Jesus in the Eucharist, we would probably not have lasted *one* hundred years. But Jesus triumphed. He filled the early Fathers of the Church with the Holy Spirit, and enabled them to wage major war in defense of Christ and the Church. They were triumphant. Christianity not only survived; it became the major religion of the world, spiritually and geographically. Through the intervention of the Lord's powerful Legions of Angels, the followers of Jesus had held back hordes of invaders attacking from the four corners of the earth. Then it was time for a rest, a little respite from the fight for survival. It had been going on since Our Lord Jesus ascended into Heaven. But there is *no time* for rest. The enemy never rests! Satan sleeps with one eye open all the time, just waiting for a chance to slip his knife into the small of our back.

We, the body of Christ, got comfortable, as humans tend to do, living on our laurels, and our newfound respectability. Keep in mind, it had been less than three hundred years since the Church had become legitimate. Persecution for the most part, had ceased. In the Fourth Century, the Lord had touched Emperor Constantine through an Apparition, in which he saw a cross in the sky with the words inscribed: *"In this sign you shall conquer."* He said, Jesus appeared to him and told him to use the symbol, Chi-Rho (the Greek Monogram for Jesus), on his shields and banners. He took that as a sign that the Lord would aid him to win the Battle of the Milvian Bridge. The Lord did! Constantine converted to Christianity, and the whole world pretty much became Christian. In short order, the persecutions of the past, the living underground, the fear of being dragged out in the middle of the night, never to return,

Above: ***Moslems at prayer***
Below:

***The Cross appears to Constantine. Inscribed across the ray of light
are the words, "In this sign you shall conquer." Constantine,
through this apparition which aided him in the battle of the Milvian
bridge, brought Christianity to the whole world.***

became a dim memory, a part of our history, rather than a part of our being. We had to try on our new coat of respectability. We basked in the sunshine of our newly acquired freedom. However, we became fat, while our enemies remained lean and hungry.

Another thing may have happened; the extremely large and ugly head of jealousy may have surfaced among our enemies. They may have become so covetous of the success and almost total acceptance of Christianity throughout the world, that they decided to imitate and destroy us.

Mohammed, a man with a vision

We had many enemies in the 7th Century. Among them were Hindus and Buddhists. But there was another group which had not yet been accounted for, because at the beginning of the 7th Century, they were not a big group. They were just germinating. The sons of Ishmael had scattered all throughout the middle East and had become separate little splinter groups, very individual, very self-centered little rulers of little kingdoms. Because of their individuality, they were very weak. They were completely ineffective as a people because they were not united.

A man with a vision was born into this society, in Mecca, in the year 570. His name was originally Mahomet, but was later changed to Mohammed. He was a simple man, of simple background, a camel driver. He never learned to read or write, but that was not unusual in those days. But he was brilliant. He belonged to one of many nomadic tribes, which the Romans never thought worthwhile conquering.

Mohammed did not initially set out to start a religion. Actually, he was intrigued by the tales of the Christians he heard from camel drivers and passing caravans. He used to listen to the Jews and Christians in the marketplace. He was fascinated with their philosophy, but he knew he would have to simplify it for his people. They would never understand it.

He spent a lot of time thinking. He couldn't read, but he could *dream*. He said, he had a vision from an Angel, the Angel Gabriel, who taught him how to read. Mohammed received a message from the Angel. He went home and told his wife. She encouraged him to go back to the foothills, to see if the Angel had anything else to say to him. So Mohammed went, and the Angel continued to speak to him. This was beginning to be exciting for Mohammed. Now, the thought came to him that he might actually be a prophet. He claimed the Angel gave him the religion he projected to his people, the religion which ultimately united them, and it was: *Believe what you want; what you don't like throw out.*

It was a very simple religion! He began to teach his first real groups of followers:

> *Give up Idolatry;*
> *Do not steal;*
> *Do not lie;*
> *Do not slander;*
> *and never become intoxicated.*

He called his new religion *Islam*, which means the Acceptation of Allah, who is God. He called his flock, *Moslems*, which means *true believers*.

We just want to stop here for a moment. The claim of Mohammed that he was visited by the Angel Gabriel, who told him this and that, out of which evolved a religion, can be very manipulative. The same may be said of Joseph Smith, who claimed to have been given divine revelation by the Angel Moroni, who spoke to him, and the Mormon religion evolved.

Today, sadly, inside our own Church, there are claims of Apparitions of Our Lady, Inner Locutions, and much more. Some of it may be true. But there are cults cropping up, based on supposed apparitions and inner locutions. When the alleged visionary or locutionist wants something, she or he simply says, "Our Lady told me she wants this." If you say no, it is as if you are saying no to Our Lady. At times, this manipulation has been known to spread its wings to political, as well as prophetic areas. When the messages begin to take on the personality of the visionary or locutionist, you know we're in trouble.

Outside the Church, we have cultists in this country who have gathered thousands of people, and millions of dollars, because they tell their followers that a major nuclear war is right around the corner; the only safe place is their little haven [where you can buy a time-share program on a bomb shelter]. We all remember Jim Jones, and the mass suicide he manipulated in Guyana, because the Federal Government was threatening to close him down and stop sending the Social Security checks to his followers.

I guess what we're trying to say here is be careful. Prudently, the Church is slow to act, that's for sure. But you can also be sure that when Mother Church makes a decision, you can put it in the bank. Be open to the Holy Spirit working in the lives of individuals, but don't let anyone steer you away from what the Magisterium is teaching you. If something sounds strange, like it's not coming from Our Lord Jesus, or our Mother Mary, but from an individual, or groups of individuals, back off. You are always safe in Church, at Mass, with the Eucharist. You don't really need more than that. Everything else is whipped cream topping on the cake. We love Our Lady, the Angels and the Saints, but they all point to Jesus.

Okay, back to Mohammed and the Moslems. Mohammed created a lifestyle, a way of life. If a brother owed a sum of money, as long as he *submitted*, became a follower of Islam and Allah, his debt was forgiven. Don't ask me what happened to the one to whom he owed the debt. He was out of luck, or so it would seem. But there was an outrageous epidemic of *Usury*[1] that had spread throughout the world, and we believe Mohammed or his family might

---

[1]Lending money at an extremely high rate of interest, so high that most people can never even make the interest payments, much less the principal.

have been victimized by this evil practice, at a given point in his life. Only one thing was for sure. The Arabs were ripe for a prophet and a religion. They were wandering around aimlessly, and the answer was to mimic Christianity.

The religion we know today as Islam *evolved* more than anything else. It's based on Christianity, Judaism, and holdover beliefs from the old Arab rites. Mohammed paid close attention to the teachings of the popular religions of his time. *Christianity* was the newest and most popular. It had spread like wildfire throughout the world. Why not take from *Christianity* and use it for his design of a new religion? That is exactly what Mohammed did. He created a doctrine based on a *distortion* of the Catholic Faith. For example, Mohammed taught:

> *There was one God; His name was Allah.*
> *Allah was all powerful.*
> *Allah was all circumspect.*
> *Allah was all good[2].*
> *Allah is the Creator of all things.*
> *All things exist through the power of Allah.*
> *Allah has always existed, and will always exist.*
> *Angels do the bidding of Allah.*
> *Man's soul was immortal*
> *There was a heaven and hell.*
> *Those who followed Allah would be rewarded;*
> *the enemies of Allah would be punished.[3]*
> *Islam has its own version of the Bible; the Koran.*
> *Moses was a prophet.*

---

[2]This can be disputed to a degree. We know from present Islam beliefs that a man who kills his enemy goes to Heaven, and a man who dies in defense of Islam goes to Heaven, immediately. To encourage killing does not sound like a god who is good.

[3]Mohammed said: "*I, last of the prophets, am sent with a sword. The sword is the key to heaven and hell; all who draw it in the name of the Faith will be rewarded!*"

Elijah was a prophet.
Mary was blessed among all women;
she may have been born without sin.
John the Baptist and Jesus were prophets;
but Jesus was not God.

If we were to not look *carefully* at everything listed above, we might say that Islam was close to Christianity, until you get to the last line. But these were the things that Mohammed chose to take from Christianity, in order to form a strong, solid, credible base. The dogmas of our faith which he *threw out* are like huge, gaping stab wounds at the heart of our religion. Followers of Mohammed, the Moslems, have some *firm* beliefs which are irreconcilable with Christianity, such as:

"Jesus was born of human estate; Jesus cannot be God. God cannot die; Jesus died, therefore He cannot be God."

We don't know if the Son of God dying for our sins was just a real stumbling block to Mohammed, an area of our Faith with which he could not reconcile. Remember, he was a simple man; he could not read or write. These dogmas of our Faith are *not meant* to be understood. We accept them in the light of faith. This is our Faith; this is what we believe. *But when it's not your Faith*, as in the case of Mohammed, and if your original course is not to lead your followers to Christianity, but to use a distortion of Christianity as a springboard, there's no big problem throwing out anything which could be argumentative or confusing. Besides, if he used Christianity in its true form, how would he be able to get people to follow him? The tools of Satan have always used this same method: change some part of the belief; give them something new, something that is more palatable for your everyday life. The Incarnation of Jesus, His death on the Cross for our Salvation, all of this was just too difficult to understand, so scrap it. In addition, he was not trying to become a

Christian; he was trying to build a *workable* theology to become the leader of his people.

Unfortunately, when *he discarded the Incarnation of Jesus*, he had to throw out a few more tenets of our religion:

There is no Trinity; there is only one God. One God with three individual Persons, who still remained one God, was too much to accept. Scrap it.

The Mass was a reenactment of the Crucifixion, Death and Resurrection of Jesus. God could not die. If He could not die, He could not resurrect. It glorified the Triune God in the Creed, which, according to Mohammed, didn't exist. *The Mass had to go.*

The Eucharist was beyond their human understanding. It was, as well, the acceptance of Jesus as God. They believed He was only a prophet. *Throw It out.*

There was no need for the priesthood. If there was no Mass, and no Eucharist, why would they need priests? Mohammed contended that all these areas of our Faith that he couldn't understand or agree with, were created by priests so that they would have power over the people. With an exclusive job that no one else could do, you couldn't have a religion without them. That would give them very *individual* powers which Mohammed didn't think were necessary, or *wise.* He eliminated them.

After Mohammed stripped away all the things he didn't like or understand, and put in all the things he did like, he used that as a foundation to actually shape and mold a religion, based on his own background, trials and tribulations, one that he and his people could live with. Above all things, he strove for simplicity in his dogma. Don't make it too hard. *Keep it simple.*

Now, can you really believe that the Archangel Gabriel gave all of this to Mohammed? Having just researched and written a book on the *Heavenly Army of Angels*, we have great difficulty accepting Mohammed's claim that it was the

Angel Gabriel who spoke to him. Can you believe that the Angel Gabriel would disavow his God, his Jesus? Could the same Angel Gabriel who announced to Mary that she would give birth to the Messiah, who said: "Hail Mary full of grace[4]" then contradict himself by telling Mohammed she was not a virgin? Would the same Angel Gabriel who spent all that time with his beloved Mary, guarded the Holy Family, who was beside His Lord during the entire period of Jesus' life on earth, then renounce His Divinity to a camel-driver in the middle east, five hundred years later? It doesn't make sense.

At least Joseph Smith, founder of the Mormons chose an angel with the name Moroni, rather than taking a Biblical name for his imagined messenger of God.

However, a curious but very interesting point is that both Joseph Smith and Mohammed picked out the most convenient parts of the Old and New Testaments, claimed they were given them *by a heavenly messenger*, and started new religions, which suited their own lifestyles and wrote their own bibles, based on these teachings. There is a great deal of similarity between the experiences of Mohammed and Joseph Smith, as well as the tailor-made religions they put together. Not bad if you can do it, and they did it.

Mohammed had a very valid reason for putting together this loosely formed structure. He wanted to unite his people. It was as simple as that. His people, the Arabs, were living in an area of the world, called Arabia, and they were spiritually bankrupt. They drank heavily; they gambled; they worshiped idols. They were completely self-centered, without ambition, which made them for the most part, an embarrassment to the civilized world. In addition to being very ambitious, Mohammed sincerely became concerned for his people, especially the more he learned about Christianity, and the

---

[4]The Blessed Mother is prophetically referred to as a virgin in Isaiah 7:14, and then more *directly* by the Angel in Luke 1:28 and in Luke 1:42

rewards of good life. He began preaching all throughout Mecca, his hometown. But he was not accepted, because he was coming against the rich and powerful.

He eventually left Mecca in disappointment and frustration. He tried to get his message across to the people of a small town about seventy miles away. But because his message attacked drinking, and the town was the center of a grape harvesting industry, he was almost killed. They ran him out of town, nearly stoning him to death. He returned to Mecca, but still had no great acceptance until a group from a far distant town appealed to him to begin a community there. He left Mecca for the town called *Yathrib*. He was welcomed with open arms. So enthusiastic were the people there, they made him a ruler of the town, and renamed it Medina, which is now the third most important shrine in Islam, after Mecca and Jerusalem.

Mohammed was in his fifties when he began his ministry in Medina. Possibly because of the almost immediate and overwhelming acceptance he received there, his ambitions and goals took on much greater proportions than he had previously imagined. In Mecca, he called himself a Prophet. In Medina, he called himself, *and was proclaimed by the people, their Ruler.* Originally, he would have been satisfied with sobering up a small section of drunks in Mecca. Now, he had grand plans. He was thinking in terms of all Arabia, and beyond. His plan to unify the entire Arab world under Islam began.

He found it to his advantage to organize an army. His attitude changed altogether. When you read the teachings of Mohammed, they are almost a complete contradiction to his actions over this period of time. Whereas he preached peace and love, his exploits were *militant*. He developed into a military leader, and even made a clause encouraging his troops to unconditional loyalty with the promise that they would go to Heaven if they died in the service of Islam.

His main goal was Mecca. He was ruler over the second largest city in Arabia, but he would not be truly a leader of the Arabs until he was ruler of Mecca. He set the stage for battle against Mecca. He told his followers the greatest place of pilgrimage was Mecca; every Moslem should go there on pilgrimage. When they complained that because they were his followers, their lives were in jeopardy if they pilgrimaged to Mecca, he vowed that he, their leader, would liberate Mecca and make it possible for them to worship at the shrine there.

He harassed the merchants of Mecca. He sent his soldiers on warring missions against the caravans that went from foreign countries to Mecca by way of Medina. Remember, he was a camel-driver. He knew the routes that would be taken. He actually forced the people of Mecca to engage him in battle. Mecca declared war on Mohammed. This gave him justification to go after Mecca. His plan worked. He attacked Mecca with a vengeance. They were no match for him. You have to realize that most of the people of Mecca, especially the religious ones, were not violent. He stepped over many dead bodies to become the ruler of this country, and that was included into the Koran, also. The Koran was actually written hands on, adding and eliminating as he went along, based on life experience.

The next ten years were to be his most formative. By the time he died in 622, Islam ruled all of Arabia, and many surrounding tribes. In addition to a large, well-oiled military machine, he had a thriving religious community going in Medina, with apostles and disciples, chomping at the bit to get out there and evangelize. His long range ambition manifested itself in a grand way. Like his predecessors Caesar, and Alexander the Great, Mohammed would be ruler of the world, or at least, his followers, the Moslems, would conquer the world in the name of Allah. Before he died, Mohammed sent word to the *Emperor of Rome* to convert to Islam. He wrote to him, "*Embrace Islam, and God will reward you twofold. But if you refuse, o ye people of the Book, Beware! We are Moslem, and our religion is Islam.*" The gauntlet had been thrown down.

Islam takes on the whole world

The growth of Islam in the hundred years after the death of Mohammed, from 622 to 732, was overwhelming. It almost defies logic. No one religion could have grown that quickly, and taken over as much of the world as this one cult did. But why? What was the big attraction of Islam? The world was ready for a Mohammed and his philosophy of "*Happy Days are here again.*" We have to get into the climate of the times. The world situation was no different than it has been down through the centuries when the power was with the few, and the masses were under the domination of slavery and financial debt. No one seemed able or willing to care for the downtrodden. People who thought they were *free men* were really under the control of the few. The wages were ridiculous; the interest rates were outrageous; and the taxes, on top of all of it, were impossible. People were drowning in their debts. There was no one who cared for them. They "*sold their soul to the company store[5]*", and they were dying.

There was injustice, to be sure. Under these conditions, the time was ripe for Islam, who promised them relief from all of their oppressions. His followers, as well as Mohammed, had been victims during their lifetimes, of great social injustices. Mohammed told the people, if they believed in Islam, their debts were forgiven. Usury was outlawed in countries ruled by Islam. Attorneys were available; courts were lenient; and judgments were in favor of the poor. *But all of this was on paper.* It was theoretical. Very often, the slaves remained slaves, and the poor

---

[5]from *Sixteen Tons* by Tennessee Ernie Ford, the singer of the 60's.

remained poor and in debt; but because they had joined Islam, they thought they were free.

Just picture millions of people enslaved by debt, all over the Arab world, given an immediate resolution to their problem, a blank check, so to speak. Join Islam, and all your debts are forgiven; you are freed. And it was backed up with strong-arm tactics of his troops. Thus began Mohammed's dream of the conquest of the world by Islam.

The Moslem conquest of all of the Middle East and half of Europe in less than one hundred years was a combination of Islam principles and sheer force[6]. The Moslems went through countries like the barbarian hordes of earlier generations. One thing that marked the Moslems was their viciousness, their hostility, and their complete disregard for human life, that is, other than Moslem human life. Those principles still stand today in the Islamic code of Ethics. One of the rules of Islam is that one Moslem cannot harm another Moslem. But any Moslem who kills a non-Moslem, is rewarded by Allah. This has changed somewhat in the past generation. In the 1980's and 90's, the Iranians and Iraqis were at war for *eight years.* The death toll was horrendous. Then we can't forget Saddam Hussein's foray into Kuwait, and the atrocities which took place there, and his wholesale annihilation of his own people, the Kurds, in the North. Nothing has changed in 1500 years with the followers of Mohammed, other than now, they are more willing to kill their own.

The Moslems just swallowed up countries. After the movement had spread throughout the Arab world, mostly by military means, but in some instances, *voluntarily* by small countries tired of being under the heel of despots, Islam set

---

[6]By 732, Islam had captured all of Arabia, North Africa, including Egypt and Libya, Spain, portions of Italy, and France as far north as Tours and Poitier, which are approximately 234 kilometers, *or 150 miles from Paris.*

their sights on the rest of the world, the non-Islam world. Conveniently, the earlier Moslem teachings based on Judaism and Christianity, went out the window, or at least any semblance of respect for each of these Faith beliefs. Invasion to the north and the west was the key word. At one point in history, Spain and Portugal were ruled by Moslems for 700 years, as was Yugoslavia and Greece. Sicily was under Moslem domination for almost 300 years.

One of the greatest clashes between Christianity and Islam took place in the form of the Crusades. Pope Urban II called a Crusade to stop the ever-moving onslaught of the Moslems, in the form of Turkish warriors. The immediate defense in 1095 was Constantinople, which was in eminent danger of being taken over by the Turks, which it was, eventually. The Crusades made as part of their quest, the liberation of the Holy Places in Palestine, which had been desecrated by the Saracens (Moslems), for centuries.

The appeal of our Pope and holy people from all parts of Europe, so touched the faithful that a highly emotional, unorganized group of 50,000 literally ran to the defense of the Holy Land. Old people, children, whole families, everyone stepped forward to dedicate their lives to the liberation of the Holy Places. It was called the *People's Crusade*. Most of them never made it past Constantinople. Those who did set foot on the shores of Palestine were slaughtered in short order.

But within a few years of this effort, organized groups of crack military troops from Europe, led by their kings or princes, or head military men, began the Crusades as we know them today. At the beginning, they were brilliant. It was as if the Lord Himself were at the helm. They captured Jerusalem from the Saracens after 40 days. But wherever the Lord is, you know the evil one is there as well.

The Crusaders became soft and comfortable, while the enemy did not. The excitement of the original goal waned.

Infighting between the various groups began. Greed for land and treasures overcame many of the noble intentions of those who had originally come over, ready to give up their lives in this honorable quest.

The Crusades lasted for just about two hundred years. In 1291, the last of the Crusaders were thrown out of the Holy Land. They did leave their mark there, however. To this day, there is a small, but strong Christian community occupying pockets of influence in various areas of the Holy Land, such as Bethlehem.

The next strong onslaught of the Moslems on Christianity took place when the Turks, under the leadership of Osman, created the Ottoman Empire, which ruled a great portion of the Christian world with an iron fist, for hundreds of years. They were responsible for rebuilding the walls of Jerusalem, and the Dome of the Rock in the temple area.

There's something we have to clarify here. Throughout history, Moslems have always been Moslems. It didn't matter whether they were Egyptian, or Libyan, or Saracens; they were Moslems. While it's true, they didn't always treat their own according to the rules set down by Mohammed, on paper, they were Moslems before they were nationals of any country. That didn't necessarily manifest itself in the actions of the leaders of the people. For instance, when the Turks barreled through Palestine or Syria, or Persia, or any of the countries they occupied, they dealt harshly with their opposition. They had no problems killing fellow Moslems who may have gotten in their way.

But once that was done, *I guess*, they all reverted back to being Moslem. Then they looked outward to the rest of the world, who became their enemy. When they fought outsiders, it was a *religious* war.

Case in point, in April of 1992, Muammar Gaddafi, the Libyan dictator, said over *worldwide television*, that we were engaged in a religious war between Islam and non-believers.

This was when sanctions were going to be taken against Libya because Muammar Gaddafi would not turn over the terrorists who planted the explosives that destroyed a Pan Am plane over Lockerbee, Scotland, killing 259 innocent people. At the time of the bombing, a statement was made claiming this horrible act was in retaliation for the mistaken bombing of an Iranian commercial jet the year before, killing 298 innocent people, by our battleship Vicennes. Now we find out that the whole thing, killing all those people on Pan Am 103, was because one man on the plane, Major Charles McKee, was going after the hostages in Beirut, and they wanted him out of the way.[7] And perhaps the saddest and most ridiculous part of the whole thing is, here we are, less than four years later, and all the hostages have been released. *On the surface, it would appear that all those people died for nothing.*

We once said that all wars are religious wars; the more we see what is going on in the world around us, we believe more than ever the truth of that statement. On a very broad scale, Christians and Moslems, the two largest and most powerful religious groups in the world, have been at war with each other for almost thirteen hundred years. There has never really been a bond of peaceful co-existence between Moslems and Christians.

We would pray that our people, the Christians in general, and the Catholics in particular, had the singleness of purpose of the Moslems. We wish that our people prayed the way these people do. Moslems, by and large, live for their religion. Because Mohammed gave them a simple religion to follow, it's very possible to be in the world and also be practicing their religion. Moslems pray five times a day. We've been in Jerusalem, and other parts of Israel, and

---

[7]Time Magazine April 27, 1992, The Untold Story of Pan Am 103 - Pg 27

heard the call to prayer 5 times a day-at dawn, at noon, in the middle of the afternoon, at dusk, and after dark [which always seemed to be just as we fell sound asleep in the Holy Land]. We've been in airports and seen Moslems spreading out their prayer rugs, going down on their knees to pray, facing Mecca. We respect our brothers and sisters for their reverence, but we pray that our people become a sign to them of the One we believe in, our Lord Jesus Christ.

However, there is also the other side of the coin. We have known Moslems who, as with some Christians, are Moslems in name only and do not follow the rules of Mohammed. Not every Moslem adheres to the rules of prayer and fasting. In Israel, many Moslems marry European women. Their wives and children are required to embrace Islam. There is virtually no conversion away from Islam among Moslems. It's got to be the other way around. Some of their customs would be difficult for us to live by. The man's mother is always the arbiter in arguments, whether between husband and wife or between the wives of sons who are all living under the one roof. When a man marries, an extension is built onto *his* family's home and he and his wife move in. Women eat as a group, separately from men. Followers of Islam would be a field day for feminist groups to attack. So there is always the other side of the coin.

The Church Fights Back!

For every splinter of the Cross, there is a triumph of the Cross. Jesus made a promise to us, that He would not leave us orphans; He would be with us always until the end of time. While we can't get into detailed stories of each of the ways God has fought the Moslem heresy over the last thirteen hundred years, and continues to fight it, we can give you thumbnail sketches of Miracles of the Eucharist that

Above:
Victory over the Saracens at the battle of Vienna
Vatican Museum - Rome, Italy

Right:
St. Francis
meets with the
Sultan in the
Holy Land. St.
Francis offered
to walk through
burning coals
with the
Sultan's priests,
if the Sultan
agreed, he and
his people
would convert.

have come about, the Saints our Lord has raised to combat this heresy, and the apparitions our Lady made to help us.

St. Francis of Assisi (1181-1226)

St. Francis has been called the Saint of the non-Christians. We know for a fact that even today, non-Christians go to the Hermitage, way up on Mount Subasio, in Assisi, to study the ways of Francis.

The Crusades had become a way of life in Europe. No sooner had one ended than preparations were made for another. This had been going on for over 100 years when Francis decided the Lord was calling him to die a martyr's death in the land of our Savior's birth. He set out three times to get to the Holy Land, but was blocked twice, once by conditions, and the other by his own bad health. Finally, in 1220, after the bodies of the first five Franciscan martyrs of the Holy Land were sent back to Europe, he forged ahead, determined to suffer a martyr's death for Jesus.

However, the Lord had different plans for Francis. Jesus guided Francis and a companion, Brother Illuminato, through the battle lines, to the Sultan of the Saracens. Francis and his comrade were caught by the Arabs, beaten, and put in chains. Then they were brought before the Sultan. When asked why they had come, Francis shared his love of the Gospel and Our Lord Jesus. He was so simple, so sincere, so understandable, the Sultan was captivated by him. Francis offered to walk through burning coals with the Sultan's priests, if the Sultan agreed that he and his people would convert. The Sultan's priests, not too happy with the idea fled. The Sultan told Francis, if he were to convert, both he and Francis would be killed.

A legend at the Church of the Holy Sepulchre is that Francis asked the Sultan to come into the Church with him, to pray at the tomb of Jesus. The Sultan replied that if he were to enter that church, the Moslems would make it into a mosque. Instead, the two prayed outside the Church of the

Holy Sepulchre, and till today, right at the edge of the courtyard of the Church of the Holy Sepulchre, stands a very small mosque, erected in honor of the Sultan, who had prayed there.

Christians were being slaughtered in the Holy Land. Franciscans had been martyred there. Yet, Francis was able to go into the jaws of hell, and not only come out unscratched, but having successfully spread the Word of God to the Moslems. Why is that? What did the Moslems see in Francis that they did not see in the Crusaders, or in the other Franciscans who went to the Holy Land to convert them? We believe Francis had the ability to empty himself almost completely, and let Jesus reflect through him. It was no longer Francis who spoke, but Jesus, *through* Francis.

The Holy House of Loreto - 1291

Our Lord Jesus loves His Mother Mary. He watches out for her, and protects everything on earth that had anything to do with her time here. And so it was, in the year 1291, when the Saracens (Moslems) decided to vent their venom and hate against Christ, and all things Christian. The Crusades were over. The Christians had been defeated and run out of the Holy Land. By destroying every holy place in Palestine, the Moslems thought they could eliminate every sign or vestige of Jesus' existence in history.

The Saracens went on a rampage. There would not be a stone left upon a stone on any of the holy places. If there were no longer any shrines where Jesus was born, where He grew up, where He taught, where He healed and called man to new life in His Father, where He died for us, where He rose giving us eternal hope that we, too, would rise, man would forget he has a Savior, and have no reason to live.

The Saracens descended on Bethlehem. They went to the church built over the spot where Christ was born. They would level it! But when they approached the building, there was a mosaic outside, depicting the three wise men. This could not be the place of Jesus' birth, they thought. *This is a mosque, dedicated to Arab kings of the past.* So they left this place, and continued looking for Jesus' birthplace.

At about the same time, hordes of Arabs rode, for all they were worth, towards *Nazareth.* They would destroy the house of Mary. Never again would Christians celebrate the Annunciation, there. Never again would they be reminded of the Jewish Virgin's *yes* that helped to redeem the world. It was well known that Jesus' Apostles and disciples began celebrating Mass in the Holy House of Nazareth soon after Jesus' death. It was a shrine from the earliest days of the Christian movement. This was an important place for the Saracens to destroy.

We believe there has always been a legion of Angels protecting the house of the Annunciation. Here, Gabriel appeared to Mary, and the Holy Family lived until Jesus began His public ministry. We believe Gabriel never left this place. But now, when danger seemed so imminent, we can visualize an *army* of Angels charging down from Heaven, their wings glistening in the sun, Michael joining Gabriel, his red cape whirling around him. In unison, the Angels raised the house from its foundation, and carried it high into the sky, resting it behind the clouds which hid it from the earth. When the Arabs arrived, with hatred in their hearts, craving to pillage and burn, they were astonished. There was nothing there! Only the grotto remained. They left it alone; it had no meaning to them.

The Angels carried the Holy House, high above the mountains and deserts of the Holy Land, across the expansive Mediterranean and Adriatic Seas to *Yugoslavia.* On May 10, 1291, it landed in the little hamlet of Tersatto, in Croatia, Yugoslavia, far from the battle cries of Palestine.

It was early in the morning, when the local people discovered, to their great surprise, a house resting on the ground. *There was no foundation under it*! Curious to see what it was, they ventured inside. They found a stone altar. On the Altar was a cedar statue of Mother Mary standing with Her Divine Son in her arms. The Infant Jesus had the two first fingers of His Right Hand extended in a blessing, and with His Left Hand, He held a golden sphere representing the world.

The villagers were awestruck, but *confused*, until a short time later, our Lady appeared to the local priest and verified that this was truly the House of the Annunciation. Pilgrimages began coming *immediately* to the Holy House of Nazareth, in Yugoslavia.

However, the joy, the Croatians had experienced at having this most precious gift in their midst, was short-lived. Three years and five months later, on December 10, 1294, the Holy House disappeared overnight from Croatia, never to return. On December 10th, 1294, in the area of Loreto, *Italy* (across the Adriatic Sea and southwest of Tersatto) shepherds reported seeing a house in the sky, flying across the sea, supported by Angels. They saw our Lady and the Baby Jesus seated on top of the house. The Angels continued inland, about four miles, and landed with their precious house and its Royal Passengers. The house moved three times until it landed in the spot it remains till today, on a hill in Loreto, where the faithful have been coming to venerate their Holy Mother for the past 700 years.

Miracle of the Eucharist of Langenwiese - 1453

Constantinople had fallen to the Turks, at the time of this miracle. They were marching north to capture all of Europe, and enslave Christianity under the sword of Islam.

In Langenwiese, somewhere between Poland and Czechoslovakia, thieves broke into a church, and stole some Consecrated Hosts, from the Tabernacle. It is believed it was to desecrate and blaspheme the Sacred Hosts. They wrapped Them in a white linen cloth. *The Hosts started to bleed profusely*, the blood pouring out of the cloth. The thieves hid the Hosts in the forest. They picked what they considered to be the most desolate spot around.

Shortly after the thieves hid the Hosts, a Polish man was traveling towards Langenwiese in a carriage drawn by four horses. At a certain spot in the road, the horses stopped abruptly, and knelt down. The driver could not understand what caused the animals to act in this manner. He got out to investigate. The horses remained in their kneeling position. As the man searched the area, he found the blood soaked bundle with the Hosts inside.

The man contacted the local priest, who went out to the place where the Hosts were buried. The priest, followed by a contingency of local people, took the bundle with the Hosts and brought Them back in solemn procession to the Church of Langenwiese. The news of the miracle spread throughout the district.

Pilgrims were drawn to the Church of the Eucharistic Miracle in Langenwiese. Prayers and petitions were offered to the Lord to halt the invasion of the Turks. The official feast was designated as the Fourth Sunday after Easter. At one time, as many as 50,000 pilgrims were reported to have come on Pilgrimage to Langenwiese, to pray for the pardon of the sins of man, and for deliverance from the Turks.

St. John Capistrano

The turning point against the Turks was at Belgrade in 1456. The Europeans had prepared for their attack. St. John Capistrano, a powerful saint of that period, near death by this time, had gathered together an army of men. Armed with prayer on the battlefield, and an enormous amount of prayer and penance at the Shrine, the Turks were defeated, and Europe was saved from them.

We truly believe that the Lord has a teaching for us in everything that goes on in the world. Historians and military leaders throughout the centuries have been instructed by their predecessors. Caesar copied Alexander the Great. Napoleon copied Caesar. Hitler copied all three. We see a resurgence today in the power and aggressiveness of the Moslem Arab world. We see European leaders mimicking their forerunners of 50 years ago, reacting with fear and intimidation to tactics of Arab terrorists with the same philosophy they used in dealing with Adolph Hitler. If we ignore him, he'll go away. If we appease him, he'll leave us alone. Deep down in our hearts, we know that will never work. There is only one way to deal with this type of enemy. *Heavy duty prayer and fasting.*

Where do we go from here?

"Communism is no longer the number one threat in the world. Militant Islam is 'number one threat' in the world." declared Cardinal John. J. O'Connor, Archbishop of New York, during his commencement speech at St. Thomas Aquinas College in Ojai, California, in June of 1989.[8] He shared that the spread of **militant Islam**, as expressed by the late Ayatolah Khomeini of Iran, *"is a very, very fearsome thing"*. He further stated that Islam is sweeping the world faster than any other religion. He projected figures which show that by the year 2,000, (7 years from now) *"Christianity will be only the second largest religion. Islam will have the most adherents."* [There are those who say this has already come to pass.] This shouldn't surprise us that much, although it should put the fear of God into us. From the time the Moslems made their big push into Christian Europe, 732 A.D., until the forward movement of the Turks was finally stopped at the end of the Seventeenth Century, beginning with the evacuation of the Crimean States, 1699, every

---

[8]The Tidings, Los Angeles, June 16, 1989

Vatican Council focused on the growing Moslem problem. They have always been a major threat to the Church, as well as to the world.

Time Magazine printed an article on May 13, 1988, which stated that by the year 2000, the second largest religion in **the United States**, grouping all Christianity together as number one, *(that means Catholics and all denominations of Protestant are lumped as one group)* will be **Moslem.** The number of Moslems entering the United States has doubled over the past decade, and while Americans are having 1.3 children per family, with a high abortion rate, the Moslems are averaging 10 to 14 children per family, with *no* abortion rate, abortion being illegal and against the Moslem religion. Although there are 800,000,000 Moslems in the world, they were pretty invisible in the United States. But the growth has accelerated so rapidly, they are becoming a major face on the American landscape. There are an estimated **4,644,000 Moslems in the United States,** with the largest concentration being in the State of California. There are more than 600 Islamic centers throughout the United States, with many more planned.

In a relatively small American town, Dearborn, Michigan, where there is a 10-15% Moslem representation, Moslem holy days are observed. We can't get Catholic Holy Days observed anywhere in the United States, and yet these people have been able to accomplish that. The girl's dress code in the public school gym class has been modified *for all students* to coincide with Moslem religious customs. In addition, no pork, *which is against Moslem dietetic law*, is served in the school cafeterias. Moslems are receiving greater and greater religious considerations and Christians cannot pray in school because of separation of Church and State. A Moslem-American recently said *"We'd like people to start thinking of the U.S. as a Judeo-Christian-Moslem society."*

This situation that you may find shocking, is by no means limited to the United States. Most European countries are finding that their Moslem population is increasing rapidly, as is the voice of the Moslems in these countries. Do I have a problem with this? It frightens me. The prospect of living under any kind of Moslem domination, in a country, a world where I cannot worship Jesus, except with a price on my head, puts me in a panic. *But is my complaint with the Moslems?* Not really! I admire their zeal. I'm concerned with the apathy of the Christians of the world, especially of the United States, and their lack of concern. Obviously, they don't see this as a real problem. Or is it that they don't see it as a problem in their time? Is our attitude one of not caring what happens to the future generations, as long as no one upsets our parade?

Perhaps they think that the Moslems don't represent a threat to our freedom of religion, or to the security of our country. I have to go back to Muammar Gaddafi's threat of April 1992, in which he said over worldwide television, that we were engaged in a religious war between Islam and non-believers. Saddam Hussein sold his war with the United States to his people, as a *Holy War*, and that the United States is the great Satan. Folks, if you don't want to believe us, believe their own people.

Jesus is trying to get our attention. Listen to Him. Listen to Mother Mary. She's been running all over the world, trying to get our attention. There's no more time. We must get on with it. *Do whatever He tells you.*

Iconoclasm: Craven Images

We're in the Eighth Century and the Church is under attack, again! The Emperors and the State have always wanted control over the Church. Think about how easy it would be to control their subjects. To disobey the Church would be tantamount to disobeying God! The faithful believed, and rightly so, that the Church was bringing them the true Word of God. They believed, as we do, that the Pope and his bishops, along with their priests, represented our Lord Jesus on earth. Now, if the Emperors could discredit the Pope and become the rightful head of the Church, they could ask any sacrifice of the people and they would have to obey! They would never question any action again.

The Emperor at that time, Leo the Isaurian, aided and abetted a group called *Iconoclasts*, who held that the veneration of all types of sacred images, whether paintings or statues or etc., was *idolatry*. He took this opportunity to wage war against the Catholic Church, using whatever false charges he could trump up. He accused the Church of advocating the worshiping of images, in place of God.

The Church fights back

The heretic sect of Iconoclasts contended that the veneration of images was *idolatry*. What was our Lord Jesus going to do about it? Raise up great Popes to defend His Church. And He did!

Seven Popes of the Church had been either Greek or Syrian, when the Lord raised up the first Roman Pope to follow them, **Pope St. Gregory II.** Not only was he distinguished in this way, but he would turn out to be the *foremost* Roman Pope of the Eighth Century! He proved himself capable and prudent, not only in handling matters of the Church, but in civil matters as well. He was a peacemaker, but never at the cost of His Lord and His Church.

He believed in *rendering unto Caesar,* as Jesus said, *that which is Caesar's.* He was loyal to the Empire, always attempting to bring about peace and reconciliation. But, from 717 until 741, when the people throughout Italy were rebelling against the unfair taxes imposed on them by Emperor Leo III, he supported *them.* All his years of loyalty, all the service he had rendered the State went out the window. The government tried to have Pope Gregory II assassinated. When that failed they tried to have him removed as Pope.

The Emperor came out with an edict! He proclaimed that the veneration of images was a stumbling block for Jews and Moslems[1] desiring to convert to the Church. [In the Holy Land, you can still see evidences of statues with their heads knocked off, dating back to the time of the Crusades, when the Saracens were destroying every Shrine of Jesus they could get their hands on.] The Emperor was able to get the Church in the East to go along. The Patriarch signed the edict prohibiting the veneration of images!

Now, had Leo III laid in wait for an opportunity to get back at Pope Gregory II? You bet he did. Leo III turned to the Pope: "*Condemn the veneration of images or be forced to step down from the Papacy.*" He not only refused to sign any such edict, but the Pope condemned *Iconoclasm* as a heresy. He issued a warning to the Emperor to stay out of affairs that are of princes of the Church, not of the world. The Pope never weakened, no matter how many threats were leveled at him. Because the people of Italy had profound reverence for the successor of Peter, no harm came to the Pope.

Pope Gregory II died and he was followed by a Syrian who took the name **Gregory III**. He began his Pontificate by

---

[1]Both believe that by praying before images that represent Saints is a form of idolatry.

carrying out that which his predecessor had begun. He appealed to Emperor Leo III to cease his persecution of the faithful and clergy who were venerating images. When he received no answer, he convened a synod. In November 731 A.D., he condemned Iconoclasm and excommunicated anyone destroying sacred images, including the Emperor and the Patriarch of the East. The Emperor responded by sending out a fleet to attack the Pope. If intimidation and threats wouldn't work, he thought, let's see how the Pope stands up to force. One way or the other, he would have him submit to his Imperial authority. I can just hear the Pope saying what we have heard Mother Angelica say so many times, "*I fear no one but the Lord, as I face Him someday, saying to me, 'I gave you a task to do and you did not do it.'*" The Pope did not back down!

Pope St. Gregory III died and **Pope St. Zacharias** succeeded him as Pope. He had been Pope St. Gregory's deacon, and was really the best man to continue the work Pope Gregory had begun. This new Pope would be remembered for his gentleness and compassion.

Now, because of the battle over Iconoclasm, relations between Rome and Constantinople were at best *strained*. The new Pope, in an act of peace and friendship, sent word to the Patriarch of Constantinople, informing him he was the new Vicar of Christ[2]. Whereas he was showing, by this action, there was no break with the Church in the East, he did not hesitate to advise Emperor Constantine that his stand on Iconoclasm was in communion with the former Pope.

Problems with Constantinople were to continue through Pope after Pope. The next Pope to have to defend the Church's position on the veneration of images was **Pope St. Paul I**. He did not back down, either, and when there was a

---

[2]He was the last Pope to do so.

Our Lady of Sorrows holding her Son's limp Body in her arms
"Pieta" by Ippilito Scalza in the Cathedral of Orvieto, Italy

debate at a synod in 767, the veneration of images was upheld.

Hadrian became Pope and he convened The Second Council of Nicea (the Seventh General Council). In September of 787 the Council condemned Iconoclasm and reinstated the veneration of Images. They proclaimed: *We worship God, we venerate the Saints, and when we pray before images (or statues) of Saints we are "paying homage not to the image but to the person depicted[3]".*

The Pope was not only able to convince Emperor Charlemagne to go along with the condemnation of Iconoclasm, but was able to induce him to return lands formerly confiscated from the Papacy. Although Charlemagne and Pope Hadrian had been at loggerheads many times, and relations were not always pleasant, when Pope Hadrian died, Charlemagne mourned his friend *"as if he had lost a brother or a child"*. He had Masses said for the Pope in all the churches of his domain, and had a monument carved, expressing the esteem and fondness he had for the Pope.

The Church fights back today!

The Second Council of Nicea cleared up the matter, they thought, for all time, but the enemy never sleeps. Our ongoing tradition in the Church, that of venerating the Saints, and paying respect to them through their images, came under attack once again, in the *Twentieth Century*. Some misguided theologians completely disregarded one of the documents from the Vatican Council II: section 125 of the Sacred Constitution on the Liturgy, *Sacrosanctum concilium*[4], and began promoting the removal of statues from

---

[3]Catholic Encyclopedia-Broderick

[4]In the Twentieth Century, Vatican Council II stated the position of the Church on the veneration of images: *"The practice of placing sacred images in churches so that they may be venerated by the faithful is to be firmly maintained. Nevertheless, their number should be moderate and*

our churches, not only of the Saints but of Mother Mary, herself. And they were discarded. They often landed on garbage heaps, broken and forgotten. And what was the result, the Blessed Mother, and the Saints, and the Angels they represented were soon forgotten.

Could millions of mothers have killed their own unborn babies, if they had first looked upon our Lady of Sorrows holding her limp Son's Body in her arms? When the statues of the Saints left, the example of the Saints left with them, and then we had a new set of heroes and heroines to emulate, only these were not with Christ, but against Him. And how Jesus and His Mother wept! The Angels were no longer visible to remind us they were with us, that we are not alone! And we often despaired! They took away all evidence of our Lord and our Heavenly Family and they left us with a new religion - empty promises and no hope. They had chosen Barabbas for us, once more, and our Lord was condemned, again!

This abuse of the *Sacrosanctum concilium*, regarding the veneration of sacred images has gone to such extremes, that, in some churches we have visited in the United States, there is not only Jesus missing from the Cross, but instead of the Cross, there are a series of metal pipes arranged in an abstract design that would have made Picasso proud.

We, as Catholics, believe that the Mass is *the supreme sacrifice*[5]. In the light of faith, and standing on the Words of Jesus Himself, we *know* we will experience *"the unbloody repetition of the Sacrifice of Christ on Calvary*[6]. There on the wall in back of the Altar of Sacrifice, where our Lord will once again come to us through the consecrated hands of the

---

their relative location should reflect right order. Otherwise they may create confusion among the Christian people and promote a faulty sense of devotion." (SC 125)
[5]Catholic Encyclopedia-Broderick
[6]Catholic Encyclopedia-Broderick

Right:
St. Michael the Archangel casting Satan into hell.
The Iconoclasts contended that the veneration of images was Idolatry.
Our Church teaches, we are paying homage not to the image, but to the Saint or Angel etc., the image represents.

Left:
Stabat Mater Dolorosa - Mary's heart was pierced with a sword. This statue is located at the 13th station of the Cross on Calvary in Jerusalem.

priest, what do we have before us to reflect upon? Archbishop Sheen boomed, at a very modern church: "*Where have they hidden my Lord?*" Where have they put *our* Lord, as they also remove statues reminding us of the loyal members of the Church who have been glorified because of their faithfulness - our Saints and our Blessed Mother?

What happened to the wood of the Cross that they nailed our Lord to? What happened to the veneration we have given to the relics of the True Cross for almost the last two thousand years? Is there too much pain, dear pastors, as you look upon the *Price* He paid for us? When you are selling the heresies of *Psychology* and *Humanism*, instead of bringing Jesus to the sheep you have vowed to feed, is the bloody Form on the Cross too agonizing a reminder of what you have been called to be, victim-priest with our Lord? As you avoid the Passion, are you cheating yourself as you cheat your congregation? Can you no longer kneel before the Crucifix, and look upon His Wounded Arms, vulnerably outstretched before you, waiting for you to love Him? Are you afraid, if you look at Him, you might turn back to Him?

One year, in Avila, Spain, our grandson called us over to look at a statue of Jesus scourged at the pillar. When we came to the statue, there were men from our pilgrimage standing there, and they were crying. Jesus looked so young! His expression plainly said: "*What did I do to you? I only wanted to love you!*"

I can remember a time when I had difficulty with Mother Mary as depicted in Michelangelo's Pieta. She looked so resigned to her son's death. I kept screaming inside, why did *she* not scream? How could she have stood silently by, as they killed her perfect and loving Son? And then, we went to the Holy Land. I saw a statue of our Lady of the Sorrows as I knelt at the eleventh and twelfth stations of the Cross, on Calvary. There was a sword piercing our Blessed Mother's heart. She was crying out in agony. Jesus'

Mother, and our Mother Mary, suffered! Her Immaculate Heart was broken as She shared with Her Son, in the Redemption of the world. I was looking at a Mother grieving for her Son. And that's when I began to discover Mother Mary. That's when I learned to love Mother Mary. This was the Mother I could relate to. She knew my pain. She had suffered just as I had. The more I searched her Heart, the more I loved Her. That's when She became my Mother, my Sister, my Confidant, the one I could turn to. I needed that image, that statue to open my heart and mind to Mary.

Mother Church was not saying, through Vatican Council II, to throw out all the statues of the Saints and the Blessed Mother, but rather to understand their place in our Church. Statues and other images, such as paintings and icons, are there as representations of Blessed Mother, the Angels and the Saints. Art is, and has always been, a means of graphically communicating God's message to us. We have heard, in the world "*that one picture is worth a thousand words,*" and we know the impact that television has had on the learning and unlearning process of our families. Christian Art is called to reflect God, the Creator. It has traditionally been for the education of the faithful. Especially in the days when only the very few could read or write, this, and the preaching of our Priests, was the only way they could learn the Old Testament, the life of Jesus and Mary, and the place the Angels and Saints have had in our lives. This is how the Church taught their children.

But, what were the abuses Vatican Council II was addressing? One time, in Sicily, in the cave of Santa Rosalia, a Saint important to my family, we were waiting for Mass to begin. Suddenly, a deacon came out onto the Altar. He announced the Mass was about to begin. People did not leave the shrine area where they were praying before a statue of the Saint. The deacon told everyone, more insistently each time that the Mass was about to begin. Finally, he scolded: The Mass would not begin until everyone was in their pews, because, he said, what was truly important was what was about to happen upon the *Altar*. When nothing else worked, he turned out the lights at the shrine of the Saint and everyone finally filed into the pews to begin the Mass.

Have there been abuses, till today, of people giving too much importance to crying and bleeding statues, to veils that have been in places where Mother Mary has reportedly been appearing and on and on? *Yes!* But is that the Church and her teaching? *No!* It is not today, and it has never been.

Santa Rosalia of Palermo, Sicily - This statue is in a cave in Palermo, Sicily. At this shrine, Mass did not begin until all the pilgrims were in their pews. The deacon said:
"The Mass is more important than the veneration of a Saint."

The Greek Schism

We were once asked, if being in Ministry was all up hill. We replied no, it was a roller coaster, taking us to the highest highs and the lowest lows. A Priest standing by answered: *"You're in ministry, all right."* Just as you hope you can take a breath, just as it looks as if there is going to be a respite from the pressure, all hell breaks loose, again.

Welcome to the ninth century

Now, we arrive at one of the worst attacks that the Church has had to face - *the Scandal of the Cross*, which had to make Jesus and His Mother Mary weep as they watched the Body of Christ break up, the beloved Church in the East leaving the Latin Church, better known as the *Greek Schism*.

It is believed by historians that Constantine's conversion to Christianity was for purely *political* reasons. With him as a convert to Christianity, he believed that *all* his subjects, in the East and West, would be *one* through membership and loyalty to the one Church he'd adopted. This was never to come about. The Greeks from the East differed from the Latins in the West. You had two different kinds of people coming from diverse backgrounds and cultures.

Constantine thought that his plan to unite the entire Roman Empire would be *insured* with the founding of Constantinople[1]. Wrong! Instead, because of his move of the Imperial capital from Rome to Constantinople, irreconcilable differences and hurts began *in the fourth century* between the East and the West that linger till today.

Now, it is true, the Pope was the leader of the entire Catholic Church, respected by the East as well as the West. But, because of the vast separation of miles, many times, out of necessity, decisions were left up to, and made by, local patriarchs in the Eastern Church. Only in extreme

---

[1]Constantinople- originally called Byzantium, and now known as Istanbul - located in modern day Turkey

circumstances, when the Patriarchs had a problem coming to a meeting of the minds, was the Pope called in to resolve their differences. This pretty much autonomous governing of the Church, in the East, would lead to split loyalties between fidelity to the Supreme Vicar of the Church and to local Patriarchs.

And then, there was the Latin arm of the Church. The Pope, as Bishop of Rome, was the *sole* leader of the Latin West, and the faithful of the Latin West looked to him *completely* for direction, vowing their total allegiance to him. Since it was true that many of the Popes were Greek, the Latins felt that their Pope should speak Latin.

There were differences! So, there were problems.

As we said before, the geographical *and* philosophical differences made unity difficult, at best. But when the Church of Constantinople, which was already separated from Rome, got cut off from the other Patriarchates of Antioch, Alexandria and Jerusalem by the Arab invasion and occupation, the rift grew even wider.

Different Rites were another factor which separated the East from the West. In the West there was the Roman Rite, while in the East they used the Byzantine Rite. As these Rites had been used from the very beginning of the Church, the West and the East both accepted the legitimacy of the other's Rite. But the sad truth was the diversity of worship made it difficult for them to pray together. Differences in the Liturgy were most felt by the laity, both of the East and the West, who could not understand the language or framework of the other's Mass. A wonderful priest once said: "*The family that prays together, stays together*[2]." They couldn't pray together, so they didn't stay together. Christ's family fell apart!

---

[2]Father Peyton

Different Languages! When a problem arose between the Latin and the Greek arms of the Church, often they did not understand each other, and so a wall of misunderstanding went up. Representatives from the Papacy found it almost impossible to learn Greek, and the most learned of the Greeks knew no Latin. They were all dependent on translators who could not always be trusted to interpret the essence or intent behind the words. [If you were ever a victim of literal translations, as we have been, you can understand the seriousness.] At the Councils, legates would only sign doctrinal documents with the condition they were not compromising themselves or their position. They did not trust, because they did not understand. This lent an air of *suspicion*, which made the chasm between the two grow even wider.

The Greeks were engulfed by all the lure and distractions of the world. Although they had been converted by St. Paul, with the remnants of the splendor that was once Greece all around them, it was almost too much to ask of them to remember that Jesus chose to be born of, and live in *humble* estate. Their ancestors had worshiped pagan gods. Now, the Greeks, although they were faithful to the Church, were often subtly being lured by false gods without being aware of it. Although they did not pray, as their fathers before them, to the gods of yesterday, were they not stirred by the splendor that once was? Deeply imbedded in their hearts, were the glorious days, the days of the Greek athletes proudly prancing before them, *victorious* after the games. They were a people who had ingrained in their memories, Aristotles and Socrates, as they tried to reconcile Philosophy with Theology. Pride was their enemy, as it has always been the enemy of the children of the One True God.

The Greeks thirsted for more and more *knowledge*. They considered themselves superior intellectually to the members of the Latin Church. This would lead to more questioning, more opinions, more need for rationalization and, consequently, less call to obey. Since ancestors had prayed to gods for everything from fertility to victory, *the* Humble God Who created them, the Jesus Who obeyed right to the point of dying on the Cross, got lost. When you put this all together, what with geographical as well as cultural miles to separate them from Rome, the seat of the Church, you have fertile ground for heresies not only to crop up, but to grow and spread.

Nationalism and *Familism*[3] played a great role in the separation, as men placed country before God and the *Eternal* Country, and *ancestral* pride before the One and Only *true* Family . [Do we not hear, today, in the United States, that we are different from our European Catholic brothers and sisters, with different needs and customs? How can a Pope rule us from Rome? What happened to the Universal Family, we belong to, the Roman Catholic Church that makes us one body, one people?] So, the infighting between good men proved Constantine's desire to *unite* all his subjects under one government impossible, and the Heart of Jesus broke as He saw His Church split in two.

Before the final break or Schism, in 1074, there were many schisms, many battles waged by the fallen angels to separate these beautiful children of Mary from their brothers and sisters in the West. But these were not enough to cause *the* break. No one could say it was because each side was not amply represented in Rome. In the four centuries following Constantine, not all the Popes were Latin; actually, most of them were Greek. *Then what caused the tragic division?* It was politics! The Emperors of Constantinople wanted and demanded that the Holy See be located in Constantinople. Although many of the local patriarchs were

---

[3]familism-a pattern of social structure in which the family unit and strong family feeling occupy a position of great importance.

faithful to the Pope, sadly, the Emperors had more loyalty from, and exercised more influence over, the majority of the churchmen in the East than did their Pope.

Emperor Constantine started it all when he transferred the capital of the Roman Empire from Rome to Byzantium (which he renamed Constantinople[4] after himself). Fifty years had hardly passed when, instead of convening in Rome, Councils began to meet in Constantinople. With some of the greatest Theologians located in the East, Christian beliefs were being defined there, and when theological questions cropped up, the East resolved them, as well. Heresies began to crop up and the Emperors in the East took it upon themselves to defend the Church, very often convening Councils for just that purpose. [I am sure, this might have begun with the good intention of preserving the true Faith.] This was *precisely* the justification, the Emperors used to proclaim Constantinople as the rightful seat of the Catholic Church. At first, the split was between Rome and *one* See of the East, that is, Constantinople, wanting supremacy or at least equality with Rome; but soon other Sees of the East followed suit and the split became a tragic reality.

It is important to keep in mind that this was mainly the work of ambitious and self-seeking Emperors, not those great and holy men of the Church of the East, not those Theologians who were, and had always been, faithful to Christ's Church and Her teaching. Most of the Early Church Fathers came from the East. They fearlessly and loyally defended the Church against heresies, as you have read in previous chapters. The Church has honored seven of these Saintly Fathers with the title: *"Doctor of the Church."* Three of them were bishops of *Constantinople*: St. John Chrysostom, St. Gregory Nazianzen and St. Basil.

---

[4]means City of Constantine

Where there is God, you will find the devil lurking in the shadows. Where there are the Holy Angels, you will find the fallen ones battling for the souls of the innocent. Heresies after heresies, over the centuries, cropped up at the instigation of the Emperors, but one by one they were put down. Nevertheless, when you chink away at the armor of the Church, you weaken it. The shield of the Church was finally to split in two, and we had what is known as the *Photian Schism* which lasted from 857-867.

The Photian Schism

How did it begin?   The avalanche that had been threatening the Church was just waiting for one pebble to be thrown down the mountain.   On the Feast Day of the Epiphany in 857, *St. Ignatius*[5], who was Patriarch of Constantinople, refused Communion to a high government official named Bardas.   Now, Bardas just happened not only to be the regent of the area, but nephew to the infamous Emperor of the Roman Empire, Michael, *the Drunkard*.   No matter who he was related to, St. Ignatius had no other recourse but to refuse Bardas the Sacraments, as he had been *found guilty of having had incestuous relations*[6].

How dare anyone insult him, or refuse him anything! Bardas appealed to his uncle, the Emperor. With the help of a Bishop loyal to the Emperor, Bardas trumped up false charges against St. Ignatius. The Emperor used this to force St. Ignatius' resignation and exiled him to the island of Terebinthos. Bardas nominated his chief secretary, Photius, a layman, as St. Ignatius' replacement. At his insistence, the week before Christmas, 858 A.D., the bishops ordained and consecrated Photius: monk, lector, sub-deacon, deacon, priest and bishop *all in 6 short days.*

---

[5]not St. Ignatius of Loyola who founded the Jesuits, but St. Ignatius of Constantinople.

[6]St. Ignatius - Butler's Lives of the Saints

Although Photius was a high ranking official in the Byzantine government, and a man of impeccable reputation, he was not acceptable as Patriarch of Constantinople, as he had been appointed by the *Emperor* Michael III. Not only was this rejected because it was coercively brought about through deceitful and devious means, it was clearly an interference of State and Church which the Church had been battling for years[7]. Photius was not accepted by all the Patriarchs of the East. They appealed to the Pope. Not only did *they* write, but Photius contacted the Pope, boldly advising *he* was the new Patriarch. The Pope, St. Nicholas I, sent legates to Constantinople to look into the situation. When they reported back to him, the Pope refused to recognize Photius. The Pope declared St. Ignatius the rightful Patriarch, and condemned Photius.

The next twelve or so years was filled with each side, the East and the Holy See of Rome leveling condemnations and excommunications at each other. Eight years after the disruption and destruction caused by Bardas, his uncle, the Emperor Michael, plotted to have *him murdered.* You may recall that Jesus warned his followers in the Garden of Gethsemane: "*Put back your sword where it belongs. Those who use the sword are sooner or later destroyed by it.*" (Matt 26:52) The following year, the Emperor was himself murdered by Basil from Macedonia. As Emperor, Basil immediately deposed Photius from his See as Patriarch and recalled St. Ignatius. But this was not done by Basil as an act for God, but for himself. He thought by reinstating St. Ignatius, he would gain the support of the many faithful who never stopped being loyal to their Patriarch in exile.

After he was restored as Patriarch, St. Ignatius asked Pope Adrian II, Pope Nicholas I's successor, to convene a

---

[7]separation of Church and State - was instituted because of abuses of State against Church, not as a means of keeping God and His Church out of our schools and everyday life.

The Agony in the Garden of Gethsemane
"Put back your sword where it belongs.
Those who use the sword sooner or later are destroyed by it."

Council to settle the matter of who was truly the Patriarch of Constantinople. *The Eighth Ecumenical Council* met in Constantinople, in 869. It condemned Photius and those who had embraced his philosophy. And although the bishops showed clemency to his followers, they excommunicated Photius!

He had fought the good fight, and like St. Paul before him, it was time. A very tired St. Ignatius went Home to Jesus and Mary on October 23, 877. With him gone, for the expediency of peace and unity, Photius was recognized by Rome as Patriarch of Constantinople.

And what do we remember of these two great men?

Photius is responsible for causing a ripple in the Church that would grow into a tidal wave which would nearly sink the Ship of the Church. Because of his widely acclaimed reputation as a scholar, his writings were very often accepted as doctrine, not only by the Greeks of his time, but long after he was dead. The charges of heresy he made against the Latin Church not only had a tremendous effect on the Schism of his day, but influenced schisms that never stopped fermenting. *One of his heresies that persists till today, separating us, is the Greek belief that the Holy Spirit comes from the Father alone, not from Jesus.*

The Early Fathers of the Church, St. Augustine being one of them, strongly wrote of the *equality* of the Three Persons in the One God. *Photius contended that because the Latin Church added to the Creed "and the Son", it was teaching heresy.* He maintained that the Holy Spirit emanated from the Father, alone! He charged that by adding "*and the Son*" to the Creed, the Church was taking away from God, the Father. How can this be, since Jesus plainly said that He and the Father were One. When Philip asked to see the Father, Jesus said: "*To have seen Me is to have seen the Father.*" (John 14:9)

In addition, when Photius made that accusation, was he not calling Jesus a liar? Jesus spoke of sending the Holy Spirit when he said,

"*It is much better for you that I go. If I fail to go, the Paraclete will never come to you, whereas if I go, I will send Him to you.*" (John 16:7) "*...He will not speak on His own, but will speak only what He hears, and will announce to you the things to come. In doing this He will give glory to Me, because He will have received from Me what He will announce to you.*"

He further states His Oneness with the Father:

"*All that the Father has belongs to Me.*" (John 16:13-15)

Whereas, each of the members of the Catholic Church, both East and West, had always respected each other's Rituals, now *Photius was saying the Latin Church's Rituals were evil.* Because of his following within the Eastern Church, soon his words were no longer looked on as one man's opinions, but dogmas. *And the rift widened!*

As for *St. Ignatius*, his personal sanctity, his relentless defense of, and unwavering loyalty to the Church (even under hardships and unfair exile), resulted in his name being added to the Calendar of Martyrs, and raised to the Communion of Saints. His Feast Day - October 23rd is still celebrated by Roman Catholics of Constantinople, as well as, Byzantines faithful to the Catholic Church, and those (Greek Orthodox) temporarily separated from us.

Although it seemed that The East and West would, again, be *one*, the fracturing of the Family had begun. The stones in the wall of the Church had been loosened, and there were those who, for their own purposes, would continue to look for weaknesses in the structure where they could strike. They fanned the fires of disobedience, as they added coals of division and discontent. A house divided against itself will fall. A movement of *separatism* - The Church of the East against the Church of the West - had begun and would continue to spread, not satisfied until Christ's Church was destroyed once and for all.

The Eleventh Century and the Church is split asunder

The year 1043 was to usher in a Schism which made that of Photius look like child play. *Michael Cerulaurius*, a very strong, out-spoken adversary of the Pope and Rome, became Patriarch of Constantinople. Upon assuming his role and responsibility as Patriarch, he immediately began writing letters of hate and division directed against the West. It was really an attack on the Pope.

As with most heresies that the Church combats, believing they have died only to see them resuscitated again, sometimes under a new name, the conflict between the East and the West of the Ninth Century would not die. As Cancer is not contained unless detected and treated in the early stages, so it was with the **Greek Schism**. The tumors that had tested benign in the past, were now showing signs of malignancy. The attacks, leveled at the Church by Photius, far from being buried with all the excess garbage of unforgiveness and misunderstanding, were now being dug up and used by Michael Cerulaurius.

The Patriarch, Cerulaurius broke off relations with the Holy See and the Latin Church! As Pastor of the faithful, instead of leading his flock to feed at Jesus' Pasture, the Roman Catholic Church, he chose to defy the Pope. He refused to accept the Pope as the final authority. *He publicly denied the Primacy of the Pope!* Here we are in another Garden and the enemy of God has tricked another son of Adam into disobeying. The devil used this man's pride, and thirst for power, to finish the work left undone by other instruments of darkness. He refused to obey! Cerulaurius was not coming against the Pope and the Papacy, he was attacking Jesus Himself. It was Jesus Who instituted His

Church with one head, Peter; and on the day He chose Peter, He chose the Popes who have followed him.

How could Cerulaurius get the faithful to follow him? He attacked the Church with false accusations and recriminations, and forced a show down by issuing ultimatums to the Pope! Called to nourish the flowers of the Church left in his care, instead, he sowed seeds of division and hatred that would grow and choke the beautiful bouquet in Jesus' Garden. Like locusts, discontent and disobedience were devouring and destroying much of the garden Mother Church had tended for centuries. Nothing would be left of the unity and love that our Lord had prayed for before He died. And so, Jesus' suffering in the Garden of Gethsemane was not enough. Now, He knelt in another garden and cried.

Cerulaurius exhumed Photius' heresies from the pits of hell, regarding the Holy Trinity, and accused the Church once again of heresy. It's amazing, isn't it, how Satan and all his fallen angels are always getting the foolish to do their dirty work? The means are as old as Genesis and that first garden: Call God by your name, *"Liar!"* or as in this case, His Church, *"Heretic!"*

Patriarch Cerulaurius added some of his own heresies. As if all his blasphemies were not enough, the devil induced him to deal *the* death blow; separate the Mystical Body of Christ: *attack the Eucharist*, the Body, Blood, Soul and Divinity of Jesus Who makes us one. As St. Paul says, *"Because the loaf of bread is one, we, many though we are, are one body, for we partake of the one loaf."* (1Cor 10:17)

He began snatching at straws in an attempt to split from the Church and become head of the Eastern Church. He claimed that the practice within the Latin Church of *fasting on Saturday* evening[8] before receiving Holy Communion on Sunday, was heretical. Not only this, but, by the Church *consecrating unleavened bread*, Jesus was not truly present in the Holy Eucharist. For the life of me, I cannot understand how he justified that. The Last Supper took place on the first night of the *Passover*. We read, in the Old Testament:

"*The Lord told Moses, 'Eat with your traveling clothes on, preparing for a long journey, wearing your walking shoes and carrying your walking sticks in you hands; eat it hurriedly. This observance shall be called the Lord's Passover...You shall celebrate this event each year (this is a permanent law) to remind you of this fatal night. The celebration shall last seven days. For that entire period you are to eat only <u>bread made without yeast</u>. Anyone who disobeys this rule at any time during the seven days of the celebration shall be excommunicated from Israel...This annual Celebration with <u>Unleavened Bread</u> will cause you always to remember today as the day when I brought you out of the land of Egypt; so it is a law that you must celebrate this day annually, generation after generation. <u>Only bread without yeast</u> may be eaten from the evening of the fourteenth day of the month until the evening of the twenty-first day of the month. For these seven days, <u>there must be no trace of yeast in your home</u>. During that time, anyone who eats anything with yeast in it will be excommunicated from the community of Israel. (*Exodus 12:11-20)

Jesus sat down with His disciples to a Seder[9] (the Last Supper). The Jews, at the time of Exodus baked and served unleavened bread. Jews, each year, remember their ancestors' flight from captivity in Egypt by eating the foods they had eaten. This same unleavened bread that Jews have

---

[8]fasting after midnight Saturday, taking in no food or drink, until receiving Holy Communion on Sunday, was replaced, by Vatican Council II, with a one hour fast prior to receiving.

[9]seder-the feast, commemorating the Exodus of the Jews from captivity, that is celebrated each year by Jewish families till today.

been eating for thousands of years, was the bread Jesus blessed and broke, saying, as He gave it to the Disciples, *"This is My Body to be given for you.   Do this as a remembrance of Me."* (Luke 22:19)

Cerulaurius' next step was to destroy the Priesthood; for, without our Priests, we have no Mass; without the Mass, we have no Eucharist. Tell the Priests they can have their cake and eat it, too. No Cross! No sacrifice! No pain! No loneliness! *He came out against celibacy of Priests.*

I recall our dear Pope John Paul II speaking lovingly, consolingly to his Priests, here in the United States, sharing, how well he knows the price they are paying, and he grieves for them; but that he must stand firm on the issue of celibacy.

As we said before, we are not here to judge our beloved priests' walk (because we do not wear their shoes), and we, if the Pope said so, would have no problem with priests marrying.   But, to those who think celibacy is an unreasonable demand upon the Priesthood, we remind you, our priests represent our Lord Jesus. What was our Lord's pain, in the Garden of Gethsemane, when His trusted three, Peter, James and John fell asleep, leaving Him quite alone to suffer?   Jesus was thrown into a dungeon, without light, without human companionship, His friends having deserted Him. The one He had entrusted the keys of the Kingdom, the rock that He would build His Church upon, Peter had denied Him. You talk of alone!

Maybe, today, we have priests leaving the Priesthood because we have removed the Cross from our churches; and in those we have not, we have removed the *Crucified Christ*, replacing him with the Resurrected Christ.   When the struggle becomes difficult for us; when we see the Judases who betray our Church, the Peters, James and Johns who fall asleep, the disciples who run away rather than share in Christ's Walk to the Cross; when we wonder what we are doing, sometimes, we only have to look at our dear Lord Jesus Crucified on the Cross, and the tears we shed are not for ourselves, but for our Jesus and his sorrowful Mother.

It is very hard for us to write this, as our hearts bleed for our Lord Who once again is rejected, bruised and battered. Patriarch Cerulaurius dealt a critical blow when he led our beloved innocent brothers and sisters away from Jesus' church with the heresies and lies he leveled against her. As he instigated the Priesthood against the Papacy, causing many to leave the Latin Church and join his newly formed Eastern Church in De facto Schism[10], he thrust another sword into Jesus and Mary's side. *He had to be certain, there would be no Church of the Latin Rite left in Constantinople.* He closed them all down!

It was as if Cerulaurius was a centurion of the Eleventh Century; only his whip was lashing out at Jesus through His Church, striking mercilessly, ripping away layers of Christ's Flesh. For it is Christ's Flesh that is on the Body of the Church.

Jesus was attacked in His Body, Blood, Soul and Divinity, as the Latin churches were closed, and as the Eucharist and the Priesthood were maligned. His children were deprived of His House, where they could come to be fed by His Word and His Holy Eucharist. Each attack upon the Church was another blow that struck Jesus, brutally, at the Pillar. But the final death blow was yet to be dealt. Our Lord was yet to receive his deepest hurt. Just before Cerulaurius closed the Latin churches, our Lord was to witness His son, His patriarch, take His Body, Blood, Soul and Divine Self out of the Tabernacle, throw the Consecrated Hosts to the ground and trample Them, underfoot. If Cerulaurius had ever believed that Jesus was

---

[10]De facto -actually existing, but not through the sanction of the Church (as in this case) or not legally approved by a government.

present in the Blessed Sacrament, what could have possessed him to desecrate our Lord Jesus in These Consecrated Hosts? He had denied Jesus was present in Hosts Consecrated of unleavened bread. It didn't matter to him, that there were faithful in his See that still believed our Lord was truly present in those Hosts. Had he no heart for the pain he inflicted upon them?

On the day of his ordination, when he professed the Creed, he vowed to uphold and teach that our Lord is truly and permanently present in a Consecrated Host, when we receive Him, or when the Host is reserved in the Tabernacle, or in a Monstrance for the Faithful to worship. In betrayal of that oath, and in disdain of Jesus' Word, he trampled his Lord's Body. The greatest of all sins is *Deicide*, the killing of God. When we desecrate our Lord in His Holy Eucharist, are we not killing our Lord in an unbloody manner, but killing Him, none the less?

The Pope at the time, Pope St. Leo IX had begun to study Greek, in an attempt to understand the arguments presented by Cerulaurius. The Pope wrote him an impassioned letter advising him of the serious sin and the far-reaching consequences of the Schism he was proposing, and reiterated the supremacy of the Papacy. Patriarch Cerulaurius rejected the Pope's mandate to submit to his authority. He countered with a demand that the Patriarch of Constantinople, who he just happened to be, be *equal* with the Pope; the Pope could remain head of the Western Church, and he, as Patriarch of Constantinople, was to have fully autonomous jurisdiction over the Church in the East. The Pope sent delegates to Constantinople to look into the matter. Cerulaurius did not show the respect due the legates from Rome, as they represented the Pope. Instead he placed his bishops above them, and said the legates did not have the authority that his bishops had, to evaluate or resolve the crisis. The legates refused to accept his terms.

Cerulaurius ended the meeting with the final blow to the Papacy; he erased the Pope's name from the Liturgy of the Mass.

On July 16, 1054, Cardinal Humbert, the Pope's spokesman, excommunicated Cerulaurius. In turn, Patriarch Cerulaurius excommunicated the Cardinal and all the legates from Rome. *The Church split in two!* As in civil court, when two adversaries seek justice, no one wins, so it was with our beloved Church. Brother against brother, did they realize, what was begun that infamous day was to have the far-reaching, devastating finality which separates us, till today?

They say, the most unforgiving are those who are part of a family; those who have loved much, sadly hate much. With God as our Father, and Jesus making us brothers and sisters, and Mother Mary as our *mutual* mother, *all* the members of the Church are family. And no matter if we call ourselves by another name, we still are family by virtue of our Baptism.

Whenever we have met someone who has left the Church, we encounter anger against the Church. Could it be they are upset because they are no longer part of Mother Church? Do they not know She loves them and like the father of the prodigal son in Holy Scripture, is just waiting for them to come back home? Do we wait as the father did, preparing a feast for those children who will return? Will the bridge they cross, be a bridge of understanding so that they can return? What do we hold out to our separated family? What gifts do we have for them? Is it bitter memories and accusations? Or is it love? Do we bring the message to them that our Pastor had once given us to pass on to those who had left the Church: "*I grieve until you return home.*"

As Pope John the XXIII had once been Papal Nuncio to the East, they were very dear to his heart. You can just hear the hope, the Holy Spirit had infused into him, of

Above: *Pope John XXIII at the Holy House in Loreto. He had once been Papal Nuncio to the East. They were dear to his heart.*

Left:
Members of the Greek Orthodox Church in procession in Jerusalem

reconciliation! Pope John declared that both sides, East and West, share in the misunderstandings that came about that day which resulted in the split.

In addition, with the Lord's ongoing call for unity, on December 1, 1965, Pope Paul VI together with Patriarch Athenagoras I, said yes to the Holy Spirit and mutually rescinded the excommunications that East and West had imposed in 1054.

Nine centuries later! How much longer? St. Augustine's words echo the Lord's Sacred Heart: "*How long, how long shall I go on saying tomorrow and again tomorrow? Why not now, why not have an end...this very hour?*' (*Confessions*, Book Eight) As he was praying, a sweet voice, coming as if from a house nearby, repeated over and over again, '*Take and read! Take and read!*'"[11] We pray, dear Father in Heaven that our brothers and sisters will possibly read this humble book and come back home!

The Church fights back!

In every century, in every period of our Church and world, you hear more of the problems and the problem-makers. Today, as probably, in all times, the Bad News seemed more exciting than the Good News. Even at Jesus' time, people killed the Good News Who was Jesus Christ, Himself. But, as with our dear Lord, the Good News lives after *eternally* and the Bad News goes where it belongs - to Gehenna[12].

In this chapter, as in others in this book, and in the news of our mainstream Church, today, you have been reading about those who disobeyed and defied the Papacy. We would like to share a homily we heard at Mass, on Trinity Sunday. It was delivered by our associate pastor, whom we

---

[11] chapter on St. Augustine-from Bob and Penny Lord's book: *Saints and other Powerful Men in the Church*.
[12] We believe Jesus meant hell.

call our baby Priest, not because of his chronological years (which are 54), but in years since his ordination, all of two. We believe, after you read his homily, you will agree that whatever he lacks in years, the Lord has infused him with wisdom and loyalty.

"This homily will explain the Creed and part of The Holy Trinity. It is a good thing we have this annual Sunday, in honor of the Holy Trinity. Most of the year, we get by without worrying about God's inner Life. We are grateful that God is God, and we don't bother too much with what He is like.

"But our God is Three in One, and we are reminded of that Mystery, every time we make the sign of the Cross. In the seminary, we studied the Holy Trinity for about a year. When we finished, they told us it was a mystery!

"God Himself enlightens us to profess the words of that Mystery, every Sunday. In our Creed, we begin by saying: 'We believe in One God' and further on we will say, 'We believe in One Lord, Jesus Christ', that 'He came down from Heaven by the Power of the Holy Spirit, He was born of the Virgin Mary and became Man.' That in part is the Nicene Creed.

"At other times, especially when we recite the Rosary, and at some children's Masses, we use the Apostles' Creed (which is much shorter), that expresses the Holy Trinity:
'I believe in God, the Father Almighty; I believe in Jesus Christ, His Only Son; I believe in the Holy Spirit.' They open up a treasury of Divine Mysteries. These Holy Mysteries call to us, and tell us to be silent, and to take off our shoes, that we are on Holy Ground.

"Both of these Creeds are very ancient, having been formulated in the first three centuries of Christianity. They were formulated in response to various heresies which arose during the Apostolic Age. The Creed became a formal expression of what the Disciples believed, a summary of the Faith which they and we profess!

"*To be wise is to face the Eternal Mysteries of life and faith, with at least enough humility to admit that we do not have the answer for everything that asks a question in life. Faith is God's gift to us, and it seeks understanding; it does not require understanding. More than a work of the mind, faith is also an act of our will. Catholics must be willing to accept the mysterious.*

"*The Mystery of the Holy Trinity is something we understand more with our hearts than our intellect. We know God through the expressions of the heart; the individual heart of each person, the heart of His Church, and the heart of His Church's authority to teach.*

"*Saint Augustine reminds us of a truth, 'God is Love'. What outward appearance, what form, what stature, hands or feet, has love? None of us can say. And yet, love has feet which take us to do good things in this world. Love has hands which give to the poor. Love has eyes which give us knowledge of those in need.*

"*The Catholic Faith is filled with mystery. The mystery is described and proclaimed in the Creed. The Creed is a summary of what we believe; it is a true expression of the Church's Heart. The Creed tells us, and the world, the Divine Plan by which we are saved in Christ. It tells the story of our salvation and is prayed universally by all believing people. The Creed unites Catholics, the world over, in a unity of Faith that gives us the only true purpose for living. When we give loving and faithful assent to the Creed, we are transported out of (the present) time and mystically united with the faithful of every time and place.*

"*As can happen with great treasures, the Creed that expresses the Trinity can be taken for granted. Our familiarity can breed negligence.*

"*There can be very little experience of God, unless there is an awareness of God. Friendship with God begins with understanding and accepting the Creed. We profess to the* world of believers and unbelievers, alike, what our God has done, what He is doing now, and what He will do in the time to come.

"It is impossible to pray to One Person of the Holy Trinity without praying to the Other Two. St. Patrick used the shamrock to explain the Trinity. St. Ignatius of Loyola understood the Trinity, by God's revelation, as a Musical Note for Each Person of the Holy Trinity, all Three Notes making a beautiful harmony.

"Years ago, in my life, at a different time and place, a little girl was asked by her bishop, at her confirmation to name the Three Persons of the Holy Trinity. She said: 'There is the Father, the Son,'...Then she looked around for a little help from her friends and asked, 'What was the Name of that Other Fellow?' What she lacked in expression, she made up for in love.

"Let us all stand, as we proclaim the Nicene Creed that tells us, and the world, about 'the Father, the Son, and That Other Fellow.'"

Father Ken Harney

Our priest freely admits he is a combination of Saints Augustine and Paul - rebellious and stubborn until the Lord captured his heart, and led him to the Roman Catholic Church. Paul was blinded that he could see; Augustine read Paul and everything he read thereafter, that was not of the Lord, was like so much straw[13]. Both these converts wrote, preached and defended the Church. This new convert, following these two heroes of the Church, is doing the same.

---

[13]St. Thomas Aquinas

Berengarianism

Berengarianism was a highly destructive heresy against the Church. It spread its poison throughout Europe for over three hundred years. The founder of Berengarianism was a member of the Clergy named *Berengarius* (or *Berengar*). He was born in Tours, France around 999 A.D. As with so many gifted people who go off course, *Berengarius* had a great start in the Faith. He studied in Chartres, under St. Fulbert[1]. Much was expected of him. How did Berengarius succumb to heresy? He didn't get it from his teacher. St. Fulbert fought the very philosophy, that of *naturalism*[2], which Berengarius would use to deny the true presence of Jesus in the Holy Eucharist.

St. Fulbert thought so highly of Berengarius, before he fell into error, he appointed him Archdeacon and Treasurer of the Cathedral of Chartres. He had seen Berengarius' great devotion to the Faith. Berengarius had great ability. He had a sound education in the Faith. What made him veer off the path of the true teachings of the Church? But wander off, he did; and sink into error, he did.

We have those theologians, today, who admit that Holy Scripture is inspired by the Holy Spirit but *insist* that the Magisterium is man's laws and not God's. They are no less guilty than *Berengarius, who ignored the analogy of faith* - which states that the same Holy Spirit Who inspires Holy Scripture inspires the Magisterium. Therefore, when studying the Bible, *we* do not interpret Scripture, we are

---

[1] St. Fulbert was highly thought of. He worked under Pope Sylvester II. The Cathedral Schools of Chartres soon became one of the greatest educational centers, under his supervision.

[2] the interpreting purely according to the principles of nature, instead of giving due weight to the spiritual, supernatural, etc.

called to turn to the *Magisterium* to discover what the Holy Spirit is saying to us through God's holy Word.

When Pilate asked Jesus "Are you a king?" he was asking about His *authority*. Pilate knew about obedience to a king or emperor. Jesus responded to Pilate's questioning of *His* authority with: "*You say that I am a king. I was born and came into the world for this one purpose, to speak about the truth. Whoever belongs to the truth listens to me.*" As with Berengarius, those who mockingly question today, "*What is the Magisterium?*", remind us of Pontius Pilate when he contemptuously challenged Jesus with "*What is truth?*". The Magisterium is in the world to bring us the Truth, Who is Jesus. Whoever belongs to Jesus, listens to the truth as found in the Magisterium.

Berengarius wrote a dissertation opposing the Church's teaching on the Holy Eucharist and sent it to Rome in care of someone named Lanfranc. Lanfranc brought it to the Pope's attention, and that's when the Popes, one after the other, got involved. Leo IX was the first pope to hear of it in 1050. He called a synod, in 1054, in which he condemned the teaching of Berengarianism which stated that *while the bread and wine in the Eucharist become Christ's Body and Blood, they do so figuratively, remaining substantially or physically what they are.* Is this not what our separated brothers and sisters in Christ believe, since the time of Luther, that the Eucharist is only *symbolically* the Lord?

Two popes during their Pontificates, called synods, to deal with this heresy. Finally, Pope Gregory VII called two councils in Rome, one in 1078 and then another in 1079. Berengarius was sent for by the first council that convened in Rome, in 1078. They called him in to answer questions about his doctrine. Although he had supposedly relented twenty years before and had sworn to defer to the Church's findings, there were doctrinal errors being taught, which smacked suspiciously of his former errors. As with some of our modern theologians who are censored for a time and then return, we *judge* repentant, but then continue to spread heresies of all kinds, it seemed Berengarius had made an oath with his head and not his heart. The issue of the true presence of Jesus in the Holy Sacrament was still being argued. The Church deemed it prudent to call Berengarius in. After careful deliberation, they required him to make a profession of faith and he complied!

Another council was called in 1079, *The Sixth Council of Rome.* Although Berengarius would promise to cease teaching his heretical doctrines, he would always turn around, attack the Church, and continue where he left off. When Pope Gregory VII convened this council, he insisted, Berengarius sign another profession of faith. After having done so, he was true to form and denied it. Being brilliant, Berengarius took parts of teachings of the great teachers of our Faith, and he used them to lead the innocent away from the Truth. God has created us to be a *member* of the body of Christ, the *total* body. When we take part of a teaching or truth, without looking at that part within the context of the total Gospel of Jesus Christ, as translated by Mother Church, we fall into error and take many with us. The judgment we must make upon ourselves on Judgment Day must, out of necessity, be harsh.

As with many of our brothers and sisters who ascertain they live by the Word alone, Berengarius interpreted the Bible using *human reasoning*, rather than relying on, and obeying, the Magisterium, the interpretation of the Word by the Church which has survived the test of time. As with some of our theologians today, he was trying to explain a Mystery with the world's realism. This has become known as a heresy of rationalism.

As is often very deviously presented to us today, in masked terminology, what he said was that since the bread and wine, used for the consecration, remained bread and wine *in appearance,* They could not be the Body and Blood of our Lord Jesus Christ. *Berengarius claimed that since bread and wine remained what they were, bread and wine, the Body of Christ remained in Heaven, and was not truly present in the Holy Eucharist.*

It was common knowledge that Berengarius was not in agreement with the oath he had taken, in 1078, so the following year, the Council required he make an even more explicit pledge of loyalty and obedience to the Church and her teachings.   Again, he agreed.   And again, with this profession of faith, although he fully knew what he was signing, he later reneged.

The Council of Rome, in 1079, played an essential role in defining Eucharistic Doctrine through this profession of faith:

I, Berengarius, believe interiorly and profess publicly that the bread and wine, which are placed on the altar, through the mystery of the sacred prayer and the words of our Redeemer are substantially changed into the true, proper, and life-giving flesh and blood of our Lord Jesus Christ. After the consecration it is the true body of Christ, which was born of the Virgin, and which hung on the cross as an offering for the salvation of the world, and which sits at the right hand of the Father. And it is the true blood of Christ which was poured forth from His side. And Christ is present not merely by virtue of the sign and the power of the sacrament but in his proper nature and true substance as is set down in this summary and as I read it and you understand it. This I believe and I will not teach any more against this faith. So help me God and this holy Gospel of God![3]

We, in the Church teach, and believe that after the Consecration, the Host is no longer bread and the chalice no

---

[3]P. 276 - The Sixth Council of Rome, 1079 - The Church Teaches - by the Jesuit Fathers of St. Mary's College St. Mary's Kansas

longer contains wine. We believe that the bread becomes the *Body* born of the Virgin Mary, the *Lord* Who suffered in the Garden of Gethsemane, the *Lord* Who hung on the Cross, The *Lord* Who died, was buried, rose and is now seated at the right Hand of the Father. We believe the wine that was consecrated has become the *Blood* that Jesus shed on the Cross, the *Blood* that flowed from His side when the tip of His Heart was pierced by the Centurion Longinus.

As we write, we can see the plan of the Lord unfurling. It is awesome, but we must admit a little frightening. We can see a glimpse of what our Lord has been wanting of us. But, as He never hands you a Cross you cannot carry, so He never asks anything of you that with Him you cannot do, today. We have said over and over again that we did not understand the full ramifications when we said yes to the Lord, and wrote "*This is My Body...This is My Blood, Miracles of the Eucharist*".

When we started to write about Berengarianism, we thought, Lord, You want us to show the connection with the Miracle of Bolsena-Orvieto, but we can see it is equally important to share the Miracle of Lanciano, and the part it played in dispelling this heresy for all time, if men have eyes to see and ears to hear.

The **Miracle of Lanciano** occurred in the village where the Centurion Longinus came from originally. When a priest, who was having doubts about the true presence of Jesus in the Consecrated Host, raised the host and said the words of consecration, the Host turned into Flesh, Human Flesh; and when he raised the chalice, the wine turned into Human Blood. The Host and Blood are still present 1300 years later, and have been scientifically tested; the results are that the Host is a Human Heart and the Blood is Human

Left:
*Miracle of the Eucharist
of Lanciano where the
Host turned into real
Flesh - a human Heart;
the wine turned into real
Blood - human Blood*

Right:
*The Miracle of the
Eucharist of
Bolsena/Orvieto
dispels Berengarianism for
all time. Berengarius
claimed that bread and
wine remained what they
were, and that the Body of
Christ remained in Heaven.*

Blood[4]. So much for Berengarius' claim that the bread remains bread and the wine remains wine.

Then, there is the **Miracle of Bolsena-Orvieto**, which brought about the Feast of Corpus Christi. In 1263 there was a priest, Peter of Prague, who was having great doubts about the real presence of Jesus in the Eucharist. He stopped in Bolsena, on the way to Rome. While celebrating Mass, when he raised the host in Consecration, the Host started to bleed. He wrapped the Host in the corporal and ran down the steps. He brought the corporal to the Pope who was staying in nearby Orvieto. *The Pope Urban IV* turned to the people and proclaimed a Miracle had truly come to pass in Bolsena that *"dispelled the heresies that had been running rampant, that of Berengarianism[5]"*.

We will, once more, see God making a positive out of a negative. Because of *Berengarius'* heresy, against the true presence of Jesus in the Holy Eucharist, the Church defined the doctrine of *transubstantiation*, affirming what the Church has believed and taught from the very beginning.

In 1562 at the Council of Trent, Mother Church defended the Holy Eucharist, one more time, against new heresies, drummed up by new heretics calling themselves reformers. It made this declaration on *Transubstantiation*:

Because Christ our Redeemer said that it was truly His Body that He was offering under the species of bread[6], it has always been the conviction of the Church, and this holy council now again declares that, by the Consecration of the bread and wine a change takes place in which the whole substance of bread changes into the substance of the Body of Christ our

---

[4]there is more on this in the chapter on Lanciano - The Heart of Christ in This is My Body...This is My Blood, Miracle of the Eucharist - Bob and Penny Lord

[5]This is My Body...This is My Blood, Miracle of the Eucharist - Bob and Penny Lord

[6] *(Mt 26:26; Mk 14:22; Lk22:19; 1 Cor 11:24)*

Lord, and the whole substance of the wine into the substance of His Blood. This change the Catholic Church fittingly and properly names Transubstantiation.[7]

In other words, the entire host which appears to be bread is changed into the Body of Christ; and the wine although it appears to be wine, is changed into the real Blood of Christ. They are no longer bread and wine; they only appear to be. It is by this *Transubstantiation* that the Body and Blood of Christ are present in the Holy Eucharist

Had Berengarius walked too far down the wrong path, he couldn't find his way home? Sometimes the false god of Pride is so enticing we think of the momentary accolades, rather than the eternal joy spending the rest of our lives in the presence of This God Who is present to us now in the Holy Eucharist, and Whose Glorified Self we will adore in Heaven. Berengarius had made a decision; he returned to Tours. They bestowed upon him the title of "*Scholasticus, Master of the schools*".[8] What title had God bestowed on him?

Compassionate mother that she is, Mother Church took him back. He died at peace with the Church; She had forgiven him one more time.

Do we not see our own dear Pope, Pope John Paul II, censuring Theologians and bishops, and then taking them back? And what is the thanks he and Mother Church receive? These dissenters continue, like Berengarius, to attack the Faith.

---

[7]chapter on Transubstantiation-Chapter 4- P.283, The Church Teaches- by the Jesuit Fathers of St. Mary's College St. Mary's Kansas

[8]chapter on Berengar of Tours-Corpus Christi-Michael O' Carroll, C.S.Sp.

Albigensianism

Constantine of Samosata has been called the founder of the Albigensians. Church historians believe they derived their name from the city of Albi, France where they first started to spread their errors. Although they began in a small area, in the Province of Toulouse, their heresies were soon to cover the entire southern part of France.

The *Albigensians of the Eleventh Century* were the revived Manichaean sect of the Third Century. Deadly weeds that had laid dormant but not dead under ground, they now shot up, choking the flowers of the Church. These revolutionaries (or *Catharists*, as they were also known), had risen once more to pose a threat to the Faith. They were a group of radical dissidents who had entered Europe through Bulgaria. They first settled in Southern France. But, not satisfied to confine their venom to the eldest daughter of the Church, they slithered into Italy and Spain.

This heresy gathered all the heresies of the past and put them into one presentation. Their philosophy or false theology used *Paganism* as well as *Christianity* to entice the unsuspecting looking for something new! Those within the Church, who are spreading errors today, are doing the very same thing as the Albigensians before them[1].

The Albigensians had an organized church, structured with ministers and rites. These ministers were called by the name, "*the Perfect*". They had a ceremony which was an abomination of one of our Sacraments. (Remember, we said they mixed Christianity with Paganism.) Whereas, with the Sacrament of Baptism, we are cleansed of Original Sin, with the Albigensians their purification rite freed the soul from the power of *matter* and from the guilt of sin. (Some of the heresies espoused that all matter was sinful.) This was accomplished, copying our Rite of Baptism, without

---

[1]chapter on New Age

211

confession or penance. Their rite was called the *consolamentum*. A *Perfect* or minister was the only one who could lay hands on a person desiring to be initiated into the sect. Once someone was purified, if he sinned, the *consolamentum* was lost, and he could not get it back. He was damned! With the Catholic Church, the Sacraments are irrevocable. We believe, once you've received them, they're yours; God doesn't take them back. Again we are looking at the heresies of the past that lacked compassion for repentant sinners. There was no forgiveness!

As in the Manichaean Sect, there were two classes within the Albigensian Sect. There were those who made a vow of perpetual chastity, subjecting themselves to extreme fasting throughout the entire year, abstaining completely from meat and dairy foods, and were strict vegetarians. They were committed to share an austere common life style with those who had made the same vows. Their charism, if you could call it that, was to live a life of strict self-denial. So far, it doesn't sound much different than some of our religious orders of the past. Those who were part of this elitist chapter of the sect were *the Perfects*.

The other class within the Albigensians, who were by far the majority, were called "*the Believers*". As with the Manichaean sect, they could have their cake and eat it, too. They were assured, they could lead a life of sin, yet still be saved through the merits of those *elect*, or the Perfects, who lived a life of abstinence and total chastity. The rigoristic life of the Perfects was abhorrent to them. Like St. Augustine, when he was ensnared by the Manichaeans, they wished to be able to sin, have their earthly pleasures, and yet gain Heaven. They were promised this could be done. What was the catch? What was required of them? All they had to do was to accept the concepts of the Albigensian dogmas, revere the *Perfect*, and promise to receive the consolamentum before they died. Again, as with St.

Augustine and the Manichaeans, they did not have to curb their passions; someone else would pay the price for them; all they had to do was adore the Perfects, worship them as gods!

They revived a heretical practice that St. Augustine helped to do away with, the custom of waiting until the point of death before being Baptized. This had been widely practiced in the Early Church, as Catechumens wished to live according to their worldly ways, and then at the last moment, have all their sins wiped away by Baptism. In this way, their souls would enter Paradise with a clean slate. Many followers of Albigensianism, because they feared losing the consolamentum, by an act of weakness or some transgression, because they believed they were doomed if they could not live up to the rigorous demands of the Perfects, chose to die by starvation or as it was called the "*Endura*". Those who committed suicide, were venerated as martyrs, a complete antithesis to Christianity which considers suicide murder!

One of the justifications for proclaiming those who have committed suicide, heroes or martyrs was, they espoused that other tired heresy: that all matter was evil; and since the body was matter, it was holy to destroy it. And since they considered life itself evil, they considered it an abomination to try to save life. As we look the other way with abortion and euthanasia, we have to ask ourselves if we look upon the body as holy, a temple of the Holy Spirit, or are we following a *new-old* heresy by condoning mercy-killing, the aiding of terminally ill loved ones to help themselves die, which is no less murder on your part and suicide-murder on theirs. I wonder, if those who are buying into Satan's lie today, realize they are condemning not only themselves to eternal damnation but the loved one whom they are assisting to die?

A dear and very holy priest said, when we, as a society, endorse any form of euthanasia, rather than being merciful, we are not only cheating that person of the gift of sharing in Christ's Passion, but we are depriving them of time they would be spared in Purgatory, through their suffering.

The Albigensians believed in two Gods: one good and the other evil. Some of the heresies of the past that also taught this error were the Marcionites in the Second Century, the Manichaeans in the Third Century, and the Paulicians in the Seventh Century.

They rejected all the Sacraments. A great target was the Sacrament of Matrimony. If you can destroy the tree, the fruit will sicken and die. To attack *Marriage*, is to attack *Family*; to attack *Family* is to destroy the world.

Wanting to appeal to the lower nature of man, which they did, they declared it was sinful to marry; however, *sexual permissiveness was not only permitted but promoted and encouraged by the Albigensians.*

Pregnancy was to be avoided at any price. As much as they were against Marriage, they hated the creation of new life *more*, as they truly believed life was evil. Do not some promote abortion, claiming it is inhuman to bring a child into this evil world, rather than change the world back to that which God created it to be? With their philosophy, the Albigensians would have wiped out the entire world without shooting a gun. Is this not what Satan is doing, today? There are some Catholic nations who have a minus-zero population growth, with more dying than are born each year; they are facing extinction. Please listen! Our future world depends on it.

They most emphatically rejected the Sacrament of the Holy Eucharist. If we believe, we are truly receiving Jesus in His Body, Blood, Soul and Divinity, then we cannot willingly be a party to sin which separates us from Him. The brand of religion they were advertising was not conducive to holiness; therefore do away with the Eucharist. Tell them there is no such thing. There is no Lord who grieves as you sin; there is no sin.

They contended that the Eucharist was not transubstantiated into the Body, Blood, Soul and Divinity of our Lord Jesus Christ if the priest was unworthy to consecrate the Host. The validity of a Sacrament depending on the worthiness or unworthiness of the Priest who was administering the Sacrament, was dispelled by Councils earlier in our Church's history.

They claimed that the New Testament was solely the work of humans, who had been inspired by the Holy Spirit. This is what is being taught today, in many of our churches; Jesus never said or did the things attributed to Him in the Gospel; words were put into His Mouth by the Gospel writers. These were situations placed in the Gospel ["of course inspired by the Holy Spirit", they protest] to draw the different societies (Gentile or Jew) to Christ. They will also say that neither Mark nor Matthew nor Luke nor John ever wrote the New Testament; it is a collection of teachings by many.

They rejected Infant Baptism. According to Canon Law, infants should be Baptized as soon as possible (c.770), and, whoever would defer it without reason for more than three weeks to a month, would sin. As we said before, their rigoristic belief encouraged only the few to partake in a very demanding form of initiation, called *consolamentum.* They rejected Baptism altogether, in favor of the consolamentum.

They preached disobedience; *they contended it was a sin to obey the Clergy or support them in any way.* No, instead they promoted revering their ministers, *the Perfects.* The true sign of sanctity is obedience.

They insisted everyone was endowed with the grace to forgive sins. Yet, Jesus felt delegating this Sacrament to his priests, was so important, after He rose from the dead, He visited the Apostles and breathed on them, saying:

"Receive the Holy Spirit.
If you forgive men's sins,
they are forgiven them;
if you hold them bound,
*they are held bound. (*John 23:21*)*
They denied the existence of the Holy Trinity.
They denied the Incarnation.
They denied we were redeemed by the death and resurrection of Jesus Christ.

They claimed it was no use to confess our sins, that Penance was worthless.

How were they able to attract so many to such an anti-social unloving religion? First of all, like cults of today, such as the Jehovah Witnesses, the *Perfects* were very generous to the Believers, providing for their bodily needs. Their demands were relatively few. The believers reveled in the easy answers to the many evils in their lives, many of which they brought about themselves. The *Perfects* delivered fiery, very dramatic sermons; in those days, our priests did not deliver *any* sermons. Many of our priests led lives of wealth and comfort, and their parishioners went hungry; whereas, the *Perfects* gave generously to their followers, while leading a very austere lifestyle. Of course, everything they gave came from other Believers.

This was a truly benevolent society for the Believer, with one arm short and one arm long; the short one (the giving one) - simply to belong to the cult and pledge allegiance to the Albigensians and their life-style; the long one (the receiving one) - they could lead a life of decadence, and salvation was theirs at no personal cost. There was only one rub. There is always a rub! *There was no resurrection.* Since the body was evil, if you lost the consolamentum, you kept coming back, *through reincarnation,* until the body was completely destroyed[2]. No wonder there were those who chose to die by suicide. Better a martyr's death (which the Perfects called suicide) than to face the possibility of falling, and losing the consolamentum.

So there was a price! There is always a price! Was Jesus going to allow these misguided children of His be lost? No, He raised another Saint!

The Church Fights Back!

During the papacy of **Innocent II**, Albigensianism was spreading like wildfire throughout southern France. Anyone could see that a major offensive had to be launched. The Pope put the job in the hands of the Cistercians. First, he sent two; when they weren't successful, he sent another two. Then he sent in *thirty Cistercians*, twelve of them abbots. These were the most disciplined, most learned religious of the times; but compared to the austerity of the Perfects, their lifestyle was relaxed and easygoing. However, it became obvious very soon that it would take more than this band of followers of St. Bernard of Clairvaux. A new pope came into power, **Innocent III**, the pope of St. Francis of Assisi and St. Dominic.

Well, the Church is in trouble; God raises up a saint - St. Dominic! The Pope turned to St.Dominic and the Bishop of Osma for help in erasing this threat from the Church. St. Dominic and the Bishop went to the Cistercians and appealed to them to live a more heroic life, a life which more exemplified that of the Savior, Whom they were called to imitate. St. Dominic and the Bishop told them that the commonfolk joined the Albigensians *more* because of the life they saw them leading, than by their preaching. They asked the Cistercians to cease traveling by horse with an entourage, to no longer stay at comfortable inns, with

---

[2]Interestingly, this is similar to beliefs of many eastern religions which are the forerunners of New Age.

Above: ***Dispute over the Blessed Sacrament***

Left:
***The Pope turned to
St. Dominic for help in erasing
the Albigensian heresy from the
Church.
The Lord used St. Dominic and
his followers to save the
southern part of Europe from
the spreading Albigensian
heresy.***

servants to wait upon them. Dominic said that after they had proved to the people that they were truly living the Gospel, then, they should use gentle persuasion and loving dialogue, rather than intimidation and dictatorial pressures to bring the heretics back to the Church.

As *Albigensianism* was now more a religion than a heresy, it was extremely dangerous to evangelize and preach against it. The Perfects did not want to lose their brainwashed followers, who would do almost anything for their god, the Perfect. And so they were not above using force.

At the recommendation of Diego, the Bishop of Osma, Dominic and his followers were sent into the area to live, much like Francis and his followers were living in central Italy. There were seventy two of them. They carried no money, no staff, no possessions. They truly lived the austere Gospel life, in an effort to convert by example. And against overwhelming odds, convert they did! The example they set bore fruit, and by the end of ten years, there were a great deal of conversions. But Albigensianism was still very strong and firmly entrenched.

By this time, Dominic was given his order, Order of Preachers, better known as the Dominicans[3]. He founded a house for Albigensianists who wished to leave the sect. Everything was going fine, until the local Count of Toulouse tried to close the house down. The Count had allowed the heretics to operate freely, to serve his own political ends. The sect controlled a considerable voting block, and was very influential. St. Dominic was causing problems for the Count; he couldn't allow him to continue. A papal legate was sent to resolve the matter quickly. He tried to dissuade the Count from supporting the heretics, to no avail. When

---

[3]Dominicans or *Domine Cane* which means God's Watchdogs.

the papal legate excommunicated the Count, he had one of his cohorts assassinate the papal legate.

All hell broke loose. A bloody war ensued, which continued for twenty years. The Count of Toulouse finally stopped supporting the heretics. But then a squabble broke out between him and the king of France, and the Count turned to the Albigensianists again for support.

Through all the battles, victories and defeats, the Lord used St. Dominic and his followers to save the southern part of Europe from the spreading Albigensianist heresy. The tide turned in 1229 when the University of Toulouse was opened, with the Dominicans as the major teaching influence in the University. It was also at that time, that the Council of Toulouse instituted an Inquisition, unlike the one in Spain, some three hundred years later, which, due to the State's interference with the Church, became more political than religious. The Dominicans were put in charge, a post they handled with the real spirit of Christianity that St. Dominic projected. The Order of Preachers grew and grew, so that in less than a hundred years, they had close to 400 convents in the area that had been infested by the heretics.

The heresy was finally put down, not so much by the Inquisition, but by the living example of the followers of St. Dominic. If we were to pick one shining light responsible for fighting for the church of that time, and putting down the Albigensian heresy, it would have to be St. Dominic. Our Lord knew who to put in the right place at the right time.

Waldensians: Tool of the Twelfth Century

There is a passage in Scripture which is extremely challenging. It is the story of the rich young man. It would touch Penny so deeply that she would cry every time the priest proclaimed that Word at Mass. We got to the point where I had to ask her to stop: "Penny," I would plead, "people will think I'm beating you!"

Peter Waldo was a wealthy merchant from Lyon who lived in the Twelfth Century. He, too, was touched by that passage: *"Go and sell what you have and give it to the poor; you will then have treasure in Heaven. After that, come and follow Me."* (Lk 18:22) He acted on it immediately. He sold everything he had and gave it to the poor; he would live an austere life, in keeping with the Gospel. By 1176, he had divested himself of all his earthly goods. This accomplished, he took a vow of poverty. Now, whenever someone is a radical sign in the world, as Jesus calls us all to be, there will be many who will see the light in that person's eyes and they will want it! Something happens! There is a joy, a peace, a freedom; that's when they follow.

At first, the townspeople probably took a wait-and-see attitude. They most likely thought he was a little crazy. But, as he was consistent in this new lifestyle, before you know it, others flocked around him. They, too, sold everything and gave it to the less fortunate. They took to the streets to spread the Good News. The only problem was, with little or no education in the Church, they became self-proclaimed preachers. They went off in the wrong directions.

Peter Waldo believed the Church was in need of reform. Evidently, Jesus felt the same way; He directed St. Francis to: *"Go and rebuild My Church, which, as you can see is in ruins."* It would seem we have another St. Francis, here. Why did one end up a Saint and the other a heretic?

We will discover throughout this, and any book written about the Church, the key word is *obedience*! Maybe, as with

Right:
**The Pope had a
dream, where he
saw St. Francis of
Assisi holding up
the Cathedral of
the Lateran.
St. Francis was
the greatest
reformer in
Church History.
Jesus told him:**
*"Go and rebuild
My Church, which
as you can see, is
in ruins."*

Left:
*St. Francis and his
Friars meet with
Pope Innocent III
to discuss the
approval of their
Rule.
St. Francis was
directly under the
Pope, but always
obedient to the
bishop who was in
charge of the area
in which he had
been asked to
preach.*

Francis, Waldo started out wanting to do good, but when we disobey and place ourselves above the Church and her teachings, one error leads to another. He and his followers were very committed to their way of life, that of extreme poverty and non-ownership. They went around the countryside, preaching this philosophy.

Now, it is true with St. Francis (1181-1226), when he began, they were a small remnant of the Church, and his followers had no need of housing or institutional structuring. But, as St. Francis and his band of poverellos (poor ones) started to grow, a Rule became necessary; food, clothing, places to live became an issue he had to face. The difference between Waldo and St. Francis is *obedience*. St. Francis worked within the Church; he presented his Rule to the Pope, and *waited* for his approval.

Waldo and his followers, however, went off the deep end with their teachings. They began to preach that the Church should have no property, either. It was one thing for them to preach poverty for themselves, but when they began to impose their beliefs on our Church, that's when the Archbishop of Lyon stepped in. He condemned the group and threw them out of the diocese.

As a natural progression of their belief, they condemned the practice of supporting the Church by tithing. Now, we all know the Church, right from the very beginning, has needed funds to bring Jesus and His Word to the faithful. As no family can exist and grow without a roof over its head, without nourishment, without education, so it is with the Church. As we journey through the centuries of our Church's existence, we can see the critical *necessity* of education and evangelization, the passing on of the Church's doctrines to all of God's children. Those faithful, whom the Lord has called to give up their lives to serve Him and His Church in the spreading of the Faith, *must* be supported by the faithful who are part of the Church but are not called to that walk. Each member of the Mystical Body of Christ has a walk and a calling. We are all called to different vocations within the Church. No segment of the Church can exist and grow without the other. During the Offertory, we hand back to the Lord that which He has given us, because without Him we would not be able to move our arm to give. The Judeo-Christian tradition has always included tithing.

Now, there were excesses at that time. When Francis and his friars, who had also given everything they had to the poor, went to Rome for permission to build their community, they saw a church laden down with materialism. But they did not attack it. They purified *themselves*. The Church was reformed as a result more of their *behavior*, than their words.

The Waldensians rejected the Pope's demand that they not preach in the Diocese of Lyon, against the orders of their Bishop. They turned *completely* away from the Church and embraced a form of Manichaenism which had not yet died. They threw out all but two Sacraments: *Baptism* and The *Holy Eucharist*. Each Sacrament is a special and unique Grace given to us from *God*. To deny any one of them, is to tell God, we reject the gift He desires to give us that we might have eternal life. Now, either we are saying we know better than God what we need, or we just don't care about Him and His Gifts of eternal life.

They accepted the Sacrament of Baptism which was given to us by Jesus when He told the Apostles, and consequently all the Priesthood that would follow, to "*go therefore, and make disciples of all the nations. Baptize them in the name of the Father and of the Son, and of the Holy Spirit. Teach them everything I have commanded you. And know that I am with you always, until the end of the world!*" (Matt 28:18-20)

They accepted the Sacrament of Baptism which cleanses us of Original Sin. Through this Grace we are made part of the family of Christ by virtue of Christ's death and Resurrection. Through Baptism we become adopted children of God and therefore heirs of His Kingdom. (Rom. 8:15-17) Vatican Council II said *"through Baptism we are formed in the likeness of Christ."*

They accepted the Sacrament of the Holy Eucharist. The Church teaches that the Eucharist is the *sacramental sacrifice* of the Mass where the same offering that Christ made to the Father, that of His Crucified Body and Blood on the Cross is now being offered through the hands of the priest, who is representing the entire Church. The Eucharist is the Real Presence of Jesus in His Body, Blood, Soul and Divinity. And St. Augustine said when we receive Holy Communion, *we do not consume the Lord but the Lord consumes us.*

They accepted two; they rejected five:

They rejected the Sacrament of Penance or the Rite of Reconciliation. In the early Church the Sacrament of Penance was known as a *"second Baptism"*. *"The Church possesses both water and tears, the water of Baptism and the tears of Penance.*[1]*"* We see this all the time, don't we; in the beginning when the love affair with God almost consumes us, we can center on no one, or nothing but making God happy. But then, the world comes crashing in on us, and we begin to compromise. One compromise leads to another, and then before we know it, the compromises become sins against the God we so passionately loved. We have traded our original Love for the empty promises of the world and *its* king. Because of the temptations and our human weakness, the Lord instituted a special Sacrament of Penance for the pardon of sins committed after Baptism (Jn. 20:21-23), and the Church has faithfully dispensed this healing Sacrament throughout the centuries.

Pope John Paul II points out, *"to acknowledge one's sin, indeed-penetrating still more deeply into the consideration of*

---

[1]Catholic Encyclopedia-Broderick

one's personhood-to recognize oneself as being a sinner, capable of sin, is the essential first step in returning to God."

Anyone receiving Holy Communion unworthily, *"sins against the Body and Blood of the Lord. He who eats and drinks without recognizing the Body, eats and drinks a judgment upon himself."* (1Cor 11:27-29) Therefore, if we receive the Holy Eucharist without the Sacrament of Penance, we are either claiming, we are not sinners, going against the Word, or we are receiving unworthily, as we are in sin and our sins have not been forgiven. Jesus entrusted this faculty to forgive men's sins, first to Peter, and, through him, to those who would follow: *"I will entrust to you the keys of the Kingdom of Heaven. Whatever you declare bound on earth shall be bound in Heaven; whatever you declare loosed on earth shall be loosed in Heaven."* (Peter 16:19)

They rejected the Sacrament of Confirmation. Baptism is that part of the initiation into the Church which is completed through *Confirmation.* Therefore, by rejecting Confirmation, they were rejecting the Grace necessary to be a full member of the Church. They were, in effect, rejecting Baptism. This highlights the fact that the Waldensians were not really well versed on the doctrines of our Church. Whether it was willful at first, or not, they wound up causing a tremendous amount of problems for the Church, which took centuries to correct.

The effects of Confirmation are an increase of sanctifying Grace and the Gifts of the Holy Spirit, *a seal placed on the soul*[2], (that's why this Sacrament cannot be repeated) which strengthens the *confirmandi* and empowers them to profess our Faith and fight the temptations of the world as " *Soldiers of Christ*[3]", not only on that day, but for

---

[2]Catholic Encyclopedia-Broderick

[3]when we were confirmed, before Vatican Council II, the bishop would slap us (gently) on the face and proclaim we were now "*Soldiers of Christ*". And, we can remember till today the feeling this gave us.

the rest of their lives. This Grace remains with us forever, whether we tap into it or not. In these days of heresies and attacks upon the Pope and the true teaching of the Faith, we certainly need to call upon the Grace received on the day of our Confirmation.

They rejected the Sacrament of Matrimony. Jesus believed this Sacrament so important that His first public miracle was at Cana, at a wedding! *"Jesus raised the marriage contract between two baptized Catholics to the dignity of a Sacrament. The two most essential properties of this Sacrament are unity, that is one spouse, and indissolubility, that is, a contract for life[4]."* It really seems inconceivable that any reasonably intelligent group could reject an institution in the name of Jesus, which was so important to Jesus.

We will never forget our Marriage Encounter weekend, when the priest called us holy, when he said this is the *only* Sacrament that comes to us directly from God. Our Sacrament is a lifetime contract between three: the husband, the wife and Jesus. He said, we have a vocation no less holy than that of the Priesthood. It changed completely how we looked at each other and our marriage. We really believe that on that weekend we became disciples of Jesus through His Church. We not only fell in love with each other, once again, but we fell in love with Jesus and Mother Church in a new and more meaningful way.

The Waldensians rejected Holy Orders. We don't find that unusual at all, when you consider that it was the authority of the priesthood, as manifested first through the Bishop of Lyon, and consequently through the Pope and his Council, which condemned Waldo and his group. He rejected the Pope's decision; it follows he would have to deny the priesthood.

---

[4]Catholic Encyclopedia-Broderick

"*Holy Orders is the Sacrament of the New Law instituted by Christ, through which spiritual power is given together with the grace to exercise properly the respective office[5].*"   Jesus believed the Priesthood was to be His sign, an everlasting sign of His Royal Priesthood in the world.   It was so important to Him, he so believed in His Church and His Priests, that on the night before He died, He gathered His twelve and showed them *how* they would bring Him to the faithful until He returned.   He entrusted to them, through their consecrated hands, the special Grace to bring Him, in His Body, Blood, Soul and Divinity to the faithful.

They rejected the Sacrament of Extreme Unction (now called the Sacrament of the Anointing of the sick).   This Sacrament is given to Baptized Catholics who are ill, suffering from old age or in danger of dying.   It is to be conferred by a priest or a bishop.   It completes the Sacrament of Penance; it wipes away any sins that *unintentionally* have not have been confessed.   In addition, it strengthens the suffering soul to unite his or her pain with that of Jesus Christ on the Cross.   There have been cases where the person was healed *physically*, as well as spiritually.

Something happens during this Sacrament!   When my father was dying, long before I knew much about the Sacrament of the Anointing of the Sick, he asked me to remain with him while the priest gave him *Last Rites[6]*.   I was standing beside my dad.   I cannot explain it, but at one point, I felt a pressure on my shoulders; it was as if some powerful Hands were forcing me down on my knees.   I can still remember the room filled with a sweet, almost overpowering love.   It was as if we had been transported to another place. I knew God was there!   I could feel a blanket of peace cover my dad.

---

[5]Catholic Encyclopedia-Broderick
[6]now called Anointing of the Sick

Something that never ceases to puzzle me is why would we reject *any* of our Lord's Gifts. If I were offering you a delicious meal, would you only eat part of it when you could enjoy the entire meal? If I were handing you a priceless diamond surrounded by precious rubies and emeralds, in a magnificent setting, would you settle for some of the rubies and emeralds or just the diamond without the precious stones, or maybe just the setting? I don't think so, but over and over again, we allow people to play the shell game, and cheat us of our heritage.

As they rejected Holy Orders, it is logical they would insist that a layman without faculties could forgive sin. But listen to this, a sinful priest could not. These faculties bestowed upon a *priest*, the day he was ordained are *perpetual*; they have nothing to do with the worthiness of the priest. The Waldensians taught that a priest's sinfulness negated the grace he had received on the day of his ordination. They claimed that a host, consecrated by a priest in sin, would not become the Body, Blood, Soul and Divinity of Jesus in the Holy Eucharist. Our Church teaches that the validity of any of the Sacraments are not based on the worthiness of the priest. This heresy was a rerun of a heresy of centuries gone by.

They rejected indulgences, fasts and all the ceremonies of the Church. It is obvious that they were not only going against the Word of the Lord and the Church of their time, they were throwing away 1200 years of tradition passed down by Peter and the Popes that followed him.

"The granting of indulgences is founded upon three doctrines of Catholic Faith: the treasury of the Communion of Saints, Christ Himself and the Blessed Virgin and the Saints[7]." Indulgences, under the proper conditions, are granted for

---

[7]Catholic Encyclopedia-Broderick

the pardon of temporal punishment due for sins. They can be gained for oneself or for someone in purgatory.

Fasting goes back to the Old Testament. Fasting is well grounded in our Judeo-Christian religions. *Jesus fasted for forty days. And yet, they rejected fasting.*

All the ceremonies of the Church raise up our consciousness to things above and not below. They are there to remind us what we are called to be, what we can be, and where we are going, the ultimate journey to Paradise. *And yet, they rejected* the *ceremonies of the Church.*

To the heretics, mortal and venial sins were all the same. Sounds familiar, doesn't it? Are there not some within the Church who are saying there is no sin, just psychoses?

They rejected the veneration of sacred images. I bet, you thought that the charge of idolatry, connected to the veneration of sacred images, was put down once and for all, but it resurfaces because the faithful do not know this heresy[8] has already been condemned by a Council.

Setting up their own set of laws, *they declared all oaths unlawful.* I am sure, it most certainly included (and probably was aimed at) the Creeds passed down to us by the Apostles and the Council of Nicea. It's no wonder, they rejected taking oaths; they had denied five of the Sacraments and tried to do away with every dogma of the Church. It would stand to reason they would *refuse* to profess the Creeds which are an oath of faithfulness to Christ's Church. They had not really rejected the taking of oaths; they had made an oath, not to the Truth, but *against* the Truth.

The Church fights back!

Synods gathered and many councils were convened. Peter Waldo and his followers were condemned as heretics, over and over again, but especially by the Third Lateran Council, in 1179. **Pope Alexander III** presided over this

---

[8]see chapter on Iconoclasm

Council. Cardinals and bishops came from the four corners of the Universal Church. *It called for the punishment of heretics, which included the Albigensians and the Waldensians.* It not only condemned these heresies, it ended a schism caused by factions who wanted Pope Alexander to be excommunicated (because he had not been elected unanimously to the Papacy). The Council not only voted for Pope Alexander, but passed a decree that all that would be necessary to elect a Pope would be a 2/3 vote of cardinals present at the voting. This is in effect until today.

Peter Waldo and his followers were excommunicated. Disobedient until the end, they refused to accept the ruling of Mother Church. Not only did they reject her findings, they became more zealous and insistent. They were not past using violent means to bring about their own brand of theology. When they affected the civil peace of the state, the government stepped in, and the Waldensians fled to northern Italy. They did not remain confined to that part of Europe or to their century. They continued to spread their heresies until the Fourteenth Century. They started to lose much of their following. Even though they were small in number, these false prophets continued to spread their poison throughout southern France and northern Italy, right up to the Protestant Revolution[9].

Satan devised a new plan. He couldn't finish off Jesus' Church with the Waldensians, as they were. They needed new ammunition, a new name, a fresh coat of paint. The Waldensians joined the Calvinist movement. And because the faithful did not know this was an old heresy which had been condemned, this attack did what the others had failed to do; it pitted brother against brother, causing hurts and wounds, although long forgotten, still dishearten and divide. *But, Jesus is coming, and we will all be one.* This, we know!

---

[9] we'll be covering that whole sad period in our next book

Right:
*The Papal Palace at Avignon.
St. Catherine of Siena met
with the Pope here and
convinced him to return to
Rome.*

Below:
*Siena has always been a place
of great art and culture. The
Piazza del Campo in the heart
of Siena. Notice the symbol
of the Eucharist (IHS) on the
front of the building next to
the tower.*

Renaissance:
New Beginnings or New Age?

Calamity struck Europe on a major scale in the middle of the Fourteenth Century, in the form of a violent epidemic, called *The Black Death*. It was given this name because victims of this disease died within a few days of contracting it, and turned black. It was later named *the Bubonic Plague*. It was a malady caused by progress; it was transmitted by rats on ships, traveling all over the world, in pursuit of commerce. Today, we have what we call man-made diseases, such as Cancer and Lukemia, another form of Cancer. There is always a price to pay for progress, either physically or spiritually, or both. In this instance, the price was devastation.

In a period of 100 years, some sixty million people were killed by this dread disease, for which there was, *and there is still no cure*. Nobody wanted to care for the sick or bury the dead. People were afraid to touch the bodies of the dead, for fear of catching the infection. Does it sound familiar at all? Do we have any epidemics running around the world today, virtually unchecked, wreaking havoc? For Europe, this loss of so many people, in such a short period of time, was an enormous problem, in that it represented anywhere from 30% to 50% of the population. The work force was considerably depleted, if not almost totally wiped out. The best minds of the century were lost. There was a great shortage of people to manage countries, operate farms and factories, supervise monasteries, or do any of the things necessary for survival of body and soul. The world needed something to bring them out of that black period.

Sea routes were opening up, as a result of the adventures of Marco Polo and his family to China. Italian seaports were becoming major centers for importing and exporting. A great need arose for workers to handle the influx of commerce that had come in. Couple that with the lack of people available, due to the Black Death, and the shortage became even worse. The feudal lords had become rich; they had other people doing their work. The serfs were tired of giving everything over to their feudal lord. Employers from the city had no problem luring workers into the cities from the rural, farm areas, to handle the work load that was stimulated by this new way of life that was evolving. *Industrialization* took place in the cities.

They had gone through generations of hard times just defending themselves from hoardes of barbarians who were trying to take over their countries. The period commonly known as the Dark Ages had been very austere and depressing, from a religious and cultural point of view. Only the monks and nuns in the monasteries and convents were able to take advantage of the great works of literature handed down by their ancestors.

With the Black Death, the Church suffered greatly. The religious orders were the first in line to help the victims of the Plague. Therefore, they were also the first to die. Their replacements, alas, were not of the same caliber intellectually as those they replaced. These new recruits were much younger, and less educated. The rules had to be relaxed to accommodate the new breed of religious; in many instances they were never brought back to their prior standards. Another problem, which was not meant to be a problem, was that too many people were leaving too much money to the religious orders. The combination of the two does not make a good formula for Chastity, Poverty and Obedience. Perhaps the suffering of doing without for so many centuries had been too demanding.

The Church wanted us to center on God and things of Heaven. We wanted an earthly source of inspiration and entertainment. With the influx of newfound wealth, the upper classes and the intelligentsia had lots of money and nothing to do. Man wanted to focus the world's attention on man and things of the earth. Man wanted to be *free*! He didn't know when another plague would strike, and all would die, and so, the time was ripe for Renaissance.

The Renaissance

The literal translation of Renaissance is Rebirth. You will read in a later chapter that one of the beliefs of New Age is Rebirth. We're not trying to make a comparison; it's very obvious. However, the *New Age* philosophy defines Rebirth with a twist, as follows; *one is conditioned to believe that all wisdom is contained within oneself.* The fourteenth century definition of Renaissance (Rebirth) is a *rebirth of the classical culture and civilization of ancient Greece and Rome.* It was *supposed to be* a rebirth of culture. *And there was a great deal of that, too!* But in addition, there was a rebirth, according to Satan's plan, *of a pagan,* very "I-centered" culture, a lustful and erotic culture. This *Culture* would explore *humanism* in all its lowest forms.

How did all this interest in Greek and Roman come about all of a sudden? Well, for one thing, the Turks were overrunning the old Byzantine empire. The Greek scholars were running for their lives. They found themselves in Italy, which was a perfect breeding ground for them to introduce the culture and art of the Masters of Greece. It also provided a place of safety for them from the Turks.

The people were told, what they needed was literature and art to enlighten their minds and lives, to lift their spirits out of the darkness of the past, a rebirth from the austere to the sublime. The proponents of Renaissance advocated the *human aspect* of mankind in art and literature, as expressed by the ancient Greek and Roman civilizations, rather than that of the *spiritual,* as portrayed by the Church.

The *Humanists* were broken into two categories, Christian and Pagan. The Christians were supposed to amplify the *good* in humanism. The Pagans emphasized the evil and apathetic.

Whereas one philosophy's intention was to explore the beauty of the languages, the sculptors, the artists, the philosophers, another stronger philosophy's focus was to delve into the subculture, the perversion of ancient Rome and Greece, with its open sex, permissiveness, radical homosexual activity, materialism, self gratification and personal advancement, a philosophy of, *if it pleases you, go for it!* We may have said it before, but just looking at what began in mid-Fourteenth Century Italy, and then spread over all of Europe, the parallels are frightening with what's going on today.

We see Satan repeating himself again as he has down through the centuries. You may recall a TV commercial of a few years ago, for a fast food chain, where a little band of very bored people are going out for lunch. They walk in a huddle like robots. One of them says *"Same place?"* They all repeat, *"Same place"*. Then he says, *"Same thing?"* They all repeat *"Same thing"*. With Satan, it's always the *"Same place"*, hell, and always the *"Same thing"*, disobedience.

He has this one plan that he's been working on since the Garden of Eden, bringing as many souls as possible, to hell. He's sure it's going to work someday, because he keeps trying. Give him credit, however. He has made *some* progress; we can see that huge cracks have fractured the walls of our Faith. Each time, this particular plan goes into effect, we lose many brothers and sisters, usually to the sin of pride and intellect. This concerns us greatly, because as John Donne, a 16th century poet said,

> *Any man's death diminishes me,*
> *Because I am involved in mankind*

We are called to be involved in mankind, you and us. That's the task of Evangelization. By our Baptism, we are called to evangelize. We are concerned with death of the soul as well as death of the body. It's not an option; it's a command. We are required to be keenly aware of the wiles and wickedness of the enemy. We have to be able to discern the glamour of evil. Satan feeds off company. He would have all of us down in the pits of hell with him. Our job is to bring everyone we come in contact with into the kingdom. We can do it because Jesus has given us the power to do it. But we have to be aware of the ongoing plan of Satan in all its insidious, seemingly beautiful forms. We have to see the trap, be sharply aware of it, and avoid it, for the salvation of our souls, and those of our brothers and sisters.

Sometimes, history has a way of smoothing out rough edges, so that heresies don't seem as menacing four or five hundred years later. Also, sadly, inventions or ideas which could allow us to recognize the glory of God as given to us through His artists, writers, sculptors, etc., are *slanted* and *distorted* by the enemy. While the original desire may have been to glorify God through His creation, our humanity and sensuality often got in the way.

Such is the case with the **Renaissance**. One aspect of it was: it laid a strong groundwork for the 17th & 18th Century **Age of Enlightenment** and the official introduction of Pantheism in 1705, which is the cornerstone of the Twentieth Century New Age Movement. It fanned the flames for the Protestant Revolution and went on to achieve its greatest strength during the French Revolution.

Renaissance was a time of boldness, of challenge, of adventure. Great accomplishments were made in all fields. Questions demanded answers; nothing was accepted on face value. Any accepted set of values was open to challenge. It was exciting. Renaissance was accepted by the elite of Europe with open arms. They wanted something new, something different, supposedly to challenge and stimulate their intellect. The pendulum swung wide, too wide! When all the experiences had been experienced, when all the challenges had been met and conquered, they found themselves in the middle of the fifteenth century, walking around in Roman togas, celebrating *pagan* Roman holidays, using pagan forms of revelry and debauchery. As happened in the Greek and Roman civilizations before them, they just needed an excuse to wallow in the erotic excesses of the Greeks and Romans.

But Renaissance also brought us the beauty and softness of God, as seen in His creation, manifested in the inspired work of such people as Michelangelo, Raphael, Da Vinci and Dante Aligheri. Great heights were reached in the areas of architecture, engineering, literature, art and sculpture. We must look at the tangible rewards we received through the contributions of those who lived in and through the Renaissance, and who glorified His Name.

Michelangelo:
Creation of the World & Last Judgment - Sistine Chapel
Pieta - St. Peter's Basilica
Raphael
The Stanzas[1] of the Signature
The Stanza of the Borgo Fire
The Stanza òf Helodorus
The Stanza of Constantine
all of these are in the Vatican Apartments
Dante Aligheri
Divine Comedy
Leonardo da Vinci
The Last Supper
Mona Lisa

This is just the tip of the iceberg. There isn't enough space in this book to list all the contributions these great artists made to the world, nor do we have room to mention

---

[1]Room

those other greats whose inspired works contributed to the Church and to the world.

Paintings by the great artists were used to teach the people the truths of our Church. Even today, when we bring pilgrims to the Basilica of St. Francis in Assisi, we use the magnificent frescoes by Giotto in the upper Basilica, to tell the life of St. Francis.

We have been criticized over the centuries for the elaborate paintings in our Churches. However, prior to the Gutenberg press, and a renewed interest in reading, not that many men, and virtually no women knew how to read. A point in fact would be St. Catherine of Siena, Doctor of the Church. She had to be taught to read by Jesus.

If you can agree that television is blamed, to a great degree, for much of the problems of our world in the second half of the Twentieth Century, it may be said of the Gutenberg printing press that it was responsible for spreading much of the decadence of the Renaissance. The printing press caused a revolution in its time, much the same as television has in our time. *But that was not at all the original intent!* The first book ever printed on the Gutenberg press was the *Bible*! In fact, the Gutenberg Bible is the most valuable book in the world. The Gutenberg press was fulfilling God's plan for it. It made the written word available to almost everybody, that is, everybody who could read. It was definitely an incentive for people to learn how to read. Unfortunately, at that time, only the *intelligentsia* could read, and they used this marvelous invention as a weapon to get their *poison* distributed to as many people, as quickly as possible. As the written word became available to the common man, there were no limits to what could be achieved for the glory of God. But it was not.

Man became his own god. *The focus of the age was completely on man, his potential, and his accomplishments.* A group called the *Pagan Humanists* are responsible for beginning and spreading Renaissance. *Pagan humanists taught that man was everything.* Beyond man, there was nothing. There was no God. Man was enough.

They also envied the powerful position the Church held in the secular as well as religious world. *Renaissance* was a perfect excuse to fight the Church, to weaken the Church, and, if possible, to destroy the Church. The upshot was that much of the temporal power of the Church was taken away, or gravely limited. The morals of the Church were in complete disagreement with the immorality of the Pagan Humanists. Thanks to the Gutenberg press, the Humanists had a vehicle, their colleagues could use to sway the minds of the people into trading in the Gospel life for a lewd, uninhibited, lustful philosophy. They especially went after the young and succeeded in trampling many moral beliefs that had been instilled in them as young people.

But at least the art of the Renaissance glorified God through the concept that *Grace perfects Nature*. What have we done with our art today? Can we compare the Masters of that period to some of the extremely offensive material we're financing with our American tax dollars through the National Endowment for the Arts, a government funded agency?

During the Renaissance, the method used to discredit the Church was very interesting. First, they went out of their way to lure the clergy. They set their sights on the upper echelons of the Church; they got them to embrace Renaissance. There were many easy avenues open to entice the clergy. The proponents of Renaissance promoted relaxing what they called "*the tight grip*" that the Church had on them. The philosophy of Renaissance was, if the Church won't let you be the way you want, simply change the Church. *The Renaissance ridiculed the concept of religious celibacy.* It was completely unnecessary, they said. This made a switch to Renaissance much easier on the religious.

The Renaissance turned the focus from God to man. And what man was saying and doing was more palatable to many of the clergy. Okay. Now that they've done all that, and gotten some clergy in high places to accept the new way and embrace some of the Pagan Humanist's scandalous behavioral patterns, they were openly exposed to the faithful, ridiculed, maligned and disgraced. The end result was that the clergy lost much of the respect the faithful had held for them.

We have a tendency to criticize the Church of that day for falling into the trap of the Renaissance. There was *so much* peer pressure, it would have been harder to believe that the Church would *not* have been weakened by the world. The movement adopted the principle of the informal father of the Renaissance, *Machiavelli*, whose philosophy, simply put is, *the end justifies the means, and a ruler must do whatever is necessary to be a powerful and successful ruler. If it means he should appear to be a good man, it's okay to give that impression. If, however, he should be a liar, thief, and cheat, then go for it. The results are what counts.*

St. Teresa of Avila, one of only two women Doctors of the Church, born into the Renaissance, contradicts Machiavelli, when she tells us that *the greatest good cannot justify the smallest evil.* And now, five hundred years later, who knows the name of Machiavelli as anything other than a little known cologne?

There were those who just wanted to enjoy the physical and material benefits derived from embracing the Renaissance movement. Then there were others, and we have to believe they were sincere, who truly thought they could explore these new horizons available to Man, and integrate them into the Christian synthesis[2]. They preached

---

[2]the putting together of parts of an element to make a whole. In this instance, completing the Christian likeness by integrating the naturalism of Renaissance.

that through the melding of the two philosophies, Christian and Humanism, they would emerge with a better concept of Christianity, for the new age.

We would really like to believe this, because we don't want to be accused of trying to uncover satanic plots under every bush. But if you would just take the expression "*Eastern Religions*" and substitute it in the places where we have used the words *Humanism* and *Renaissance* in the above paragraph, you'll see that what they were trying to sell in the Renaissance is the same theology, they're trying to sell today. Even though their intentions were pure, and I want to believe with all my heart that they were; the aftershock of their philosophy was felt for centuries afterward.

Let's say, they really felt this loosening up was in our best interests. How do they know what we can handle? How do they know what gets us through the night? Maybe we need that strictness in our lives to keep us on the straight and narrow. It's like telling an alcoholic or drug addict, a little of *the horse that bit you*[3] is really all right. It might even be medically beneficial. It might also lead you down the path to your death. So while it may be okay for some, those who are strong enough to handle it, the intelligentsia, what about us weaklings who can't handle *a little permissiveness*, *a little pornography*, *a little booze*, *a little snort of cocaine*? Must we die to feed your ego?

Renaissance brought us papal figures like the Borgias (Alexander VI) and the Medicis (Leo X) who were clearly influenced by the world they were born into. Pope Alexander VI unwittingly brought us to the edge of revolution, by instituting the practice of selling indulgences to fatten a depleted Vatican treasury. Pope Leo X was involved in a power play to gather as much property for the

---

[3]An expression used when someone suffering alcoholic hangover is given a drink the next day. The benefits are supposed to be medicinal.

Medici family as possible.   He spent more time as a commander-in-chief than as Pope.   He reintroduced the policy of selling indulgences, becoming a target for Martin Luther. He was also the Pope who bestowed upon Henry VIII the title: *Defender of the Faith.* Enemies of the Church love to point accusing fingers at the clergy of this period. Did we have religious, priests and cardinals who did not follow the mandate of Jesus? We surely did. Are we still here? We surely are. Jesus made a promise, *"the gates of Hell will not prevail against you (My Church)."*

The Renaissance is not totally to blame for the revolution, commonly known as the Protestant Revolt. But the Renaissance was the greatest single factor that made fertile the ground where Satan would cultivate this next great attack on the Church Christ founded, from which we are still reeling, five hundred years later. The Renaissance put a huge chink in the armor of the Church. It lost some of the prestige and respect of the people. Because it had been weakened badly by Renaissance popes and hierarchy, the Church became ripe for the likes of Martin Luther, John Calvin, and all those who instigated the revolution, which brought about *the Scandal of the Cross.*

It's possible in this chapter, that we may have shown a one-sided view of the Renaissance, and portrayed it as all evil. This was not our intent. We do believe that some of the treasures which were left behind from the Renaissance, are gifts from God, and are meant to glorify His Name. I guess if we were not in such serious times, we could afford to be more generous, or open-minded. We would even try to justify their viewpoint. *But these are such serious times.* I have to ask the question. *What price Renaissance?* How much did it cost in lost souls for us to be free spirits, to have a Michelangelo, or a Raphael, or a Leonardo da Vinci as a part of our heritage?

Was it, is it, worth the price?

The Church Fights Back!

God is in charge. He's always with us, in there fighting for us. Very often, we have to wait a few hundred years, and look back in retrospect, to realize just how much He has been working for us, sending Angels, Saints, and Miracles to lift us up, prove His power and glory to us, and thwart Satan in his attempts to destroy us.

In our century, we have been privileged to see some of the Powerful People of the Church in action, people who dare to be Catholic and to be persecuted for their stand. It includes faithful bishops who have been maligned by their fellow bishops, as well as priests, for their loyalty to the Pope. Our own Mother Angelica is a perfect example. She took the instrument Satan had decided he'd use to destroy the Church, Television, and solemnly offered it back to God, as she battles anyone or anything that would attack that Church she so dearly loves. She has been so under attack from those who are supposed to be on our side, she needs a score card to tell who are the good guys and who are the bad guys.

Our dear Pope John Paul II who is not only the head of our Church, but a sign of hope and fidelity in this hopeless, unfaithful, uncaring world. He is not only a great Pope, but a great humanitarian. We know we get bashed for our bad Popes, but do we get special credit for these extraordinary Popes? History will honor these future Saints, and their contribution to the Church of this Century.

Looking back on the Renaissance, at first, we're so overwhelmed by the damage done by the movement, we wonder how we weren't *completely* overpowered by the enemies of Christ. But then we take a closer look. Dear Lord Jesus, we were fighting neck and neck with them, and I believe we beat them. If only for the fact that we're still here, hanging by our thumbs, but we're here. However, it's uplifting to behold all the ammunition, the Lord sent us.

Our Lord Jesus counterbalanced the assault by way of Miracles, and Saints. There were those who were in direct combat, attacking the obvious problems of the day, and others, who dealt indirectly, attacking our weaknesses, by which Renaissance was able to exist at all.

The fact that there were so *many Saints and Miracles*, we can't possibly bring them all to you in this book, is so exciting. It would be just too huge for you to even carry around with you. But that will give you just a microscopic idea of how much God loves you and is involved with your life. But let us touch on some of them.

Miracle of the Eucharist of Volterra, Italy - 1472

During the Renaissance period, most of the cities in Italy were little City-States. Provinces, like Tuscany, Venice and Milan were small Kingdoms. There was constant backstabbing between the various provinces and cities. The Medicis, the Borgias, the Pittis, the Sforzas, and the like, were all trying to take over smaller areas to build their individual empires. Caught in the middle of these intrigues were little republics like Siena, Lucca, and Pisa, of which Volterra is a part.

One of the Medicis, the great Lorenzo by name, had decided that the small mountain town of Volterra would be a good addition to his Florentine empire. He hired a group of mercenaries.

One of the mercenaries came into the Church of St. Francis in search of gold. He headed immediately for the tabernacle, where we know the most precious "Valuable" in the world lives. His goal was not our Lord, though, but treasures of the earth. Inside the tabernacle, he found a box, most likely a pyx. It was made of ivory, and contained the Blessed Sacrament. Either he was not aware that Our Lord was in the box, or didn't care. In any event, he threw the box into his bag, and started to leave the church. The priests in the church prayed feverishly.

A strange thing happened. He couldn't find the door of the church. He staggered around several times, cursing and threatening the priests. Then his sight left him completely. He was blind. He flew into a rage. Panic overtook him. He withdrew his sword, swinging it wildly as if to hit some invisible force that had taken over his body. The more helpless he became, the wilder he acted, and the more he cursed.

The priests must have felt the presence of the Lord in their midst. They gathered up courage. They told the soldier that if he would give back the box with the Body of Our Lord Jesus, perhaps his sight would be given back to him. The thief hesitated, cursed some more, then plunged his hand into his bag to feel for the case he had stolen. As he grabbed it, he began to rant and rave, as if he were possessed by Satan. He let out a blood-curdling scream. His face contorted grotesquely. He flung the box against one of the columns of the Church.

At the instant the box struck the column, the earth began to shake throughout the city. It sounded like a groan from heaven. It was reported as the worst earthquake ever to hit that city. It calls to mind the Gospel account of the events following the Death of Our Dear Lord Jesus. In Matthew 27:51, "*Suddenly the curtain of the sanctuary was torn in two from top to bottom. The earth quaked, boulders split, tombs opened....The centurion and his men who were keeping watch over Jesus were terror-stricken at seeing the earthquake and all that was happening, and said 'Clearly this was the Son of God.'*"

The thief was completely distraught. Between his blindness and the terrible earthquake, he fell to his knees in tears of sorrow and fear. He confessed all his sins and asked for forgiveness. The Franciscans prayed with him. The thief regained his sight. The ivory box had shattered all over the floor, but the Sacred Host remained intact. It was picked up by the priests, and placed back into the tabernacle.

Why do you think this miracle was so important for the Renaissance? The Lord was showing this soldier, as He showed St. Paul, where his treasure lie. These two men had to become blind so that they could see. Is the Lord asking us to close our eyes to the glamour of evil, so that we can see the Glory of God? Is that how he was trying to combat the enticement of Renaissance?

Powerful Men and Women in the Church

We speak often of Holy Clusters. We have seen clusters of holy places and events that seemingly have no connection with others, except that they were all instituted by the Lord. The chronological sequence may be centuries apart. But time is a limitation put on us by man, not by God.

In Italy, San Giovanni Rotondo, where Padre Pio lived for the first half of the 20th century, is only twenty miles away from Monte St. Angelo, where the Archangel Michael appeared towards the end of the 5th Century. Both places are within a hundred miles of Lanciano, where we have the oldest recorded Miracle of the Eucharist in our Church, which took place in the 8th Century.

Our Lady appeared to St. James the Apostle, while she was still alive, in Zaragoza, Spain. Zaragoza is also the location of a Miracle of the Eucharist. If that's not enough, within 50 miles of Zaragoza in two opposite directions, there are two more Miracles of the Eucharist.

So, it's fairly established that the Lord gives us Holy Clusters of places. But we have never realized that *He also gives Holy Clusters of people!* He raises up Saints to do battle with the enemy, in these special times. *He uses people; He uses us!* There should never be a doubt about that. If you have ever felt alone, rejected, unloved, don't believe it.

That's a gift from the evil one. All you have to do is look at those who came before us, to see just how much your God loves you! Clusters of holy people, saints of the same time period, worked together to bring us closer to the kingdom. We want to share how the Lord used clusters of Holy People to do battle against the *Renaissance*.

Catherine of Siena & Raymond of Capua

Although the Renaissance began in the middle of the 14th century, the seeds of hate and disobedience were planted long before. The enemies of the Church went after the Papacy before the 14th Century began. The Pope was unsafe in Rome. A particular family was trying to take over the property of the Popes. It came to a head at the turn of the century. In 1304, Pope Benedict XI fled to Perugia, near Assisi, where he died the same year. The new Pope, Clement V, accepted an offer from the French King, to rule the Church from France, in Avignon. This was the beginning of a 68 year period when the Church was virtually in exile. It has been nicknamed "*The Babylonian Captivity*".

For the enemies of the Church, this was perfect. The Church was seriously weakened. Its authority was virtually non-existent. No wonder it was so easy for a movement like Renaissance to flourish in Italy during this time.

Renaissance began, and the Lord raised up a powerful woman in the Church, Catherine Benincasa, twenty-third child in a family of twenty five. The Church was in such desperate need, the period so crucial, the Lord gave us a woman of great spiritual strength, who would one day be declared a Doctor of the Church[4].

Catherine's entire life was one long battle. It was as if the Lord gave her the gift of struggle so that she would be prepared for the major battle, she was to wage against the

---

[4] She and St. Teresa of Avila are the only women to be so honored.

satan of the Renaissance. She knew from her earliest childhood that her life was to be committed to the Lord.

One night she had a dream. All the founders of the different Orders in the Church were there. St. Dominic stepped forward and said, *"Do not worry. You will wear this habit."* Having said this, he handed her the black and white habit of the Mantellate[5].

She privately took the vows of Nuns who belonged to *Religious Orders*, poverty, chastity and obedience, although as a Third Order Dominican, it was not required of her. She stayed in her room, except to attend Mass. For three years she lived this solitary life. Although she allowed no one in her cell, she was never alone. Jesus, sometimes with His Mother and, at other times, with the Saints and Angels, would come and instruct her about God His Father, the Truths of the Gospel, about salvation and sin.

Catherine wanted to be able to read. A friend from a noble family, lent her a book of alphabets. Hard as she tried, she could not learn how to read. Frustrated and upset, she turned to Jesus and complained, *"If You want me to read, You'll have to teach me, Yourself. Otherwise, I'll remain the ignorant fool I am."* From that time on, reading came easier and easier to Catherine, until the day she was to master it completely. She never learned to write, however; *she dictated* all her marvelous writings, which later earned her the honorable title, *Doctor of the Church*.

Raymond of Capua was assigned to Catherine as her spiritual director. He would give her *daily* Communion, which the other Dominicans would not allow her to receive. He was forty-four years old. Catherine was twenty seven. The first time she saw him serving Mass on the altar of the Church of St. Dominic, she heard a voice in her heart, saying, *"This is my beloved servant. This is he to whom I will*

---

5 Mantellate - Third Order of St. Dominic, a lay or secular Order.

entrust you." He was not really sold on Catherine. Although the Lord chose Raymond to be her spiritual partner, he had some growing up to do, some dying to self. He didn't come that way; he had to develop. Actually, it took the Black Plague to do it.

Siena was rampant with the plague. Raymond came into town and worked tirelessly beside Catherine day and night. Because he, as a Priest, was urgently needed to administer the Sacraments, Raymond got very little, sometimes *no* sleep. This went on until one day he felt a pain and a swelling in his groin. His head began to ache and burn with a raging fever. With what little strength he had left, he dragged himself to Catherine's home.

When she returned from doing her rounds of patients in their homes and at the hospital, she found Raymond on a cot, *delirious*, more dead than alive. He had all the signs of the Plague. Catherine placed her hands on his head and prayed for an hour and a half straight, without stopping. As she prayed, he could feel the heat leaving his body, his old vitality replacing the weakness left by the disease. He later wrote, *"It was as if something was being pulled out of me at the ends of all my limbs."* Catherine finished praying; Raymond was completely cured.

Catherine *trusted* Raymond. She had never met anyone like him, with his wisdom, intelligence, and ability to listen. She felt, at last, she had met her *mentor*. She talked to him endlessly, words pouring out of her, of the Visions she'd had of our Lord Jesus, of her thoughts on sin and sanctifying grace. He was having a problem absorbing all she said; it was too much. He had never heard of revelations such as the young visionary was sharing. He was having trouble believing in them *and* her.

The next morning, he reluctantly returned to Catherine, *thoroughly convinced* she was not reliable. Upon arriving, he found her too weak to move, but not, to his dismay, too weak to talk incessantly. He found himself getting *agitated*. All this endless talk of hers was very annoying and irritating. He bent down, disbelieving, anxious to get this over with. Instead of seeing Catherine's face, the Face looking back at him was That of Jesus Christ. Startled, he blurted out, "Who is this looking at me?"

"It is He who is," Catherine responded. Raymond was *now* convinced she was *genuine*, a true follower and disciple of Jesus. He became her most zealous champion and strongest advocate.

Raymond was Catherine's right hand man for the most important years of her life, her last six. It was during this time they took on evangelization outside of their immediate area. He gave her credibility. With him by her side, she could go out and do the Lord's work, as He had commanded her. They went to Pisa and other areas of Italy, preaching against Renaissance, for the Church and the Pope.

Catherine receives the Stigmata

Blessed Raymond of Capua was with her in Pisa, when he saw her transfigured into the Image of Jesus Christ. He had just finished celebrating Mass for Catherine and her companions when she went into ecstasy, *"her soul separating as much as it could from the body."* They saw her body, which had been prostrate on the floor, rise. Mid-air, she kneeled, her face aglow with the fire of Jesus' Love inside of her. Then with a tremor, her body fell in a heap onto the floor. Her companions waited for her words, as she came out of the rapture. Catherine awoke after a few moments, and went directly to Raymond.

"Father, I must tell you, that by His Mercy, I now bear the stigmata of the Lord Jesus in my body."

Those were glorious times for both of them. But they were to be short-lived. First Catherine went to Avignon, and then to Rome, to help the *new* pope fight the Western Schism.

Catherine goes to Avignon

The Popes in Avignon lived in unbelievable wealth and luxury, using their power for their own benefit and that of family and friends. The papal court had become "*a fountain of affliction, a house of wrath, a school of error, a temple of heresy*[6]." Catherine had a fierce loyalty to the Pope, teaching that we should love and respect him as "*sweet Christ on earth.*" When the Florentines were rebelling against Pope Gregory XI, she wrote to them, scolding them.

The Florentines did not heed Catherine. They taxed the clergy. The Papacy of Avignon sent a Nuncio to straighten them out. They dragged him into the street and beat him up. Avignon excommunicated Florence.

Catherine wrote *many* letters to the Pope, pleading the case of Florence. She felt the answer to the solution was for her to go to the Pope in Avignon. So, at the invitation of the Pope, and with the hopes of Florence, Catherine set out for Avignon as a *peacemaker*. She and the Pope met, at last, face to face in the year 1376. She was twenty-nine years old! Catherine remained in Avignon for four months, at the express wish of the Pope, advising him how to deal with the crisis in the Church.

Catherine was a woman *who got a thought and forged ahead, barreling through all opposition.* The Pope vacillated between the different *cliques* in his court; one day he was going to Rome, encouraged by those who agreed with Catherine; the next day he was remaining in France, swayed by those who insisted he and the Papacy belonged in Avignon. He asked Catherine to pray for a sign from Heaven showing him what was best to do. She did as he asked and, after Communion one day, Catherine's body became taut. She was lost in prayer for about an hour. As

---

[6] quoting the Italian poet Petrarch

she came out of her ecstasy, they heard her say, *"Praised be God, now and forever."*

A few days later, the subject of whether to remain in Avignon or to go to Rome, came up again. Catherine replied, *"Who knows what ought to be done better than your Holiness, who has long since made a vow to God to return to Rome?"* Pope Gregory *knew* it had to be the Lord; no one knew of this vow outside of himself and the Lord. There was the *sign!* He would act!

The Pope went to Rome. He was received and accepted by everyone. Not only the Roman citizens, but the clergy, the Bishops, the Cardinals, the most influential and the humblest welcomed their Pope *back home*. He was their hope for peace, but the peace he and they sought was never to be realized in Pope Gregory's time. On the 27th of March, 1378, the Pope died. On April the 18th, a new Pope was elected. Pope Urban VI was to prove himself hard and uncompromising. Sadly lacking was the mercy and gentleness of the Savior; so, attacking indiscriminantly, the Pope made many enemies in the Church.

The situation became so serious, the French Cardinals asked the Pope to meet with them. They asked him to resign. *He flatly refused*. They declared him an illegitimate Pope and calling him the *Anti-Christ*, they elected a *French* pope on the 20th of September. The French pope illegally took the name of Clement VII. The Church was *split in two*. The Great Western Schism, that Catherine had foreseen and *prophesied*, was here!

The Pope called Catherine to Rome. She left Siena, and arrived there on the 28th of November. At the insistence of her Pope, Catherine remained in Rome, meeting with him and writing to different heads of state, begging them to remain loyal to the Pope. Raymond was sent to France to preach against the French impostor Pope,

Clement VII. It was the last time Catherine and Raymond ever saw each other alive.

Raymond went to Genoa, on his way to France. He was not too keen about the prospects of going into France. All he really needed was half an excuse for not going into France, and he would have stayed in Italy. The excuse came in the form of a threat against his life, or so he proposed. He decided to stay in Genoa, and work with the Dominican community there.

When Catherine found out, she sent him a blitz of a letter, accusing him of every form of cowardice. Had she known she would never see him again, would she have been so harsh? We don't know. She was a very stubborn girl, but on the other hand, she loved Raymond dearly.

Catherine, the Eucharistic Faster

For the seven year period prior to her death, she took no food into her body other than the Eucharist. Her fasting did not affect her energy, however. She maintained a very active life during those seven years. As a matter of fact, most of her great accomplishments occurred during that period. Not only did her fasting not cause her to lose energy, but became a source of extraordinary strength[7].

Catherine gave her last ounce of blood for her Church. Near the end of her painful journey on earth, her friends heard her say,

"O Eternal God, accept the sacrifice of my life for the mystical body of Thy holy Church. I have nothing to give save that which Thou hast given to me. Take my heart then and press it out over the face of Thy Spouse!"

She saw God take her heart from her body and squeeze it out over the Church. As long as Catherine had a breath of

---

[7]excerpt from Eucharistic Fasters from "*This My Body...This is My Blood, Miracle of the Eucharist*"

life in her to give, she prayed and sacrificed for her love on earth, Mother Church. She told her companions, she would continue to fight for her Church even after death.

She had a Vision in the early part of 1380, in which the ship of the Church crushed her to the earth. At that moment, she offered herself as a willing sacrifice. She was to be ill from this time until April 21 of that year, when she suffered a paralytic stroke from the waist down. On April 29, she went to her reward.

As she lay on her death bed, one of her greatest sorrows was not having Raymond, her *"Friend of her heart"*, as she liked to call him, by her side. On April 28, 1380, the day she died, Raymond was in Pisa, some 240 miles *away* from Rome. Physically, they were separated by many miles. But spiritually, they were in communication. He heard in his heart, *"Tell him never to lose courage. I will be with him in every danger; if he fails, I will help him up again."* A short time later, when he was informed of the death of his great partner in the Lord, Catherine, he was told that she said those words on her deathbed. She had forgiven him; she had asked him to forgive her.

It was only natural for Raymond to take over her work. He did her justice by working day and night to end the Great Western Schism. He became well-known as a result of his association with Catherine, and his work to end the Schism.

Raymond died in Germany, away from his homeland. But he didn't have a homeland anymore. He was a pilgrim, going from place to place, until he arrived at his home in Heaven; he was waiting to be reunited with his Catherine. His work finished, in 1399, at age 69, Raymond was reunited with Catherine.

St. Bernardine of Siena 1380 - 1444

St. Bernardine is considered one of the most powerful men in our Church. He is given all these unofficial titles;

Left:
St. Catherine dei Ricci
Dominican
Had the Stigmata
Mystically married to
Jesus
Received a wedding ring
from Jesus
Shared in the Lord's
Passion for 12 years

Right:
St. Bernardine of Siena,
second founder of the
Strict Observance of the
Franciscan Order,
reformer of the
Franciscan Order,
great preacher, and
Defender of the Eucharist

Apostle of the Holy Name of Jesus, Second Founder of the Strict Observance of the Franciscan Order, Defender of the Eucharist

St. Bernardine of Siena was born in Massa Marittima, a suburb of Siena. There were virtues in Bernardine which the Lord needed to use at this point in history. He had the same tenderness and compassion for the sick that Catherine of Siena and Raymond of Capua had. The *plague* resurfaced in Siena when Bernardine was only twenty years old. He threw himself into the job of taking care of the sick, and burying the dead. He had a great charisma. He was able to get many of his companions to work by his side. As some of them died during the plague, other young men stepped forward, eager to serve the Lord through Bernardine.

He worked at high speed during the plague. It was as if the Lord provided him with super energy (or 1,043 Angels) to handle a necessary mission, and when it was completed, He allowed him to collapse and then recover. But these were serious times. There was not the luxury for Bernardine to pamper his body. There were two major assignments he had to handle. He had to evangelize all of Italy; he had to reform the Franciscan Order. Either job was more than one man could handle in a lifetime. Bernardine was taking them both on, and he would also do other things for his God.

The Franciscan order had been the strongest weapon the Lord could use in the Middle Ages to reform the Church. And they were successful. Under the banner of St. Francis of Assisi, the Poverello[9] of Jesus, reform came about. Satan tried in so many ways to break up the community. He was powerless, until he sneaked in the old standbys of *pride, envy, self-pity, and the like*. Division crept into the fraternity. Even during Francis' lifetime, the Rule was changed. After

---

[9]The poor one

his death, it was just a matter of time until everything he had stood for, would crumble and blow away by a strong wind.

The adherents of the strict observance rule had dwindled down to a handful, about three hundred. The Lord chose Bernardine to become the defender of the Rule of St. Francis. However, at the beginning, Bernardine had no grand illusions about his future role. His early days as a Franciscan remind us a lot of St. Anthony of Padua. He chose seclusion. His friends had been too available in Siena. It led to too much distraction. He asked to be transferred to a more remote place, where he could grow in spirituality and contemplation. The Lord granted his wishes, just long enough to prepare him for the job ahead.

He was a brilliant speaker, although he never thought so. In a short time, his name was well known. His fame as a preacher spread. He began his missionary journeys preaching the word of Jesus, especially Jesus in the Eucharist. He became so popular, they had to have his meetings outside, in the open air, because there wasn't enough room inside the Church. And he didn't patronize anyone! He attacked the wickedness of his day, our good old friend, the Renaissance. He gave credit for all the gifts in his life to the Holy Name of Jesus.

He had a symbol made, which he wore around his neck. It was big, about 7 inches in diameter. I H S[10] was in the middle, emblazoned by rays of blinding light. He had a way of zeroing in on the important values. He would go to the members of an important family, especially in Florence and Siena. He would point to their family crest, which adorned their palaces, homes, and offices. *"Take down that symbol. You don't belong to the family of Borgia or Medici. You belong to Jesus. Put up the symbol of Jesus!"* And they did it. Just go to the *Palazzo Vecchio* in Florence, or the *Piazza del Campo*

---

[10] the monogram of His Holy Name

in Siena. You will see the symbol of St. Bernardine. Go to the private residences all throughout the area of Tuscany. You will see the symbol of St. Bernardine.

Bernardine became famous for his missionary work. But it was time to get onto his next important work, saving the Franciscan Order. Bernardine was a firm believer in the original Rule of St. Francis, which was not being practiced by the Franciscan community by and large. They contended from the time of Francis that it was too strict. There were a small group of stalwarts who still practiced the original Rule of Francis, but they were very small. Bernardine became their champion and trail blazer. He traveled the countryside, recruiting fervent young men to the Strict Observance Rule of St. Francis. He was so sincere, so full of love, that he was able to get entire convents to switch from the Conventuals to the Observants without causing a world war.

Bernardine spent the rest of his life encouraging a modified form of the original Rule of St. Francis. He was a very rational man. Francis was against learning of any kind for the Friars. Bernardine was a learned man. He knew the necessity of knowledge. So he pushed for education of the Friars, and he got his way. But by and large, he was for the Rule as Francis had written it.

"As he got on in years, he could feel the pressure of the Lord. He had to get back out on the road, to his missionary work. The advocates of the Renaissance were making great footholds in the Church, as well as in government. Bernardine had to fight them. But now he had an army of almost 4,000 Friars of the Strict Observance. One of them, **St. John of Capistrano**, will be the subject of our next saint of the Renaissance. You see how the Lord works? *Remarkable!* You know how they pass the gauntlet from one runner to the other in those Olympic Team Racing events? The current runner strains at the bit to go as fast and as hard as he/she can to make it to the goal. Then, waiting to take over is a fresh racer, also eager to take off like a shot and run his/her heart out. That's how the Lord works with us. He raises up Saints who, somehow, train or affect another saint, who does the same to another saint. Here you have Francis of Assisi, who affected Bernardine of Siena, who affected St. John of Capistrano, and on and on.

Bernardine wore himself out at age 64. He had just given a fifty day series of Lenten sermons. He had gone back out on the road preaching. He was headed towards Naples. He got as far as Aquila, when he collapsed. He died on the evening of the Ascension, and is buried in Aquila. You have to know that there was a big crowd waiting to welcome him into the Kingdom, with Jesus and His beautiful Mother Mary at the front. Probably somewhere in the back of the line, a short, big-eared, rumpled Friar was smiling. Father Francis was proud of one of his boys.

St. John of Capistrano 1386 - 1456

Enter a young man called John the German, or better known, especially by Californians as San Juan Capistrano, John of Capistrano. He was called John the German because his father was of Germanic background, and although John was Italian, he looked like a German count. His hair was blonde, and thus the nickname, *Capi strano*, which means in Italian, *Head of a Foreigner*.

A brilliant man, he received a degree in law in Perugia, near Assisi, and became Governor of Perugia at the age of 26. His priorities were anything but religious, until he was taken prisoner during a local war between the Perugians and the Malatestas. His story inside prison is much like that of St. Francis, although it took place some 200 years later. He began to consider the values of his life, and upon being released from prison, he embraced the Franciscans.

St. John's life is so exciting! Possibly because he was a late vocation, his novice master treated him brutally. But every time he was mistreated, the Lord gave him the gift of spiritual consolation. As some of his sister saints after him, St. Therese of Lisieux, and St. Bernadette of Lourdes, said, the harsh treatment they received from their Novice Mistresses was a source of Sanctification for them.

He lived a life of physical discipline. He was really very hard on himself. Considering his background, and all the comforts he was accustomed to, he forced himself to live as a pauper. He wore threadbare clothes, shoes with huge holes in them, ate very little, and slept less. But it was this severity which allowed him to put his old life completely behind him, and focus clearly, on what the Lord had for him to do.

He was greatly helped during this time by St. Bernadine of Siena. John became one of his students. Through Bernardine's influence, he developed his passion for the Eucharist, and our Dear Lord Jesus. John worked with St. Bernardine in the reform of the Franciscan Strict Observance Rule. He was his right hand man. Wasting nothing, the Lord used his brilliant mind, and his skills in government, to put the Franciscan Order back into shape. You see how the Lord utilizes everything, wastes nothing?

After he and Bernardine were finished with their mission, he struck out on his own to fight for the conversion of heretics, and to correct the grave errors that were being spread. Keep in mind, they were in the thick of the Renaissance. The enemy was developing strong roots all over. It was almost impossible to keep track of their activities, because they struck from many sides at one time. Does that sound like the New Age movement of today?

John developed a reputation for holiness. Crowds of faithful gathered to hear him wherever he spoke. He had great healing powers. Over the years, he was given uncommon authority by the Vatican to do battle with

Heretics, Schismatics, and those involved with Witchcraft and the Occult. He was very stern in his dealings with enemies of the Church, and was considered an apostle, a prophet. No matter where he went, the faithful flocked to hear him, touch him, ask him to heal their sick. He gave credit for all healings to the intervention of the relics of St. Bernardine, which he carried with him.

Towards the end of his life, the Pope sent John to the areas of Bavaria, Austria, and Poland to defend the faith. A group of heretics led by John Huss, called Hussites, were forerunners of Luther. Among the errors they spread, was a denial of the Real Presence of Jesus in the Eucharist. This heresy had become very strong in the area of Austria and Poland. St. John spent all his time fighting these heretics. As if that was not enough, he also recruited an army to stop the onslaught of the Turks, which was building up. St. John was indirectly involved with the **Miracle of the Eucharist of Langenweise**[11].

The turning point against the Turks was at Belgrade in 1456. The Europeans had prepared for their attack. St. John Capistrano, near death by this time, had finally gathered together his army of men. Armed with an enormous amount of prayer, John and his men, in addition to many other troops, defeated the Turks.

John had been successful, or rather the Lord had been successful through John. But he was completely worn out. Like his role model before him, St. Bernardine, it was time for him to go home, to be with his larger family, in Heaven. After a life of turmoil in the name of Jesus, for the love of Jesus, he died very quietly, very peacefully, the same year the Turks were stopped at Belgrade, 1456. Who would be the one to take John's place? Who would be the next? You can

---

[11]which is covered in our chapter on the Moslems

be sure there were many, and are still many, who are willing to answer the call, *"Here am I, Lord, I come to do Your will."*

St. Philip Neri 1515 - 1595

In Philip's time, the Church was at a low point. Renaissance had taken its toll on the spirituality of most religious in Rome. The Medicis controlled the College of Cardinals. Choice candidates became princes of the land, rather than of the Church. The writings had become extremely secular and pagan. Morals and morale were at an all-time low. Severe abuses were occurring, as a result of giving into the worldliness of Renaissance, and all it stood for. *Everybody knew all about these abuses, but nobody did anything about them.* Is this not happening today? Martin Luther was brewing a kettle of discontent in Germany.

Philip left his home in Florence and came to Rome, based on an inner locution, or mystical experience. He converted from a good young man, interested in the world, and all it had to offer, to a deeply spiritual man, willing to throw caution to the wind, and go without hesitation, wherever the Lord sent him. He spent two years in Rome, in virtual seclusion, giving himself over to prayer, almost completely. Then, he burst forth from his little room to become a brilliant student in philosophy and theology. He worked at a feverish pace in this direction for three years, and then, as compulsively as he had begun, he just *stopped!*

Possibly the reason behind his sudden 180 degree change in direction was the sorry condition of the Church. We have to believe that he had a very special relationship with Our Lord Jesus, because he made radical modifications in his life at a minute's notice. He would never be content with just going through the motions. If he would have been made cardinal, he would be a prince of the *Church*, not a landowner. He felt the call to do something extreme. So, he went out and stood on the street corners of Rome and

**St. Teresa of Avila received the Transverberation of the Heart.
Born in the middle of the Renaissance,
she contradicted Machiavelli, when she said:**
"The greatest good cannot justify the smallest evil."

talked to people. In short, he was answering the call to evangelize Rome.

Something very interesting is that people were really anxious to hear about doing good. Not everyone was caught up in the paganism that had become so prevalent. But they didn't know where to go, or whom to ask, or what to do. They didn't want to join in the permissiveness that was rampant. But they needed someone to say it was all right not to want those things, but to want something of a higher level. Philip gave them that. He had a beautiful personality, and a great sense of humor. It didn't take long before he had them listening to him. Pretty soon, he had them joining him in corporal works of mercy, visiting hospitals, prisons, the elderly and the sick. They realized more gratification and self-worth from this, than from all the Renaissance perversion which was being thrown at them.

He had a mystical experience, which is so very similar to that which *Padre Pio, St. Teresa of Avila* and *St. John of the Cross* had written about. Theirs was called *Transverberation of the Heart*. Padre Pio and St. Teresa of Avila, actually saw an Angel, who pierced their hearts, one with a lance, the other with an arrow. For the rest of their lives, they literally burned with love of Jesus. Both felt a largeness of the heart.

Philip was sleeping at the Catacomb of San Sebastian out on the Appian Way outside Rome, which he did very often. At one point during the night, while he was praying, he saw a globe of fire, which came closer and closer to him. He felt it go through him, into his mouth, down his throat, all throughout his body, finally resting in his heart. The heat burned like an inner glow. He began to convulse in emotion. He was so full of love, he thought he would explode. Every part of his body tingled. He finally had to cry out to the Lord to make it stop.

On a negative side, from that day on, he never knew when he would be overcome with fierce fluttering of the heart, so much so that his whole body would shake. On the positive side, he was so filled with the love of Jesus, he radiated from it. All this took place before he was ordained a priest. He never felt worthy to be a priest; he was finally convinced, however, and was ordained at age 34. He continued his apostolate of speaking to people, and in that way bringing them back to the Church. However, the vehicle he used was the Confessional. He spent hours and hours each day counselling penitents.

He began a practice of having dialogues and interchange with the large group of penitents, who spent long hours at the church, waiting to go to confession. A big room was set up above the church. Followers of the community of Philip Neri would flock there in great numbers to hear these lectures and dialogues.

Now keep in mind, this was during the Renaissance, when there were so many distractions of every kind available down the block, or around the corner. Yet these people would rather be in church, listening to Philip Neri talk about Jesus.

When the congregation was called to prayer in the oratory, a bell was rung to get their attention. Thus began the tradition of the Oratorians, which actually became a community. Fr. Philip Neri was its founder. Some years later, when Philip drew up a modest Rule for a small number of devotees who had become priests, they were called the Oratorians.

His community blossomed; more and more disciples joined. The Pope gave them a run-down church, which they tore apart, and built a new, beautiful facility, from which they could glorify the Lord. However, when it was ready, everybody moved into it except Philip Neri, the superior. He wanted to stay in his secluded living quarters, where he had spent so much of his life, where the Lord had worked so powerfully. *But obedience is the keyword.* It really didn't make much sense for his whole community to headquarter out of this beautiful building, and for him not be with them. So, out of obedience to the Pope, and his community, he finally joined them.

For the last twenty years of his life, he ministered to many people from his room at the church of Santa Maria in Vallicella. A veritable *Who's who* of the Church, and the country, passed through those doors, asking for guidance. It was in this way that he was most successful, and felt most comfortable. It was the same as he had done from the beginning, speaking to one or two in the streets, or one in the confessional. He was able to fight the evils of the Renaissance most powerfully from this intimate vantage point. The royalty of the world and the royalty of the Church came to him for advice, as well as his community.

On May 25, 1595, forty four years and two days after he was ordained, at age eighty, Philip Neri gave his body and soul over to his Lord. He joined the Communion of Saints in Heaven. But here on earth, his work continued vigorously. His followers begat more followers who begat more followers, and on and on, and so the Lord was able to keep His promise to us, "*I will be with you until the end of the world.*" Thank you, Lord, for Philip Neri. Thank you Philip Neri, for saving the Church.

St. Catherine dei Ricci 1522 - 1590

Alexandrina dei Ricci took the name, Catherine as she entered the Dominican Order at age thirteen, influenced by her heroine, St. Catherine of Siena. Catherine was from a noble family of Florence. We have to take a moment here and point out some more of the Lord's sense of humor. Most of these people we're writing about, from this period of the Renaissance, are from Florence, where Renaissance originated. Catherine dei Ricci was from a noble family in Florence; Philip Neri was from Florence; Catherine of Siena was from Siena, while St. Bernardine, born of a noble family, was from Massa Marittima, a suburb of Siena. Siena is about fifty miles from Florence.

The point is that these areas, Florence and Siena, are and have always been extremely worldly, artistic, cultural, knowledgeable. When Renaissance hit, Florence and Siena were the first areas to embrace it. The Medicis, who ruled the Papacy during part of this time, were from Florence, as were the Pitti family, and the Sforzas. And yet, the Lord chose some of His greatest defenders, and fighters from among the people of this area. And if that was not enough, many of them were either from royalty or nobility. God is hilarious, *sometimes.*

Catherine dei Ricci was a very holy girl, but very ill. She was given the gift of turning her afflictions into Redemptive suffering, and used these sufferings to develop virtues, such as unearthly patience, considering the extent of her physical agonies. She is said to have been able to accomplish this virtue by constantly contemplating on the Passion of Christ.

Here, we run into the Holy Cluster of Saints we talked about before. The Lord put Catherine into the path of *St. Philip Neri,* in a very unusual way. They had corresponded about matters of the Faith, but had never actually met. It would have been difficult, because Catherine was cloistered in Florence, and Philip's workplace was Rome. However, she bilocated to Rome, where she appeared to him; they had long conversations. St. Philip verified this, as well as other witnesses, who actually saw the two saints conversing.

In the life of Catherine, we see the Lord fighting the evils of the Renaissance in a completely different, indirect way, through a *suffering servant.* While it's true that her mysticism, her ecstasies and her Stigmata attracted the attention of many, she was basically a cloistered nun. She didn't go out into the world and spread the good news of Jesus. She showed the power of God, as manifested through this one ailing daughter. Through Catherine, the Lord showed another way of life, another set of values, an option to the debasement being offered through the Renaissance. The Lord was telling these people, *"There is another way. You don't have to buy into this lifestyle. Come to Me. I prove to you through My people that you can live a wholesome life, a life close to me, and be happy. Where your treasure lies, there is your God. Make Me your God."*

Catherine was given the gift of the Stigmata, in her hands, feet and side. The Stigmata refers to the wounds, scars, or skin abrasions that appear on the flesh of individuals. They correspond to the wounds suffered by Christ in the Crucifixion. Catherine was given an additional gift, in that she experienced the Crown of Thorns. She actually experienced in a mystical sense, the agonies prior to the Passion of Our Lord Jesus Christ. This began when she was in her early twenties, and continued on until her mid-thirties. It took place every week, and then repeated itself the following week. It was a truly amazing experience. She actually went through the events from Holy Thursday evening at the Agony in the Garden, to the Crucifixion on Good Friday. She was in deep meditation the entire time. The only time she came out of it for a short period was when she received the Eucharist every morning. She regained consciousness, received her Lord, and went right back into the events of the Passion.

This went on faithfully for twelve years. It was witnessed by hundreds, possibly thousands of people. However, looking at it in the light of the commotion it caused, when word got out about it, it became a real cross for the rest of the sisters in the convent. Prayers and penance were offered by all, *including Catherine*, for it to end. Finally, in 1554, as an answer to prayer, it came to an end. A gentle sigh of relief was breathed by all concerned. However, this did not mean, by any stretch of the imagination, that her ecstasies ended. They were just not so dynamic.

Catherine was given a very special gift by Our Lord Jesus, which became a source of conflict, and a major problem in her cause for Beatification. She was given a wedding ring by Our Lord Jesus on Easter Sunday, 1542, the same year that her Passion experience began. He came to her on that morning, brilliant in light, and presented her with a *gleaming ring*. It was an actual gold ring, with a diamond. It was seen in that form by various members of her community, all of whom were very reputable.

Then it was seen by all the other members of the community in a different form. It became what they termed a red lozenge, or quadretto. Catherine never saw it in that way. She always saw the ring. But the rest of these ladies saw the red lozenge at different times during Catherine's life.

Catherine's superior tried to find a way to remove the cause of the problem, which was this red mark on her finger. Catherine was agreeable to any ideas the superior had to remove the mark. But all the time, she insisted she couldn't see any mark on her finger. What she could see was the magnificent ring of gold and diamond that Our Lord Jesus gave her.

She was a very holy lady. The ring, her stigmata, and ecstasies, tended to cast a shadow on what would otherwise have been considered a very holy life. When her cause for Beatification was opened in 1614, most of these sisters were dead. The Devil's Advocate was a very renowned priest, who went on to become Pope Benedict XIV. He was disturbed about what appeared to be confusion, and unrest over the ring. However, the Lord worked through the distraction, and Catherine is a member of the Communion of Saints. Jesus used her in an indirect way to battle the Renaissance. She was a contradiction to the values of the day. She suffered greatly all her life, but she accepted her role as a redemptive sufferer with unusual joy, which was seen by everyone with whom she came in contact. She reacted to the great gifts the Lord gave her, with humility, love and thanksgiving.

†

There are literally hundreds of canonized saints or beatas who lived during the period of the Renaissance. We have just chosen this few to bring you, in order for you to be secure in the knowledge that your God loves you, and is taking care of you. When you look at the problems of today, look at the parallels you saw in this chapter. Don't for a minute take for granted that God is going to make it all go away. But one thing you can count on is a little saying that sits on our prayer room wall. It says simply, *"Lord, there is nothing that will happen to me today, that You and I together, can't handle."*

Pope St. Pius X   *Pope John XXIII*

Pope Paul VI   *Pope John Paul II*

Left:
**Archbishop Sheen said
that, *"Satan's greatest
achievement in this
century is to destroy the
belief in his very
existence."***

Modernism: a Twentieth Century Heresy

We have to believe that as long as we have hot and heavy attacks against our Church, we're doing the right thing, we're on the right path. It's not bad enough that we have all the powers of hell coming at us from outside the Church, we have to have homegrown heretics, apostates, whatever you want to call them, attacking us from within. A hot, burning flame rose from the pit of hell towards the end of the Nineteenth century. It was given the name, *Modernism*, a black heresy of the Twentieth Century, and the first major attack against the Catholic Church by the New Age movement. The flames were fanned by a group of priests, philosophers and critics of the New Testament, who came up with a new way to destroy the Church, from within its ranks. The movement was spearheaded by a French Abbé, Alfred Loisy, and an English Jesuit, George Tyrrell.

The charges against our Church were so outrageous, just to listen to them makes you want to stutter. But there is a truism, here. If you're going to make a noise, make the biggest one you can. If you're going to be a crook, rob the biggest bank. Don't do anything in half measure. That's exactly what these people did. They aimed for the jugular of the Church, Sacred Scripture, and all it represents. They began by denying the four Gospels. They claimed they were manipulative concoctions, designed to coerce the ignorant masses into following a lifestyle, pre-ordained by Church leaders (I guess they're talking about Popes), under threat of eternal damnation into a Hell that also doesn't exist.

Let us say this. If you want to fight an evil, using the truths of our Faith: the words of Jesus and the dogmas set down over the centuries, and your opponent doesn't want to listen, all he has to tell you is that everything, you're basing your beliefs on, is a lie. How do you defend your

convictions, when your *bases*[1] *in fact* are denied?   For
instance, in Math, we have certain truisms, bases on which to
build our blocks. We accept that $2 + 2 = 4$; $5 \times 20 = 100$.
But if someone, whom you're trying to teach, tells you that
all your math formulas are false, how do you convince them
that they're true?

This is what these Modernists did. They attacked the
very foundation of the Church. *They maintained that Jesus
was only a prophet, born of a time, for that time, not the
Second Person of the Trinity, not the Son of God.*   They
denied the Trinity, itself! Remember the philosophy, go for
broke. *They denied that Jesus instituted any Sacraments.* They
insisted, He didn't found our Church. They gave credit to
St. Paul for having begun the Church, as a cult to Jesus. Let
me tell you up front, St. Paul does not want anybody to
believe he started the Church. All you have to do is read his
letters. *Were they discredited, too?* They don't say. But they
do say that the Nicean or Apostle's Creed was an attempt to
force the people to believe in all these lies.

If you're stuttering, just think of how our dear Pope St.
Pius X must have felt. These were his people. He had to
deal with them. He did the only thing he could, under the
circumstances. He wrote a strong encyclical condemning the
heresy, and its adherents. There were sixty-five points, all of
which were condemned. The heretics, Frs. Tyrrell and Loisy,
made a lot of noise, as they refused to accept the Church's
ruling on the Modernist heresy.   They were
excommunicated, and never reconciled with Mother Church.
However, one really good thing came out of it. An anti-
Modernist oath, or Loyalty Oath, was required to be taken
by all Clergy. In it, the clergy had to denounce Modernism,
and all its sixty-five points. The authors of the oath felt
certain it would keep the Modernists out of important posts

---

[1]Plural of basis

in the Church, and thus, for all intents and purposes, kill the heresy. This remained in effect until 1965, when Pope Paul VI did away with the taking of the oath. There are those Modernists, today, who explain away their refusal to pray the Creed, with the excuse, *"if they didn't believe all the things in the Creed, they wouldn't be here at Mass."*

Before 1965, the only way Modernists could get around the oath would be to lie, to commit perjury. Did our dear saintly Pope St. Pius X or his advisors or, for that matter, all the authority in the Church, really believe that a little thing like lying would keep the Modernists out of the Church? This is one area we find so difficult to understand. Were we that naive? Everybody praised the swift actions of Pope St. Pius X in nipping this heresy in the bud, and ridding the Church of it. Didn't they think something was strange when the movement was put down, virtually without a battle? There were even statements made, implying amazement, to the effect that never in the history of the Church had we intoned such a swift death knell to a heresy.

The advocates of Modernism fell into a category, which we have seen down through the ages, but very strongly in this century. The term is *elitist*. They were extremely intelligent and very proud to let you know about their superior intellect. *That aspect, pride, that powerful weapon of Satan's, which first manifested itself in the Garden of Eden, has never been stronger than in this century.* They held high positions in the Church, key, strategic positions which could be very instrumental in the event of a takeover, and very effective tools to pervert the beliefs of the people of God. Now, for a moment, let's just look at some of the words we've just used: *key, position, takeover, effective tools, pervert.* What does that sound like to you? *To me, it smacks of war!* It might very well be the type of war we've fought in the last half of this century, *Guerrilla warfare,* but it's still very much war.

The Modernists did not die; they did not blow away; they went undercover. They were a small, select group. They stayed that way. Their clandestine modus operandi proved to be quite exciting to those "*highly intellectual, chosen ones*" who were recruited to join the now, super secret society. They very smoothly turned a negative into a positive. There was a new in-club in town. It was the Modernists. *Swell!* They took their anti-Modernist oaths whenever they had to and maintained a strong silence. The key word was *inconspicuous*. Now we're sure these enemies of the Church were chomping at the bit to show Satan's hoof of pride, to let the world know what they were doing undercover, to destroy the Church. But they maintained the discipline to keep everything under wraps until the day they could shout to the world what they were doing.

They were so good at being low key, they actually put us into a lull. Well, to give credit where credit is due, most rank and file Catholics had never heard of Modernism. Even those clergy in Church were confused when they first read, *Pascendi dominici*, and *Lamentabili sane*. They didn't know what it was, and now that it was gone, why bother even exploring it. So whatever clamor Modernism brought with it, went away quickly. We went into a period in our Church, which was completely out of character. It was a period of peace, or so we thought. There were no outward signs of any severe heresies on the horizon. Of course, we may have been pre-occupied with World Wars 1 and 2, and the Communist takeover in Eastern Europe. We may have been trying to save our lives. At any rate, for those of us born between 1900 and 1940, we lived in an unreal world in our Church, a world of unity. We thought this is how the Church had always been, and always would be. We became victims of the strange events emanating from Vatican II down to today, and we didn't know what to make of it. Then a priest told us that we were the exception rather than the rule. The

Church had always been in turmoil. Our forty years, which is like a teardrop in the ocean, was a contradiction to what has always been, and will continue to be. We were in limbo.

But we're not sure that's exactly what happened. Too much of what first came down the pike after Vatican II, came too quickly. It was only one or two years after the Council, and we were breaking Rosaries and throwing them down the aisles of Churches. Statues of Our Lord Jesus, Our Lady, the Angels and Saints were discarded which by the way, if you've forgotten, is a heresy called *Iconoclasm*. This was caused by Modernists who were building and planning, building and planning. Had they been dormant, waiting for the moment when they could strike, or had they *already* sewn seeds of dissatisfaction? Were the negative events which took place after Vatican II a culmination of all the work the Modernists had been doing for decades before?

It could be a coincidence, although we don't believe in coincidences, but the year the Modernists came out of hiding and started to flex their muscles, 1962, is the same year the Scottish community of Findhorn was founded. Findhorn is the Vatican city of the New Age Movement. It was founded to help anchor "The Plan" on earth, *the Plan being the universal takeover by the New Age Movement.*[2]

You see references to New Age sprinkled throughout this book. There's a reason for that. You would have to be blind not to see the influence Satan has had over the centuries, using the principles we see manifested in what is called today, the New Age Movement. There are good people who would like us to believe that there is nothing about New Age that is conspiratory. We can't see that. We see, big and bold, a plan which has been executed at various times in the history of our world and our church. It has always been somewhat successful, because we've lost souls,

---

[2]*Hidden Dangers of the Rainbow* - Constance Cumbey Pg 51

and if you consider losing one soul as serious, we have to admit the plan is working.

The Church fights back!

However, as we have said and said and said, *God is in charge*. He is always in charge. Don't take Him for granted; but don't ever get the idea you're alone down here. The Holy Spirit worked powerfully through the Ecumenical Council, or Vatican II. It's very possible that the Ecumenical Council, initiated by Pope John XXIII was something he had worked on for years, but if that's so, he kept it a big secret. We know he must have had a reason not to announce it from St. Peter's Basilica, or at one of his great General Audiences, or at a Mass at St. John Lateran, the Cathedral of Rome. He had to have had a purpose, or did the Holy Spirit have a purpose, to choose the Feast day of St. Paul's Conversion, January 25, 1959, for the Pope to make this momentous announcement, from the Basilica of St. Paul outside the Walls. He attributed it to a sudden inspiration from the Holy Spirit, and we believe that's what it was!

When he made the announcement, he didn't immediately give his reasoning for the decision. After having made the statement, it appeared, he was somewhat indefinite as to what his goals were. It wasn't until later that he stated, he was looking towards a *New Pentecost*, a means of regeneration for the Church. We still remember his opening wide the windows of the Church, to let the Holy Spirit fly in. If you add to this, the fact that it took everyone by surprise, that he was not able to arouse a great deal of enthusiasm from the curia right away, you know this was not man's work. This gift of insight was given to the Pope alone.

Pope John XXIII was well known for his somewhat impulsive methods. We believe that he knew much more than he shared about the immediate threat to the Church from the Modernists who were working feverishly underground. We believe that, because he enlisted the greatest powers in existence to aid him with Vatican II.

On October 4, 1962, just one week before the opening of the Ecumenical Council, he took a trip to the Santa Casa, the Holy House of Nazareth, in Loreto, Italy. He camouflaged it as a pilgrimage to Loreto and Assisi, for the feast of St. Francis. But if you look at his schedule for 1959 through 1962[3], you will see very little traveling outside the Vatican. Remember, he was preparing one of the most monumental historical events, the Church had ever known. He knew the seriousness of what was about to take place. He could not allow himself the luxury of leaving Rome. Yet, the week before the Council was to begin, he went off to Loreto. Don't kid yourself. He knew what he was doing. He was recruiting aid from the Queen of the Angels.

He celebrated Mass in the little house where the Angel Gabriel had announced to Mary that she would be the Mother of God. At this time, he consecrated the Ecumenical Council to her Son, under her protection. Part of the prayer he said to her is as follows:

"O Mary, O Mary, Mother of Jesus and our Mother too, we have come here this morning to pray to you as the first star above the Council that is about to be held, as the light that shines propitiously upon our way as we proceed trustfully towards the great ecumenical gathering which the whole world awaits.

"In almost sixty years of priesthood every step of ours on the ways of obedience has been marked by your protection, and we have never asked anything else of you but the obtaining from your divine Son of the grace of a holy and sanctifying priesthood.

---

[3]Journal of a Soul - Angelo Roncalli - Chronology

"Even the summoning of the Council came about, as you know, O Mother, in obedience to a plan that seemed to us truly to correspond to the will of the Lord.

"Today, once more, and in the name of the entire episcopate, we beg you, most sweet Mother whom we hail as Help of Bishops, for ourself, the Bishop of Rome, and for all the Bishops in the world, to obtain for us the grace that will enable us to enter the Council chamber of the basilica of St. Peter's as the apostles and first disciples of Jesus entered the room of the Last Supper; one single heart, one single throb of love for Christ and men, one single intention to live and sacrifice ourselves for the salvation of individuals and peoples.

"So, in future years and centuries, may it be said that through your motherly intercession the grace of God prepared, accompanied and crowned the work of the Twenty-first Ecumenical Council, imparting to all the children of the Holy Church new fervor, generosity, and firmness of intention."[4]

One week later, to the day, October 11, 1962, Pope John XXIII opened the Second Ecumenical Council, with this prayer:

"Almighty God, in Thee, distrusting our own strength, we place all our trust. Look kindly upon these pastors of Your Church. May the light of Your supernatural grace be with us as we deliberate, and as we draw up its laws; and be pleased to grant the prayers we utter with one faith, one voice and one mind.

"O Mary, Help of Christians, Help of Bishops, whose love we have recently experienced in a special way in your church at Loreto, where it pleased you to cause the mystery of the Incarnation to be venerated, bring everything, by your aid, to a joyful, favorable and successful conclusion. With St. Joseph your spouse, with the holy apostles Peter and Paul, with St.

---

[4]Journal of a Soul - Angelo Roncalli - Pg 400

John the Baptist and St. John the Evangelist, pray to the Lord our God for us.

"To Jesus Christ, our most loving Redeemer, the eternal King of all peoples and all ages, be love, power and glory for ever and ever. Amen."[5]

We believe that despite the barrage of attacks on Vatican II, Our Lady and Our Lord Jesus were there, guiding and protecting the Pope and his bishops. It is a *dogma of the Church* that the Holy Spirit surrounds a Council from making any kind of formal error. The Lord may allow us to go through our paces, but He will always be there, until the end of time.

The Battle rages

If we were to go through the documents of Vatican II and read what they actually said concerning various aspects of the Faith; if we would then compare *them* with what the Modernists brought to the laity of the Church, and what was subsequently put into practice, we would swear that the two had nothing to do with each other. It's like when we read what our Pope John Paul II is supposed to have said, in one Catholic newspaper, and then read the *direct translation* in the *L'Osservatore Romano*, or some other traditional Catholic source, you would vow you were reading two different speeches by two different people. And so it went with Vatican II.

Just to take some random quotes from the documents:

† *"Popular devotions of the Christian people, provided they conform to the laws and norms of the Church, are to be highly recommended."* (Sec. 13)

† *"Regulation of the sacred liturgy depends solely on the authority of the Church, that is, on the Apostolic See, and as*

---

[5]Journal of a Soul - Angelo Roncalli - Pg 401

laws may determine, on the bishops[6]....Therefore no other person, not even a priest, may add, remove, change anything in the liturgy on his own authority." (Sec. 22)

† "Catechesis must impress upon the minds of the faithful the distinctive character of penance as a detestation of sin because it is an offense against God." (Sec. 109)[7]

It's the most amazing thing we've ever read. As you can see, the documents are 180 degrees from what actually was practiced as a result of Vatican II. It was as if the Modernists were on the mark, ready to run their hearts out, when they were given the whistle by the powers that be. It took years before the actual message of Vatican II found its way into the churches. We praise God, our Pope consecrated this Council to our Lady's protection and guidance. Only such a perfect, loving mother could turn around her children's errors, and make the Council work to glorify God, which was its original intent.

The Battle Lines are Drawn

In these last thirty years, all masks have been removed, all cloaks have been taken off. The only thing they won't accept is if you call them *Modernists*. Quote anything they say, which is party-line Modernist, and it's no problem. In fact, they love to give newspaper and television interviews where they use shock value to attack the church. They play the game, but don't dare give them the name. We're trying to come up with a few words that would accurately describe this behavior. *Pride* is way up there. My mother used to love the word Gall, which also translates into *Arrogance, Audacity,* or *Insolence*. Who do they think they are? Why do we, the

---

[6]In union with the Pope - Not part of the quote, but our bishops get their authority from their union with the Pope.

[7]Quotations taken from Battle for Vatican II - Richard Cowden-Guido Page 30-31. Most quotations in this chapter have been taken from Battle for Vatican II, with appreciation to Richard Cowden-Guido, and Jeffrey Mirus of Trinity Communications for permission.

Church, allow them to preach their venom, while wearing Roman collars, using the title of Father? We're not going to make judgments on any of them, in particular. We just want to pass on some quotes, and allow you to come to your own conclusions.

Fr. Hans Kueng - Openly denies the Divinity of Christ:

"While Christians have the obligation to abandon all belief in Christ's physical resurrection, they should nonetheless 'hope that Jesus is somehow with God and therefore that life has an ultimate meaning.'"

"I do not wish to engage in cheap polemics against persons, but "Ratzinger[8] is...just like Fyodor Doestoevski's Grand Inquisitor..."

"...medieval usages and conceptions again recommended by Ratzinger as essentially Catholic...include not only indulgences, Rosary, Corpus Christi processions and celibacy, but also the exaltation of Mary."

Fr. Edward Schillebeeckx - A dissident priest who has devoted himself since Vatican Council II to attacking the Divinity of Christ, and whose police record in Holland for public nudity and exposure was revealed in the *National Catholic Reporter, January 10, 1986.*

"Even if Jesus' body could not be found after He died, that fact 'had merely a negative effect: it did not lead to triumphant hope in resurrection, but to confusion and sorrow.'"

On June 13, 1984, Cardinal Ratzinger wrote to Fr. Schillebeeckx, insisting he disavow an argument in his book, *Ministry of the Church,* which stated that an ordained priest was not necessary in every situation to celebrate the Mass!

---

[8]Cardinal Joseph Ratzinger, head of the Sacred Congregation for the Faith

Karl Rahner - This priest fashions himself high above the peasants, the 850,000,000 Catholics. He considers them with disdain[9].

He is against prayer. He claims there is no afterlife. He is the one who initially promoted the *cosmic Christ* - "*In death one does not leave the material world but enters more deeply into it and becomes what he calls an 'all-cosmic', somehow present to and in communication with all material reality, an 'open system' towards the world and a real ontological influence on the whole of the universe.*" Now I have no problem telling you that I don't understand a word I just wrote. But that's only to let you know that you're okay; there's nothing wrong with you. Moreover, Jesus never looked down on us with disdain. He came to us as a humble preacher who did not talk above the heads of His people. He spoke straight, simply, using things and circumstances they could relate to. Was this so called priest proposing a form *of reincarnation*?

The Catholic Television Network of America, which is a satellite broadcasting network under the direct control of the Bishops of the United States, chose in 1984 to sponsor a series of Lenten television interview programs wherein such gentlemen as Fr. Hans Kueng[10] and Fr. Edward Shillebeeckx explained their "*faith experiences*" and views about the impact of Christian spirituality on contemporary life.

Thomas Sheehan - Book Reviewer - New York Times

As part of a book review on Hans Kueng's book, "*Eternal Life*", Sheehan wrote: "*Jesus performed no real miracles, instituted no sacraments, ordained no priests, and*

---

[9]All quotations on Hans Kueng, Edward Schillebeeckx, and Karl Rahner are from Battle for Vatican II - Richard Cowden-Guido

[10]This, after Fr. Hans Kueng's work was condemned by the Congregation for the Doctrine of the Faith on December 15, 1979. In addition, it was determined by German Bishops that he was not qualified to teach Catholic theology.

consecrated no bishops, since 'he did not know he was supposed to establish the Holy Roman Catholic and Apostolic Church with St. Peter as the first in a long line of infallible popes. '"

"New Testament exegetes[11] argue that the authors of the Gospels used...apocalyptic tropes[12] not to describe historical events but to express in imaginative and symbolic language their belief that Jesus was somehow alive with God and would someday reappear."

"A growing body of Catholic exegetes think the gospel stories of the empty tomb originated in a cult legend."

"Virtually all modern theologians agree that the Resurrection is a hermeneutical[13] symbol rather than a historical event."

In reviewing Hans Kueng's book "Eternal Life", Sheehan opens with "The dismantling of traditional Roman Catholic theology is by now a fait accompli[14]."

One of the most amazing things about all of these people, and many more we haven't mentioned, mostly all priests, is how much they actually *hate* our Lady. That really has to say something. It's not just apathy, or indifference. It's downright hostility! How could anyone hate our Lady? What has she ever done to anyone, other than love them, that would cause them to hate her? But then, how can you hate Jesus? These people hate Him with the same passion as their heretic brothers and sisters down through the centuries. They try to destroy Him by belittling who He is, what He's done, the sacrifices He's made for us.

John Fowler, a former managing editor of the *Catholic Eye*, said of his college education:

---

[11]Biblical Scholars

[12]figures of speech used in the Medieval Church

[13]The science of interpretation, esp. the study of the principals of Biblical Exegesis (critical interpretation of the Bible)

[14]accomplished fact

"At Catholic colleges, with few exceptions, traditional Catholic values are not only being ignored, but also attacked. This was the last thing I expected from a Catholic education when I decided to attend my now alma-mater, the Jesuit College of Holy Cross in Worcester, Mass.....

"....My professors, priests included, followed the now-patented solution: they took a "neutral" position towards Catholicism in their classroom lectures....many teachers showed that they were not so much 'neutral' towards the faith as prejudiced against it; a prejudice which held Catholicism to be more harmful than meaningless.

"On the other hand, the Religious Studies department did deal passionately with Catholicism", though "courses on Church Fathers or Church History were rarely taught, never mind stressed. Instead I was....encouraged to venerate....Kueng, Schillebeeckx, Rahner, Teilhard, Father Drinan and the Berrigans. I learned little about Catholic History, dogma, original sin (or any other kind of sin)....Nor about the early Church Councils, Augustine, Aquinas, Pascal, Dante, the Church Fathers, the Saints, Xavier or Chesterton....Incredibly, a student could graduate from Holy Cross without ever having heard most of them mentioned, never mind knowing or reading about them.

"To receive an education at Holy Cross...meant being unfamiliar with Catholic doctrine or theology, being told to recognize Catholic traditions as meaningless and superstitious, being taught the dark incidents of Church history, true or alleged, and being cut off from the moorings of 2,000 years of Catholic history and culture[15]."

What we have just read brings tears to our eyes. That is possibly the saddest thing we have ever heard. What have we allowed to happen to our Catholic institutions? Where can you go to receive a solid Catholic education? Why are

---

[15]Battle for Vatican II - Richard Cowden-Guido Pg 94-95

we amazed when our young people graduate .
institutions and know nothing about our Faith, o.
have a twisted, distorted image of what Catholicism i.

In the mid-70's in our part of the country, we
exposed to more young people who had graduated from u.
Jesuit university in our state, who were atheists, or agnostics,
or just turned off to the Church. It seemed like everyone,
who was churned out of one of these schools, was completely
against the Church. Well, if what we read above is indicative
of what is being taught, no wonder they're coming out as
anti-Catholic. Your money and mine are supporting these
institutions. They in turn are attempting to destroy our Faith
through our young people.

What hurts tremendously is when we see the word *Jesuit*
before any of these names. We have always had such great
respect for the Jesuits. Ignatius of Loyola, father of the
Jesuits, has been a hero of ours for years. We have some
very close friends who are Jesuits, whom we believe to be
solid, well balanced priests. And yet, we hear about *this*
Jesuit school, *that* Jesuit theologian, and it devastates us.
We know that St. Ignatius would turn over in his grave, but
the question is, *would anyone care?*

The Church Fights Back!

We don't like to bring you negatives. This chapter hurts
a lot because these are our own, our priests who are
attacking us. Again, they're not trying to destroy the
organization of the church, only the Body of Christ. They
would like to eliminate our Pope, and then dust off his chair,
try on his robes, maybe make an adjustment in the tailoring,
look around at the marvelous, well-oiled organization they
have stolen, and go on with business as usual. But as you
know, that's not going to happen.

"You are Rock, and upon this Rock I will build my Church, and the gates of Hell will not prevail against it." (Mt. 16:18)

And so what does the Church do in times of trouble. The Church fights back. How does it fight back? We go back to the introduction of this book.

In times of Crisis, God sends us special grace. This grace may come from Eucharistic Miracles, Apparitions by Our Lady, and Saints and other Powerful Men and Women in the Church. It may come in the form of Angelic intercession. It will come from anywhere the Lord deems necessary. The only thing we have to be assured of is, it will come. He will use whatever or whoever it takes, whenever it is needed, in order to protect us from anything or anyone, who would bring us anywhere near the brink of hell. Very often, even if it means protecting us from ourselves.

We want to share with you some special people the Lord has given us. With the exception of Padre Pio, they are still alive, and so we can't give them a lot of praise, because they get upset with us. But when the Lord gives us a gift, we have to glorify Him in that gift, we have to praise His Holy Name, or He will not continue to give us the gifts. So here we go.

Padre Pio of Pietrelcina

We wrote of Padre Pio in our book, *Saints and Other Powerful Men in the Church.* At one point, we stated:

"To many of Padre Pio's adversaries, he was a throwback to the Middle Ages. Everything that he represented was pulling us back to where we came from, rather than bringing us into the modern age of Science and Technology, this Twentieth Century. Perhaps that's true. Very possibly, we've high-teched ourselves right out of the Kingdom. Padre Pio represented back to basics, to those values which made our Church and our world, grand. He fought all his life to preserve the beliefs of Our Lord Jesus, the Apostles, and the early Fathers of the Church.

"Could Padre Pio see into the future? Was he aware of what the world was becoming during his lifetime, and would deteriorate into after his death? Did he sacrifice his 81 years of life, being physically as well as spiritually tortured by the fallen angels of Satan, so that the common man, the simple believer, would have something to hold onto? Did he allow himself to be a crucified Christ to give us strength?

"We'll probably never know the extent of sacrifice that Padre Pio made for us during our lifetime. We may not even understand it in what time is left of this world of ours. Perhaps he was a Twentieth century Don Quixote, the Man of La Mancha, who wanted nothing more than to save the world, and was willing to sacrifice himself in the process. Doesn't that sound a lot like Jesus? We believe the Lord gave Padre Pio the *impossible* dream, that Padre Pio *held onto* that dream, *fought* for that dream, and *died* for that dream. Did he live in vain? Were his 81 years of agony for nothing? That, my brothers and sisters, depends entirely on us."[16]

If you were to ask any of the Modernists, what they thought of Padre Pio, they would rear back like a vampire who sees a Crucifix. They may even hiss. This is an exaggeration, of course. But you must realize Padre Pio reminded them of the very things they wanted to bury. He was representative of a time of holiness, of obedience, of love and fervor for Our Lord Jesus, our Mother Mary, and all the Angels and Saints. *His crime, as far as they were concerned, was that he brought these things into the Twentieth Century. They didn't belong here. They weren't cosmic; they were medieval! They belonged in the time of St. Francis and St. Anthony. What were they doing here? It's not part of the plan!*

---

[16]Saints and Other Powerful Men in the Church - Pg 493-4

Padre Pio was a suffering servant, a reminder of what Our Lord Jesus went through for us, and for those who hate Him. Padre Pio will be standing there, arms outstretched, vulnerable, a sign and a symbol, until the end of time.

John Cardinal O'Connor - Archbishop of New York

Cardinal O'Connor is a fighter, a man who doesn't back down from a good brawl. He is the Pope's hand-picked representative for a difficult area of the United States, in a time of turmoil. We will not go into a biography of Cardinal O'Connor. We will just share how he attacked his job as Archbishop of New York with a fervor, a zest, that was completely against what his fellow bishops were advocating.

When the bishops of the United States convene in the National Catholic Conference of Bishops, they try to be as much in agreement with each other as possible. And while it's good to present a united front for the world, when falling in line with the rest might mean waiving your principles, you have to come to a screeching halt.

Such was the case with Archbishop O'Connor. He had just been appointed Archbishop of New York, but hadn't taken over the See, yet. It was 1984, the year of Mondale, pro-choice, and Geraldine Ferraro, the first female candidate for Vice President in the history of the United States. She proved herself to be Catholic in name only, changing her loyalties at the slightest opposition. Add to that Mario Cuomo, an Italian-Catholic governor, and a most outspoken pro-choice advocate. This is what *big John O'Connor* walked into. But he was up to it.

Cardinal Bernardin had made a speech as the new head of the Bishops' committee for Pro-choice activities. He enraged many, when he suggested that pro-lifers were not as concerned over other social justice issues. The New York Times, which is the most *anti-Catholic* and pro-Modernist newspaper in the United States, gave it front page coverage.

Archbishop O'Connor came into New York from Scranton, Pennsylvania, where he was still Bishop, and together with Archbishop Law of Boston, bore down on the Bernardin stand, without actually throwing any punches at the Cardinal Archbishop of Chicago, until the issue was completely dead. Archbishop O'Connor received quite a bit of flack from the NCCB[17], not necessarily because he was defending the pro-life people, whom Bernardin was supposed to be pasturing, but because he didn't stand in line with the rest of the bishops.

We know Pope John Paul II knew what he was doing when he appointed John O'Connor to the post of Archbishop of New York, but we don't know if the rest of the church in the United States was ready for him, at least not the city and state of New York. Archbishop O'Connor has been at the center of every controversy which attacks our Church. He balks at nothing, not even taking on, and threatening excommunication to the Governor of New York. As with so many of our martyrs, dry and wet, should you ever stand trial for being Christian, Archbishop John O'Connor, the verdict would be overwhelmingly guilty! John Cardinal O'Connor, you are a true defender of the faith.

Bernard Cardinal Law - Archbishop of Boston

Our Lord Jesus placed another powerhouse in one of the most Catholic communities in the United States, Boston. However, it has been bombarded by all the elements of hell, including abortion, Modernism, New Age, permissiveness and the like. After his appointment on March 23, 1984, just four days after Archbishop O'Connor had been installed in New York, he immediately let the people, the press, and his fellow bishops know exactly where he stood. In August, 1984, he told the Knights of Columbus, "*The right to life is not*

---

[17]National Council Catholic Bishops

a 'one issue' tenet of our institutions. It is the issue - primarily and predominant."

At the beginning of the Bishops' Conference, in 1985, everybody seemed to be feeling everybody else out. No one wanted to make any definite statements until they had some idea of what the climate was going to be. Cardinal Law let them know right up front who he was, and where he stood. On the evening of the second day, he got up, and spoke *in Latin.* He cut to the heart of why Pope John Paul II had called this synod:

"Ideas have consequences....today there are negative consequences flowing from a secularization of the Church's teaching and mission. We must attend to our responsibilities as doctors and masters of the Faith.

"Very often there is open dissent, even in theological faculties at Catholic universities. I understand the difference in linking the theologians and the magisterium, but the difficulty cannot justify open dissent....I propose a Commission of Cardinals to prepare a draft of a Conciliar Catechism to be promulgated by the Holy Father after consulting the bishops of the world. [18]*"*

It was definitely Holy Spirit, but it was almost uncanny. It's as if he shot an arrow into the proceedings, and while we're not suggesting that this proposal became the focus of the Synod, it was picked up by the bishops and journalists as a strong topic for discussion throughout the Synod.

Karol Wojtyla - Pope John Paul II

Here is another, no, possibly the *best* example of a man, chomping at the bit to restore the traditions of the Church, and protect her against all her enemies. Karol Wojtyla is the man for all seasons, our true Vicar and *"Sweet Christ on earth* [19]*"*. Like Jesus before him, he has always had a humility,

---

[18]Battle for Vatican II - Richard Cowden-Guido
[19]St. Catherine of Siena

a shining love that has touched not only members of the Church, but people of all religions and all nations on earth. He is the future Saint that Jesus has raised up for this day and this time, with the Church in this crisis.   When he became Pope, he was immediately able to win over the people of the world, not only Catholic and Christian, but by and large, *everybody.* He used everything the Lord and Our Lady had given him, and armed with his shield of "*Totus Tuus*[20]", he went out to do battle with the enemy.

The first challenge, he accepted was from the Liberation Theologians, and secular humanists in Mexico. He knew the people revered Our Lady under her title of Our Lady of Guadalupe. This devotion kept the country out of civil war on more than one occasion. Pope John Paul II went to Mexico, and *the people went wild.* While he was attempting to turn the tide of *Modernism* which had found its way into the Mexican Clergy, he was also giving a message to the world, *loud and clear,* that he was a power to be reckoned with, not just in the local church, or the church of Rome, but in the worldwide arena.

He went after Poland, supporting Solidarity there, pushing and pushing to get human rights recognized by the government. There are those, especially in the former Soviet Union, who will swear that John Paul II was a major factor in the fall of Communism.   That belief is widespread. Testimony has been unearthed from a KGB defector that a plot was formulated to assassinate the Pope after the first attempt was bungled. Obviously, it never succeeded. Praise God! Thank you Mother Mary.

He took on the mass exodus of priests from their vows. During the 60's and 70's, thousands upon thousands left the priesthood and were given dispensations.   John Paul II turned off the faucet on dispensations. He sympathized with

---

[20]All yours

his priests who have, all of a sudden, after two thousand years of faithfulness to the priesthood of their brothers before them, felt it impossible to keep their commitment to Christ.   But compassionately, in a letter to the clergy, he stated, "...*the priesthood cannot be renounced because of the difficulties that we meet and the sacrifices asked of us.   Like the Apostles, we have left everything to follow Christ; therefore we must persevere beside Him also through the Cross."*

He had barreled through the enemies of the Church like a bull in a china shop. He never let up, even in the debilitating period after his assassination attempt on May 13, 1981.   He was constantly in a mode of check and countercheck.   An example of that took place in August, 1981, when Pope John Paul II took over the Jesuit order. The head of the Jesuit order died suddenly, and the normal chain of events would have been to replace him, at least temporarily, with an American Modernist. Pope John Paul, still very weak from his wounds, actually took command of the Jesuit Order, became its head, until a proper chapter meeting could take place. He effectively blocked the strong Modernist movement which has run rampant in the Jesuit order, at least temporarily.

The previous year, 1980, he removed Archbishop Jean Jadot as Apostolic Nuncio in the United States. Nothing has ever been said about the Archbishop or his loyalties, but during his tenure in the United States, Modernism flourished in every area of the Episcopate, from seminaries to Diocesan headquarters.   After his replacement by Archbishop Pio Laghi, a very liberal Catholic magazine, *the Catholic Reporter,* said what many people were thinking. "*U.S. Catholics owe him (*Jadot*) much; more than any other person, he shaped the face of today's US Episcopate."*   As we know, the U.S. Episcopate was in a sorry state in 1980.

Pope John Paul II just keeps going. He reminds us of this great leader, wearing a silver coat of armor, charging on a white charger, gleaming sword in the air, cutting down every enemy who gets in his way. His shield is his dedication to Mary, "*Totus Tuus*". The Lord gave him, early in his ministry, a strong right hand man, Cardinal Ratzinger. He is unquestionably "*The Pope's Man*". A great indicator of this is how much he is hated by the enemies of the Church. We're reminded of the Scripture passage, "*If you find that the world hates you, know it has hated me before you. If you belonged to the world, it would love you as its own; the reason it hates you is that you do not belong to the world.*" (John 15:18-19)

Mother Angelica - A voice crying out in the desert

In a time, when our women *religious* and women as a whole are complaining they are not allowed to play a meaningful role in the Church, and in the world, a cloistered nun, a Poor Clare, so like her baptismal name Rita, is standing up and being counted. She is making the news, not with disobedience and defiance of the Pope and the Church, like many of her fellow religious, but with her eyes on Jesus, obedient to Him, His Vicar, and His Church, even to death on the Cross. She, like our dear Pope John Paul II will not sell out Jesus and His Church, not even for her apostolate. Always ready to stand up for the Church, no matter what the price, what the threat, she forges ahead and tells her *family* what is really happening, what is the true teaching of the Church, the orthodox teaching of the Magisterium.

As there are those who would dare call our Pope "*that old man, that old Rip Van Winkle who has been asleep these last twenty years*", so there are those (sometimes the same ones), who say "*we're going to put that nun back where she belongs in the cloister*". What they do not know, because they have eyes but do not see, and ears but do not hear, is that she is in the Cloister. Her charism is not television but the perpetual adoration of her Spouse and Savior, our Lord Jesus. And He is the one Who is the Head of Eternal Word

Television Network, the only true Catholic voice, the John the Baptist of the Nineties.

Our St. Paul of the Twentieth and soon the Twenty-first Century is spreading the Word to the four corners of the world *fast*, with the means the Lord has given her (television and short wave radio) to combat the enemy who is racing against the clock to take as many poor innocent souls into hell with him.

It's Not Over till it's over

Major attacks on the Church continue to take place. In 1984, every tenet of our institution was being torn asunder. Pope John Paul II was able to feel the pulse of what was going on. The Modernists were so out of the closet, it was ridiculous. When they have a podium like the New York Times to espouse the entire Modernist philosophy, it's time to make a move. A particular attack by Thomas Sheehan: *"the folk religion of most practicing Catholics still lives on the pre-revolutionary fare that generally is served up from their local pulpits and especially from the one currently occupied by the conservative Pope John Paul II."*

We said at the beginning of this chapter, as well as at the beginning of the book, "*In times of Crisis, God sends us special grace. This grace may come from Eucharistic Miracles, Apparitions by Our Lady, and Saints and other Powerful Men and Women in the Church.*" They're here. We had Fulton J. Sheen; we have Fr. Harold Cohen, Fr. Ken Roberts, Mother Teresa, Mother Angelica, Sister Briege McKenna. It goes on and on. *We have you; we have us!* We can't get the job done without us. Archbishop Sheen said "*Don't worry about the Church. The laity will save it.*"[21] That's all well and good if we do it. It's a real warm fuzzy. *But we have to do it, and we have to do it now!*

---

[21]Paraphrasing a quotation of Archbishop Sheen, made to Fr. Shamon, while Archbishop of Rochester, NY

New Age:
Through a Shattered Mirror

We are created in the Image and Likeness of God. Before the fall, our world was meant to be a Garden of Eden. After our redemption by Jesus, it was supposed to be a New Jerusalem. However, Satan, the master of deceit and perversion, takes the beauty, the Lord visualized for us, the life and the world He would have for us, and reworks it, but masks the change so that what we see is just the slightest, deformed resemblance of God's vision for His children. We call that twisted image, *New Age*.

We look at the New Age philosophy, and see Christianity through a shattered mirror, a warped parallel universe, much like Alice in Wonderland's topsy-turvy world. If you examine any aspect of Christianity through the misshapen image of a shattered mirror, you will find things that are remotely recognizable, but everything looks alien, unfamiliar, bizarre, as if it were twisted out of proportion. That is part of what New Age is. You keep saying to yourself, "*It's almost like what we believe in.*[1]" For instance, we believe in God; they believe in "Ascended Masters". We believe in Angels; they believe in spirit guides. We believe in

---

[1]We'd like you to do an exercise. Put the index fingers of both hands together. Extend your arms all the way out in front of you. The line is straight. Now take those two fingers; put them together, and then turn both fingers just a hair outward. Now follow the line the fingers make, moving your hands out to the end of your arm. You will see that you are at a triangle. That *slight* deviation from the straight line, that *almost*, is the same as the pathway to Hell.

Resurrection; they believe in Reincarnation. We believe in being born again of the Holy Spirit; they believe in the law of Rebirth[2]. But then, we believe the snake is a symbol of satan; they believe the snake is godlike. We believe 666 is demonic; they believe 666 is a religious symbol. We believe man is created in the Image of God; they believe man created God in his own image. We're not sure which man, and which image at this point, but you can be sure they'll tell us[3]. It's a distortion of the truth; it's almost like... a parallel world.

New Age claims that every two thousand years, we enter into a *new age*, ergo the name, New Age. The two thousand year period before Jesus, that of the Old Testament, is referred to as the *Age of the Bull*. These last two thousand years are called *The Age of Pisces*. According to the New Age philosophy, we will enter into the *Age of Aquarius* in 1997. They claim that each new age brings with it, a new Messiah. Jesus was the Messiah of the Age of Pisces. The New Age Messiah is called Lord Maitreya. According to New Agers, Jesus is history; Maitreya is in.[4]

We *Christians maintain* we are not going into a new age, but into the end times, and the New Age Movement is Satan's last, most desperate and deadliest attack on the Church. It is a systematic subtle seduction of God's people, designed to confuse the average person, and at the same time, appeal to the pride factor of the pseudo[5]-intellectual.

"Make no mistake about it. The New Age Movement is a religion, complete with its own bibles, prayers and mantras,

---

[2] One is conditioned to believe that all wisdom is contained within oneself

[3] George Orwell, *a New Ager* (Constance Cumbey in her book-Hidden Dangers of the Rainbow), said in his book, Animal Farm, "*All animals are created equal, but some animals are more equal than others.*"

[4] This is the philosophy of the New Age Movement. It is not by any means our philosophy.

[5] pseudo - sham, false, deceptive

Vatican City/Jerusalem equivalents, priests and gurus, born-again experiences (they call it 'rebirthing'), spiritual laws and commandments, psychics and 'prophets', and nearly every other indicia of religion."[6]

One major contradiction of New Age is that it's not new at all.   New Age, in its most basic form, *(Pantheism and Pride)* goes back to the Garden of Eden, when it was used by Satan to tempt Eve into eating the forbidden fruit in Genesis 3:1-6.

"The serpent was the most subtle of all the wild beasts that Yahweh God had made. It asked the woman, 'Did God really say you were not to eat from any of the trees in the garden?' The woman answered the serpent, 'We may eat the fruit of the trees in the garden. But of the fruit of the tree in the middle of the garden, God said, 'You must not eat it, nor touch it, under pain of death.' Then the serpent said to the woman, 'No! You will not die! God knows in fact that on the day you eat it **your eyes will be opened and you will be like gods**[7], *knowing good and evil."'*

Pride has been Satan's most effective weapon against man since the beginning of time. It is so insidious; it works so well. He used pride on Eve. *Eve ate the fruit; the rest is history!* Pride is also one of Satan's major hooks in reeling in victims to the New Age Movement. Expressions like *"You are superior; you are enlightened; you are one of the specially chosen"*, and *"It's not for everyone, only the intellectual few"* are among the catch phrases commonly used when reeling in people *(fish)* into the movement.

Now, knowing what we do about Satan, Lucifer, Beelzebub, the snake, call him what you like, do you really think he wanted Adam and Eve to eat the fruit of the forbidden tree because he liked them? Do you think he

---

[6]*The Hidden Dangers of the Rainbow* - Constance Cumbey, P. 40
[7]*"You will be like gods"* - Pantheism

wanted to be best friends with them[8]? Do you think he wanted them to be gods? Not really. The most likely scenario is that he fully intended to drag them down into the bowels of hell. He wanted to show God up, *(pride)* to prove that he was better than God *(envy)*.

New Age appeals to all the seven deadly sins. At a glance, it would seem that these seven capital sins, *Pride, Covetousness, Lust, Anger, Gluttony, Envy, and Sloth,* would constitute a New Age manifesto, much as the Ten Commandments comprises our rules of Judeo-christian behavior. In addition to pride, which is how it hooks its disciples initially, there is also *envy.* Envy is a major tool of New Age groups.

New Age has taken so many forms over the centuries, the list is endless: Hinduism, Buddhism and Confucianism. From the end of the Middle Ages to the French Revolution, movements such as *Renaissance,* the *Age of Enlightenment, Age of Reason,* were all strong precursors to New Age.

Some of the more modern versions include, but are not limited to, Yoga and Transcendental Meditation, Feminism and Wicca Witchcraft. When one name goes out of vogue, new, slicker, better packaged, sugar-coated terms are invented. Today, we have high-tech pseudonyms like *The New Spirituality, Creation Spirituality, Secular Humanism*[9], *Third Wave, Holistic Movement, Transpersonal Psychology, Planetary people, Centering Prayer, Enneagrams,* all very cerebral, all very chic, all engineered to lead you gently down the primrose path to hell. New Age is designed to allure many, *and betray all!*

St. Paul was truly inspired. He saw it coming, and warned us about this cult two thousand years ago, in

---

[8]Jesus wants to be best friends with you
[9]Although Secular Humanism is a takeoff on a Renaissance term, Pagan Humanism

Colossians 2:8.   In this warning, Paul, in the *First Century*, gives us the most encompassing definition of New Age.

"*See to it that no one deceive you through any empty, seductive philosophy, that follows mere human traditions, a philosophy based on cosmic powers rather than on Christ.*"[10]

Seductive *(to lead astray, tempting, enticing)* - It rouses the pride factor.   It promises what it can't deliver, power and divinity.   The New Age movement recruits members by appealing to intellectual superiority.   It also strongly arouses the sensual, the animal tendencies within its victims.   Sex, free sex, sex of any kind and perversion, is acceptable. People with obsessions for sex, and the need to justify these obsessions are perfect candidates for New Age.   Just think of it.   You can take part in any perverted act, and *it's a religious experience, part of your religion!*   As a matter of fact, those who frown on illicit sex, especially homosexual activities, are condemned as being neurotic, and psychotic.   They've even coined a new term, **Homophobia**, devised to harass and intimidate.   There is no definition in the dictionary[11] for Homophobia.   *The word doesn't exist!*   And yet, it's all the latest rage for New Agers.   Their definition of it is: if you don't approve of homosexual activities in any way, it's your problem; you are homophobic.   You have an *attitude,* and you better come to terms with *your attitude. Terrific!*   They insist: there's nothing wrong with homosexuality, or homosexual behavior; you're the problem.   We've heard that the best defense is a good offense, but this is ridiculous.   You are now labeled; you are *Homophobic.*   Learn to live with that!   If you have an aversion of any kind regarding homosexuals, it's because you're repressing homosexual tendencies in yourself.   Remarkable!   They even give workshops on *our* problem.   It is the most deceptive,

---

[10]New American Bible - Catholic version
[11]Webster's Dictionary - Second College Edition

manipulative, dishonest scheme we've ever seen, but brilliant. Where will we go from here? How about *Adultery-phobia*, or *Euthanasia-phobia*? The possibilities are endless.

Basically, anything that is frowned on by society, is acceptable with New Age; anything that is respectable by society at large is objectionable to New Agers. New Age is a distortion of Christianity. Its champions attempt to take microcosms of our faith belief, and distort them, twist them, stretch them, turn them upside down, inside-out. It can lead to great confusion, and they count on that. It's about weakening or destroying our belief in the concept of the Triune God, Father, Son and Holy Spirit. New Age is out to destroy Catholicism from without and within, but mostly from within. Sadly, a significant number of proponents of the fostering of New Age are by and large, members of the Catholic, Protestant and Jewish churches. The New Age will betray all of them. Right now, New Age is extremely anti-semitic[12]. In addition, Christianity has no place in the new world movement in its present form. They'll keep the shell, but the guts have to go.

Human - New Age teaches that *man* is divine. The definition of Pantheism is that each of us is God. There is no personal God in Heaven. God is within us, and all things. That's why you will hear people saying, "*God is everywhere. He's in the trees, in the sand, at the beach....*" The term *God Immanent* means that God is diffused in His creation; creation is diffused in God. He's not in Heaven; He's out there, in here, a part of everything.

"*A classic explanation of Creation, according to Confucius (5th Century B.C.), was that the world started with nothing. After a long time of nothing, something appeared[13]. Out of*

---

[12]Dangers of the Hidden Rainbow - Constance Cumbey

[13]We have a problem with *something* all of a sudden coming from *nothing*. Anyone who believes in Divine Creation, has a problem. Sounds like Darwin's theory of Evolution and the Big Bang theory!

something, P'an Ku[14] evolved. No one knows how long P'an Ku lived, but when he died, 'his last groan became the thunder; and his last breath became the wind. His left eye became the sun; and his right eye, the moon. The blood of his veins became the rivers; his hair the forests, and his flesh became the earth[15].'"

This is nothing other than **Immanence**, a New Age belief, which teaches that God is part of creation, and creation a part of God. The only difference is that Confucianism actually put together a body, the parts of which became creation. Other than that, they're about the same. But there has always been something that neither New Age nor the monkey-trial Darwin evolutionists or Confucius can explain satisfactorily: *where did it come from*; where did it begin; how did nothing become something? We call that process, *Creation*, and it's *Author*, God!

Secular Humanists claim "*Humans are responsible for what we are or will become. No deity will save us; we will save ourselves.*" **Yeah, right!**

Rosemary Ruether, Catholic theologian of the feminist movement, states, "*Nobody can save the world by himself. The only way you can save the world is by all of us together.*"

We believe that God *created* everything. It is true that everything is created in the Image and Likeness of God, but that doesn't mean everything is God. We believe in the "**I AM**" of Yahweh, rather than the "We are". Let's be honest. If everyone is God, what is God? He's just one of us. In Randy England's book *Unicorn in the Sanctuary*[16], he uses a short story by J.D. Salinger as an example of the absurdity of our being God. "In J.D. Salinger's story, 'Teddy', a ten year old boy recounts his realization of the pantheistic god. *'I was six when I saw that everything was God....it was on a Sunday, I*

---

[14]We have no idea who or what P'an Ku was
[15]Gaer, Joseph, How the Great Religions Began, Pg. 113
[16]TAN Publications, P.O. Box 424, Rockford, IL, 1990

remember. My sister was...drinking her milk and all of a sudden I saw that she was God and the milk was God. I mean all she was doing was pouring God into God, if you know what I mean."

If you look at the track record of the people of God, (us) in salvation history, we haven't done very well at all. *The possibility of Humanity being responsible for the salvation or destruction of the world is extremely depressing and completely mind-boggling!*

New Age also preaches Reincarnation. This is a very big part of the movement. It is defined in two ways: 1) Rebirth of the soul in another body, and 2) the soul reappears after death in another and different bodily form. Simply put, it means we're all coming back after we die, again and again, in another form, *until we get it right?* It could be as a dog, or a mouse, or a snake, a giraffe or ostrich. I'm not sure just what the requirements are not to have to keep coming back again. If you follow the line of Hinduism to its theological conclusion, they maintain that the highest level of reincarnation is becoming a Brahman bull, at which point, Divinity is attained. Maybe then we can stop coming back. Is that supposed to be my vision of Heaven, being a Brahman bull?

Another strange facet of New Age is its worship of created things, rather than the Creator. They maintain there is more power in crystals, pyramids and the like, which are creations (some of them man-made), than in God, who *created* the things they're worshiping.

They reject a Superior Being, Whom we call God, and yet they attribute god-like qualities to humans who have died. These are called "*Ascended Masters*". We have always referred to humans who reflected a mirror image of God as Saints. We have only one *Ascended Master*. We call Him Jesus, the Christ, second Person of the Blessed Trinity, only begotten Son of God. But the New Agers refer to these souls of departed loved ones as *gods*.

Cosmic - I don't know where St. Paul came up with this word, but it hits the mark like an arrow. Cosmic is another catch phrase of New Agers, and Catholic theologians expounding New Age Philosophy, i.e. Thomas Merton, an *ascended*[17] Benedictine, Pierre Teilhard de Chardin, an *ascended*[18] Jesuit, Matthew Fox, a *non-ascended* Dominican, and unfortunately, many other priests and nuns who are still with us, but whom we wish would ascend or descend, or just leave our Church. *Cosmic actually means of the universe, universal.* Everything in New Age is a combination of Pan Global, Cosmic, Planetary, Galactic, Aquarian, and on and on. It reminds me so much of all the science-fiction magazines of the 30's and 40's, *Flash Gordon and Buck Rogers in the Twentieth Century.*

It really should be funny; we should have a good belly laugh, and go on with our lives. But we can't. It's too serious; it's too frightening; it's too risky. A trend was begun in the '80s to make Dracula, vampires, Frankenstein creatures and hobgoblins into cartoon characters, after the success of *The Adams Family* and the *Munsters*, TV heroes of the '60s. There's even a Dracula-type breakfast cereal on the market, called *Chocula*. The thinking was, if we make these Satanic creatures laughable, no one will take them seriously. That's fine, except then they can freely *roam the earth seeking the ruin of souls.* Sound familiar? It's the ending of the Prayer to St. Michael. Archbishop Fulton J. Sheen said "*Satan's greatest feat in this century is to destroy the belief in his very existence.*"

We believe the same applies to New Age. We can't laugh it away, because they're not laughing. They're deadly

---

[17]or descended, based on your viewpoint
[18]the same as footnote above

serious, and the stakes are high. We could lose our Church, our faith, and our souls.

Where it all Began

We have already stated that New Age began in the Garden of Eden, or better yet, it probably began when the Angels were tested, and Lucifer committed the sin of Pride and Envy. But in our modern day world, where did it begin, and how?

The New Age Movement was begun in 1875 by a woman named Helena Petrovna Blavatsky. At the turn of the century, an offshoot of her movement in the Catholic Church was called *Modernism*, a heretical group which was condemned by St. Pope Pius X in 1907. However, after staying underground for about sixty years, they surfaced strongly during and right after Vatican II, and are alive and well and with us today, working diligently to bring the Catholic Church into the New Age Movement.

We're going to attempt the near impossible. We're going to try to break through all the sugar-coated cover up, through the cosmic, trans-global, universal, galactic garbage, and tell you exactly what New Age is, what its proponents are trying to accomplish, and how successful they've been.

New Age is really a generic term. It's as if all the misfits and the powers of hell have joined forces to destroy the Church.   Every sadistic, masochistic group, including heretics, devil worshipers, feminists, Nazis, radical homosexuals, and other misfits that the world ostracized, have banded together under the banner of New Age.

It is an international network of thousands of these little factions, which form a loose coalition, but a partnership nonetheless. They are well-heeled financially, and politically very powerful. There are those who tell us these groups are not well-organized. *We believe they are very well-organized.* They specialize in befuddlement, confusion, perplexity, sleight of hand, double-talk, and razzle-dazzle.   Their philosophy, in no matter what area they choose to expound, is always on the edge of truth.

They maintain their platform to be a new world order, unity, one government, one religion, one currency, and on and on. They even advocate one credit card. *There goes the shopping mall, Mabel.* They embrace Eastern religions, mostly Hinduism spirituality, Transcendental Meditation, Yoga, Buddhism and Native American legends, supposedly 25,000 years old and older.

They're too cheap to start their own church. They want our Church, and those who are being seduced by them can't even realize that they will be the first to be axed when the new sweep takes place.

The Catholic Church is a perfect vehicle for a takeover. It is universal; it has a worldwide network; it literally covers the globe. We have a built-in organization that is the most encompassing in the world. Why destroy the guts. The New Agers would do to the Catholic Church what the advocates of the Neutron bomb would have done to the world with the bomb. The people would have been destroyed, but the basic structure would remain intact. That's a very inhuman concept.

A priest whom we trust, referred to Satan and his followers as *termites*. It's a great analogy. For the most part, you don't ever see termites, until it's too late. When your house crumbles, you know you've been attacked, no, devastated by termites, but by then, it's too late. The same applies to this long-standing cult of Satan's, in its latest form, its cyanide-sugar coating, its slick Madison Avenue packaging.

New Age is possibly the most dangerous cult we, as a Church and people, have ever been exposed to. Perhaps the reason is because it's the most difficult to define. It is so slithery, so cunning, defenders of the Faith throw their hands up in frustration, because they just can't pin down what it is.

It has so many facets; it encompasses so many areas; it is coming at us from so many directions, we don't know where to begin. Very often trying to give workshops on New Age, we end up confusing instead of instructing. This is their game: make it so baffling, people will not understand; they will just nod their heads and agree, like so many sheep.

We find advocates of the New Age everywhere we look. There are times we think we are experiencing the invasion of the body snatchers. Those who are supposed to be the good guys, the priests and sisters, are espousing Enneagrams, Witchcraft, goddesses, mother god, global unity, Hindu mantras, yoga, and on and on. They wear the right clothes; they're in Diocesan offices and Religious Education Offices; they write for Catholic textbook Publishers; they teach in Catholic Universities; they've infiltrated parishes and seminaries; they look like religious; but they've become victims of the *Satan of the New Age.*

One of the most viable targets for New Age is the women religious of our Church. They have been attacked viciously. There's a reason for that. The **feminist movement** in our country was crumbling. It had failed miserably. The great gurus had betrayed the rank and file. Women had given up much of what they had previously possessed, in the way of position, influence and stature, and had received only ridicule and rejection in exchange. The Equal Rights Amendment never got off the ground floor. The young and middle aged career women were distancing themselves from their former masters (or rather, mistresses). Anything that even remotely resembled the Feminist movement was avoided like the plague. Something had to be done, or the expressions, *Ms., ERA,* and *Women's lib* would fade into oblivion much like the hula hoop and frisbee.

They set their sights on the women religious as far back as the mid-70's. There was a weakness there, a soft spot, where a knife could easily be thrust. Satan has always been able to find the weaknesses of human nature, and exploit them. And so he did in this instance. Sadly, the weakness in our women religious was innocence. But Satan could work with that. He used their naivete, a misguided feeling of poor self worth, and turned it against his worst enemy, God.

The major role for women religious from the beginning, was to be Brides of Christ. Their sole reason for being was to adore Our Lord Jesus, and turn their lives over to Him. How they went about doing this was determined by which community they entered. Each one had its own charism. But by and large, the bottom line was the same. However, somewhere along the way, in our Twentieth Century, which is a very I-centered age, the focus changed, reversed itself. It went from *Thee* to *me!* Women Religious have bought into some very bad press, and in the process, are losing all the things they held dear, all the reasons they entered into the religious life in the first place.

There is a unique brand of brainwashing going on, based more on peer acceptance, and the glamour of evil, than on anything tangible or plausible. Sensationalism and complete disdain for morals of any kind are the highlights of this rampage of rebellion. It's almost as if we can see these victims, these beautiful daughters of a loving Father, spit in His face, as well as that of His Son. Do they choke on that first rejection of Jesus, and the Father? Does it get easier each time they have to repeat these abuses? Does a time come when they can watch the tears run down His face, and it has absolutely no effect on them at all, no remorse registers in their heart? Is there a time when they turn to stone?

Part of the methodology of the advocates of this movement is to work very much *within the Church*. Beneath some of these statements has to lie a tremendous amount of hurt. We can see the manifestation of anger. For example, an answer made by Catholic theologian, Rosemary Ruether to her own rhetorical question, "Why bother with the Church at all?" was, *"Roman Catholicism goes along the same as ever when dissatisfied people leave it, happily relieved of their critical presence."* That was the anger speaking, prompted by a deep hurt, justified or unjustified. We are saddened, however, that any of our women in the Church would feel that their contributions throughout history, have been virtually nothing, that they are second class citizens in the Church, and that they don't have a viable role in the Church of the 21st Century. Where we seem to go towards opposite poles, is the degree of the offense, the need to lay blame, and where to lay the blame, and the remedy. Reconciliation doesn't seem to enter into the picture. Total destruction is the ultimate goal.

While it would seem that nothing less than all-out separation is the objective of the leaders, their plan is not to actually destroy the Church, but to use whatever they can of the Church, i.e., its worldwide network, the ready availability of an audience, and the actual structures, church buildings. In addition, wherever possible, use the clergy wherever it's practical, to the degree they are necessary, and for as long as they are productive; then discard them. These daughters of Eve are a very hard bunch of ladies. The word *ruthless* would seem very appropriate. *Deadly* also comes to mind.

But here's the thing. Again, it's a *small group* of women, trying to take advantage of a very important, major component of our Church, our women. But they're very effective. It's as if Satan plants one or two in each community, sent there to sew seeds of dissension. And we let them do it, in the name of democracy of action, or more liberal guidelines, or self-realization. But in return, instead of happy, healthy, well rounded sisters, what we're getting is goddess worship, mother god, witchcraft, homosexual activities, rebellion, alienation and just general disquietude. In an effort to bring the convents into modern times, to make them more acceptable to a generation that is not used to the lifestyle of the religious, we're just opening the door for the enemies of the Church to walk in. And because we are not as devious and plotting, because our agenda is one of trying to get closer to our God and our Church, rather than losing God and destroying our Church, we're being systematically taken over.

We would like to ask our Sisters in Christ to go back to their early years, when life was so beautiful and exciting, when Jesus was the center of their lives, when they were willing to give up anyone and anything, just like their predecessors, St. Bernadette of Lourdes, and St. Therese of Lisieux, all for the love of their Lord, Jesus. We'd like them to remember how it was when their relationship with Jesus was so ardent, their love so strong and personal, their focus so clear.

We appeal to you, our sisters, *directly*. Don't let someone talk you out of this great joy; it's yours. You deserve it; Jesus wants you to have it. Don't buy into the bad press that you're only second class citizens in the Church. You are power in the Church. You have been since the beginning. You always will be. Don't give it up; don't let it be taken away from you by a malcontent. Fight for your Love, even if the person you're fighting is yourself.

Ask yourself and your gurus a question. Why? Why are they doing it? Is it really because they believe in women goddesses, or is it because they hate God? Are *they*, manifestations of *him*, the evil one, the enemy of God? For those who tell us they don't believe in Satan, and that sin is relative, and hell is a state of mind, do they really believe it? Satan would like you to believe he's got nothing to do with it, that he doesn't exist. But he's got that hoof, and the hoof is pride. He's got to let you know it's him. When that happens, when you see him, when you feel him in the pit of your stomach, and you know it's him, react the way you know you should, the way you were taught. Don't let yourself slither down into the bowels of hell.

Don't let anyone convince you that the things you learned as a child, the beautiful truths the sisters taught you in grade school and high school, are not true. A young priest, newly ordained, shared with tears in his eyes, that his greatest letdown, when he entered the seminary, was to find that all the stories Sister Mary Regina told him in grade school about God, Our Lady, the Angels and the Saints, were all lies. We wanted to take him in our arms, hold him, protect him, and console him. *They were not lies; they were true. They are true.*

In all of this New Age, one thing which stands out as a really sore point, a great inconsistency, is this hating of God the Father. How can you hate God? He is so good, so loving, so unconditional. He is a faithful God to an unfaithful people. We make an impossible world to live in, create man-made diseases like Leukemia and Aids, abuse our bodies and minds with alcohol and drugs, and then blame God for a terrible world.

Do they hate Jesus as well? While they're denying His Divinity, are they also denying His Crucifixion? Are they denying His total surrender for us? I hope they are. I hope they don't truly believe that He suffered and died for us. I hope they don't believe He was mortally wounded before He ever picked up His Cross. I hope they don't believe that the Cross He carried, and was nailed to, was so big for Him, that they had to dislocate His shoulder to get Him on it.

It's really better for Him, less painful, that they don't believe all those things happened. If they do believe, and still mock Him, still spit at Him, still question His Divinity, it would be worse. It would hurt so much more, if He thought the people He died for, were indifferent towards Him, just didn't care about Him. It would be so appalling if all those people, who are buying into the lies that they are disenfranchised, marginalized, and unloved, knew how they were hurting Him, and just didn't give a damn. My God, oh my God, how terrible that would be; *how terrible that is!*

We believe the New Age Movement is a major threat, not only to our Church, but to the world. Take it seriously, folks. Another of Satan's greatest weapons is *indifference.* It's a sin which can have far-reaching consequences. There are those who are trying to warn us about the New Age Movement on one hand, while others are telling us not to take it too seriously. They try to get us to reject any idea of an organized conspiracy. They actually give us the impression that if we *do believe* that there's a conspiracy afoot, we're paranoid. Are we overly apprehensive, or are there enemies infiltrated in our churches, our schools, our banks, police departments, military establishments, and major corporations? Are we doing anyone a service, especially the innocent, by playing down the seriousness of the situation?

By ridiculing and belittling those who see a real danger in this movement, we take the chance of discrediting potentially powerful allies, and turning off the alarm before the major explosion, which threatens to destroy us all. We don't diffuse the bomb; we camouflage it by making it something it is not. The New Age movement is a bomb that is ready to go off. If left unchecked, it could destroy our Judeo-Christian Heritage. It can and will definitely take over all forms of Christianity. And when it does, the Name of Jesus would be forbidden and banned.

We pray, dear Lord Jesus, that none of us become too intelligent, too much of an expert on New Age, that we allow the Satan of Pride to slither in and fritter away all the good that You could do through us. Keep us simple, O Lord; keep the garbage out of our minds so that we can be childlike enough to hear You, and act on Your instructions.

What are the Signs?

From our own personal experience, I can tell you that when you feel a knot in your stomach from something your priest has said from the Altar, which sounds like heresy, when a program has been instituted in the Church, for self-Realization, or praying skills from the great Eastern Religions, when your school children come home and tell you about the Pyramid project they did in Science[19], or your CCD students show you a book on praying, which has a chapter on Mantras as a form of Christian praying, and the book has an *Imprimatur*, when the hair on your arms and the back of your neck begins to raise, when your Irish temper begins to flare, especially if you're not Irish, you know, my brothers and sisters, your Church is under attack.

We will give you a list here of areas that we have become aware of in the writing of this book, and in the lectures we have given throughout the country, where a brother or sister tells us various war stories about how the Faith is being maligned. These are good guidelines, but they keep changing the names, and camouflaging the subject matter. So you have to rely on the whispering of the Angels in your ears. Trust only the true teachings of the Church. Be aware that while we, the people of Christ, are involved in many things, most of which have nothing to do with our Church, or our immortal soul, the enemy has only one focus, the overthrow of the Church, the elimination of the name of Jesus as Messiah and Christ, and the destruction of your soul. Be cautious when you hear or read the following:

Enneagrams
Mantras (Hindu Chanting)
Eastern Religion Meditation
Centering Prayer (Transcendental Meditation)
Yoga (Hindu discipline to unite human with divine)

---

[19]Pyramids and Pyramid power have no basis in science whatever

Homophobia

Witchcraft

Goddesses

Numerology (Method of Divining Hidden Knowledge)

Creation Spirituality (Mother God)

A Course in Miracles; Self study of spiritual psychotherapy

Channeling - Possession of a body and spirit by a foreign spirit - a more sophisticated version of seances and mediums. In Channeling, we eliminate the middle man, and the spirit that takes over a body is not usually a loved one, but some powerful spirit guide or ascended master, based on whom you ask. A key word here is *Possession*!

The Battle Lines are Drawn

The parallels are awesome. We see armies lining up on opposite sides of the battle field. On one side, there is the negative, Satan's soldiers, seducing, enticing, tempting, and dragging innocent souls to hell. All that we have shared with you in this chapter, is part of Satan's endtime plan. He is aware that the end is coming. It's been predicted. It's glaring at us from one of the walls of the Sistine Chapel in Rome, and has been since 1571. Look at the Last Judgment. It's all there. Satan's plan is to accelerate, to drag as many souls down to the pits of hell as possible, to wreak as much havoc as possible, to get as much as he can before it's all over. It's much like Hitler's *scorched earth policy*. Destroy everything possible, so that there's nothing left when it's all over. Well, where do you think Hitler got it from? To quote King Louis XVI, "*apres moi, le deluge*", "After me, the deluge". Satan knows that when it's over, he's relegated back to the smoke-filled pit of hell, with whatever winnings he has been able to amass. But that's the end of it.

Satan is very aware of the activities of his worst enemy, Mary, Our Lady, the Mother of God. According to St. Louis Marie de Montfort, during Biblical times, Mary was virtually silent. What she said was powerful, but she said very little. In the end times, St. Louis Marie maintains that Mary will be the second John the Baptist, heralding the second coming of Lord Jesus, the Christ, the Messiah, only begotten Son of the Living God. She's taken on a major role in blocking the advance of the enemy.

A very important point is that the New Age Movement is a small movement, made up of a minority of malcontents, agitators, troublemakers from various religious and ethnic groups, who have been blackballed by society. *But then, so was the Hitler gang!* Satan has always used the few to lead the many to hell. Catholicism was lost in most northern European countries because of a minority; the majority were loyal Catholics. The New Agers are united and organized. They are in key positions. They do not have a leader; they have groups of leaders. They will fail, because they have to fail. They are Satan-based. They will be destroyed. Jesus will triumph, because He said He would. It's Scriptural. We can take confidence from that. *But how many dead bodies will be strewn along the road?* How many will they take with them, and force an even greater gap in the Church than we have right now? The Church will be protected against the gates of hell. But Jesus did not say that whole nations would not be lost. And we know He's not too thrilled with the United States. Look at our track record on abortion.

When we were children, we took chances; we dabbled in the occult without knowing it: we read horoscopes; we played with Ouija boards, and nothing terrible happened to us. Possibly, as we got a little older, we began having our fortunes read from tea leaves, or had our palm read, or our skulls, and maybe even tarot cards. And we're still here, right? I mean, no great bolt of lightning came out of the sky, and struck us dead, did it? Well, let me tell you. You're in the big time now. You're playing with the pros. Little people like us have no business gambling with our lives, and more importantly, our immortal souls, for a little thrill, to live dangerously, to be disobedient. Get up now, and walk, no *run*, very quickly, to the nearest church. There's no more time to play Russian Roulette with your soul. Penny was given a word the other morning as she awoke. It was, "**Arm the people - prepare them for battle.**" Then we were given another word the same day, which affirms for us, this chapter. A priest said, "*According to C.L. Lewis, Jesus was either Lunatic, Liar or Lord.*" *Either we stand on the side of those who call Him Lunatic or Liar, or we stand with those who call Him Lord!*

We're reminded of the Scripture passage that is sadly attacking many homes today:

"*I have come to light a fire on the earth. How I wish the blaze were ignited! I have a baptism to receive. What anguish I feel till it is over! Do you think I have come to establish peace on the earth? I assure you, the contrary is true; I have come for division. From now on, a household of five will be divided, three against two, and two against three; father will be split against son and son against father, mother against daughter and daughter against mother, mother-in-law against daughter-in-law, daughter-in-law against mother-in-law.*" (Luke 12:49-53)

We have a mighty task ahead of us, and we've got to get about the Lord's work. Don't let anyone sell you a bill of goods. Our Church works. Our religion is solid. Jesus is Lord. Stay on that course. Don't stray. There may be a lightning bolt with your name on it, heading your way, or worse than that, a breathtakingly beautiful person *with a hoof!*

Epilog

If ever there has been affirmation that powerful forces of evil have been at hand to wipe out the people of God, we have seen it in this book. If ever there was a need for unity in the Church, for a strong voice and a strong arm, it's now.

We don't mean to frighten you with the fact that what exists in our world today has been attacking us from the beginning. We do, however, want you to have a healthy respect for the enemy. Don't take for granted that Jesus and Mary are going to save the Church. They need you.

What can we do, you say? We're just a small prayer group in a big parish; we're a small parish in a big diocese; we're a small diocese in a big Church. *Wrong!* You are the Church. You are the people of God. You may be the only voice of our Pope and the Magisterium in your area.

We cannot fight the adversary unless we know who he is. We pray this book has enlightened you somewhat as to who the enemy is, and how he works. God uses us to foil Satan in his attempt to destroy us, and our Church. We have to be alert; we have to be sharp. We have to listen to the Lord, and act on His commands. We have nothing to fear. Our Lord Jesus, His beautiful Mother Mary, all the Angels and Saints, are by our side to guide and protect us.

They ridicule those who would warn us, call them paranoid, accuse them of seeing devils under every rock and plots behind every corner. After the research we've done on this book, poring through volumes about heresies and heretics, the obvious and clandestine, what we've written about is only the tip of the iceberg. There are old heresies and new heretics cropping up every day.

We praise You, dear Lord Jesus. We pray that we may play a small part in the victory over those who would split Your Cross even more. We give glory and honor to You. Without You, we can do nothing. *With You, the Scandal of the Cross becomes the Triumph of the Cross.*

Bibliography

Bausch, William J. *Pilgrim Church, a Popular History of Catholic Christianity* Twenty-Third Publications CT 1989

Broderick, Robert C. *The Catholic Encyclopedia*
Thomas Nelson Inc. Publishers Nashville 1970

Butler, Thurston, Atwater - *Lives of the Saints*
Christian Classics - Westminster, Md 1980

Gaer, Joseph - *How the Great Religions Began*
Dodd, Mead & Co. New York 1929

Cumbey, Constance - *The Hidden Dangers of the Rainbow*
Huntington House - Shreveport, LA 1983

England, Randy - *Unicorn in the Sanctuary*
TAN Publications, PO Box 424, Rockford, IL, 1990

Harney, Martin - *The Catholic Church through the Ages*
St. Paul Editions Boston, MA 1980

Jesuits St. Mary's College St. Mary, KS- *The Church Teaches*
Tan Publications - Rockford IL 1973

Jurgens, W.A. - *The Faith of the Early Fathers Vol. 1*
Liturgical Press, Collegeville, MN 1970

Kelly, JND - *Oxford Dictionary of Popes*
Oxford University Press NY 1986

Lord, Bob & Penny
Saints and Other Powerful Men in the Church 1990
Saints and Other Powerful Women in the Church 1989
This Is My Body, This Is My Blood 1986

Markoe, John SJ - *Triumph of the Church*
Catholic Information Society NY 1962

The New Catholic Study Bible - St. Jerome Edition TEV
American Bible Society NY 1985

Pacwa Mitch S.J. - *Catholics and the New Age*
Servant Publications, Ann Arbor, MI 1992

Steichen, Donna - *Ungodly Rage*
Ignatius Press - San Francisco, CA 1991

Journeys of Faith

Books

Bob and Penny Lord are authors of best sellers:
This Is My Body, This Is My Blood;
Miracles of the Eucharist $8.95 Paperback only
The Many Faces Of Mary, A Love Story $8.95 Paperback $12.95 Hardcover
We Came Back To Jesus $8.95 Paperback $12.95 Hardcover
Saints and Other Powerful Women in the Church $12.95 Paperback only
Saints and Other Powerful Men in the Church $14.95 Paperback only
Heavenly Army of Angels $12.95 Paperback only
Scandal of the Cross and Its Triumph $12.95 Paperback only

Please add $3.00 S&H for first book: $1.00 each add'l book - Louisiana. Res. add 8.25% Tax

Videos and On-site Documentaries

Bob and Penny's Video Series based on their books:
A 6 part series on the Miracles of the Eucharist filmed at EWTN
A 9 Part Eucharistic Retreat series with Father Harold Cohen
A 12 Part series on The Many Faces of Mary
A 10 part series on Saints and Other Powerful Women in the Church
A 12 part series on Saints and Other Powerful Men in the Church
Many other on-site Documentaries based on Miracles of the Eucharist, Mother Mary's Apparitions, Saints and other Powerful Men and Women in the Church, and the Heavenly Army of Angels. Request list.

Pilgrimages

Bob and Penny Lord's ministry take out Pilgrimages to the Shrines of Europe, the Holy Land, and the Shrines of Mexico every year. Come and join them on one of these special Retreat Pilgrimages. Call for more information, and ask for the latest pilgrimage brochure.

Lecture Series

Bob and Penny travel to all parts of the world to spread the Good News. They speak on what they have written about in their books; the Body of Christ, through the Miracles of the Eucharist, the Mother of Christ, through her apparitions, and the Church of Christ, through the lives of the Saints both men and women and what they are saying to us today. If you would like to have them come to your area, call for information on a lecture series in your area.

Good Newsletter

We are publishers of the Good Newsletter, which is published four times a year. This newsletter will provide timely articles on our Faith, plus keep you informed with the activities of our community. Call 1-800-633-2484 for subscription information.